OBJECT-RELATIONAL

D B M S s

TRACKING THE NEXT GREAT WAVE

The Morgan Kaufmann Series in Data Management Systems

Series Editor, Jim Gray

Object-Relational DBMSs: Tracking the Next Great Wave, Second Edition,
Michael Stonebraker and Paul Brown with Dorothy Moore

Web Farming for the Data Warehouse, Richard Hackathorn

Management of Heterogeneous and Autonomous Database Systems,
edited by Ahmed K. Elmagarmid, Marek Rusinkiewicz, and Amit P. Sheth

Database Modeling and Design, Third Edition, Toby J. Teorey

A Complete Guide to DB2 Universal Database, Don Chamberlin

Universal Database Management: A Guide to Object/Relational Technology,
Cynthia Maro Saracco

Readings in Database Systems, Third Edition,
edited by Michael Stonebraker and Joseph M. Hellerstein

Understanding SQL's Stored Procedures: A Complete Guide to SQL/PSM, Jim Melton

Principles of Multimedia Database Systems, V. S. Subrahmanian

Principles of Database Query Processing for Advanced Applications,
Clement T. Yu and Weiyi Meng

The Object Database Standard: ODMG 2.0, edited by R. G. G. Cattell and Douglas K. Barry

Introduction to Advanced Database Systems, Carlo Zaniolo, Stefano Ceri, Christos
Faloutsos, Richard T. Snodgrass, V. S. Subrahmanian, and Roberto Zicari

Principles of Transaction Processing, Philip A. Bernstein and Eric Newcomer

Distributed Algorithms, Nancy A. Lynch

Active Database Systems: Triggers and Rules For Advanced Database Processing,
edited by Jennifer Widom and Stefano Ceri

Joe Celko's SQL for Smarties: Advanced SQL Programming, Joe Celko

Migrating Legacy Systems: Gateways, Interfaces, and the Incremental Approach,
Michael L. Brodie and Michael Stonebraker

Database: Principles, Programming, and Performance, Patrick O'Neil

Atomic Transactions, Nancy Lynch, Michael Merritt, William Weihl, and Alan Fekete

Query Processing for Advanced Database Systems,
edited by Johann Christoph Freytag, David Maier, and Gottfried Vossen

Transaction Processing: Concepts and Techniques, Jim Gray and Andreas Reuter

Understanding the New SQL: A Complete Guide, Jim Melton and Alan R. Simon

Building an Object-Oriented Database System: The Story of O_2,
edited by François Bancilhon, Claude Delobel, and Paris Kanellakis

Database Transaction Models for Advanced Applications, edited by Ahmed K. Elmagarmid

A Guide to Developing Client/Server SQL Applications, Setrag Khoshafian, Arvola Chan,
Anna Wong, and Harry K. T. Wong

*The Benchmark Handbook for Database and Transaction Processing Systems, Second
Edition,* edited by Jim Gray

Camelot and Avalon: A Distributed Transaction Facility,
edited by Jeffrey L. Eppinger, Lily B. Mummert, and Alfred Z. Spector

Readings in Object-Oriented Database Systems,
edited by Stanley B. Zdonik and David Maier

OBJECT-RELATIONAL DBMSs

TRACKING THE NEXT GREAT WAVE

SECOND EDITION 2

MICHAEL STONEBRAKER

PAUL BROWN

WITH DOROTHY MOORE

MORGAN KAUFMANN PUBLISHERS, INC.
SAN FRANCISCO, CALIFORNIA

Senior Editor	Diane D. Cerra
Director of Production and Manufacturing	Yonie Overton
Assistant Production Manager	Julie Pabst
Copyeditor	Ken DellaPenta
Indexer	Paul Kish
Cover Design	Ross Carron Design
Cover Image	Don and Liysa King/Image Bank
Printer	Courier Corporation

This book was typeset in FrameMaker by Dorothy Moore.

Designations used by companies to distinguish their products are often claimed as trademarks or registered trademarks. In all instances where Morgan Kaufmann Publishers, Inc. is aware of a claim, the product names appear in initial capital or all capital letters. Readers, however, should contact the appropriate companies for more complete information regarding trademarks and registration.

Morgan Kaufmann Publishers, Inc.
Editorial and Sales Office
340 Pine Street, Sixth Floor
San Francisco, CA 94104-3205
USA
Telephone 415/392-2665
Facsimile 415/982-2665
Email mkp@mkp.com
WWW http://www.mkp.com

Library of Congress Cataloging-in-Publication Data is available for this book.
ISBN 1-55860-452-9

Contents

Preface **xi**

CHAPTER 1 *The DBMS Matrix* **1**

1.1 A DBMS Classification Matrix **1**

1.2 Quadrant 1: Simple Data without Queries **2**

1.3 Quadrant 2: Simple Data with Queries **3**

1.4 Quadrant 3: Complex Data without Queries **8**

1.5 Quadrant 4: Complex Data with Queries **15**

1.6 Universal Applications **20**

1.7 Technological Drivers in the DBMS Market **24**

1.8 Summary **26**

CHAPTER 2 *Characteristic 1: Base Data Type Extension* **27**

2.1 Need for Base Type Extension **27**

2.2 A Better Way: Extensible Data Types **33**

2.3   User-Defined Functions and Operators   **36**

2.4   Fully Object-Relational Type Extension   **41**

2.5   Summary   **53**

CHAPTER 3   *Examples of Base Type Extension*   **55**

3.1   Geographic Information Systems
      Applications   **55**

3.2   Image Type Library Applications   **58**

3.3   The Quantity Data Type   **59**

CHAPTER 4   *Characteristic 2: Complex
                Objects*   **61**

4.1   Type Constructors   **61**

4.2   Using Type Constructors   **63**

4.3   Collections and Client-Server
      Communication   **73**

4.4   Base Types and Complex Objects   **73**

4.5   Summary   **76**

CHAPTER 5   *Other Type Constructors?*   **79**

5.1   A Time Series Example   **79**

5.2   An Array Example   **81**

5.3   Summary   **86**

CHAPTER 6   *Characteristic 3: Inheritance*   **87**

6.1   Data Inheritance   **87**

6.2   Inheritance of Functions   **93**

6.3   Summary   **98**

CHAPTER 7   *Characteristic 4: Rules*   **101**

7.1   Update-Update Rules   **102**

7.2   Query-Update Rules   **103**

7.3   Update-Query Rules   **104**

7.4   Query-Query Rules   **105**

7.5   Semantics: The Dark Side of Rules   **107**

7.6   Summary   **111**

CHAPTER 8   *Object-Relational Parsing   113*

8.1   How an Object-Relational Parser Works   **113**

8.2   Summary   **116**

CHAPTER 9   *Traditional Relational Optimizers   117*

9.1   How Relational Optimizers Work   **117**

9.2   Performing the Restriction on the Table emp_R   **119**

9.3   Methods for Processing the Join   **124**

CHAPTER 10   *Object-Relational Optimizers   131*

10.1   Extension 1: Operator and Function Notation   **132**

10.2   Extensions 2 and 3: B-Trees and User-Defined Comparison Operators   **133**

10.3   Extension 4: User-Defined Selectivity Functions   **135**

10.4   Extension 5: User-Defined Negators   **136**

10.5   Extension 6: User-Defined Commutators   **136**

10.6   Extension 7: Access Methods on a Function of the Data   **137**

10.7   Extension 8: Smart Ordering of the Clauses in a Predicate   **138**

10.8   Extension 9: Optimization of Expensive Functions   **140**

10.9   Extension 10: User-Defined Access Methods   **142**

10.10   Extension 11: "Flattening" Complex Object Queries   **144**

10.11 Extension 12: "In-Line" Sets   **145**

10.12 Extension 13: Indexes on Attributes of
  Sets   **146**

10.13 Extension 14: Optimization of Scans of
  Inheritance Hierarchies   **147**

10.14 Extension 15: Optimization of Joins
  over Inheritance Hierarchies   **147**

10.15 Extension 16: Support for User-Defined
  Aggregates   **148**

10.16 Summary   **149**

CHAPTER 11   *Implementation of Rule Systems*   *151*

11.1 Support for Triggers   **151**

11.2 Extension to More General Rules   **156**

11.3 Scalability   **157**

11.4 Summary   **161**

CHAPTER 12   *Architectural Options for*
Commercial Vendors   *163*

12.1 Strategy 1: Do Nothing   **164**

12.2 Strategy 2: Rewrite a Relational Engine from
  Scratch   **165**

12.3 Strategy 3: Sell Two Systems   **166**

12.4 Strategy 4: An Object-Relational Top on a
  Relational Storage Manager   **167**

12.5 Strategy 5: Incremental Evolution   **169**

12.6 Strategy 6: Write a Wrapper   **170**

12.7 Strategy 7: Write a Gateway   **175**

12.8 Strategy 8: Extend an Object-Oriented
  DBMS   **181**

12.9 Strategy 9: Glue an Object-Relational Engine
  onto a Persistent Language   **182**

12.10 Summary   **183**

CHAPTER 13   *More on Object-Relational Architecture* **185**

13.1   Calling Extensions   **185**

13.2   Middleware   **193**

13.3   Summary   **200**

CHAPTER 14   *Extension Performance: Implementation Makes a Difference* **201**

14.1   Examples   **202**

14.2   An SQL-92 Solution   **204**

14.3   The Informix 2-D Spatial DataBlade Approach   **206**

14.4   A Z Transform Solution   **207**

14.5   A Final Spatial Extension   **209**

14.6   A Comparison of the Alternatives   **212**

14.7   Summary   **213**

CHAPTER 15   *Object-Relational DBMS and Application Servers* **215**

15.1   Implications of a Thick Database on Traditional Application Servers   **219**

15.2   Two-Tier Thick Database Model   **223**

15.3   Three-Tier Thick Database Model   **225**

15.4   Summary   **229**

CHAPTER 16   *Multiquadrant Problems* **231**

16.1   A Video Service Application   **232**

16.2   An Insurance Application   **237**

16.3   Summary   **240**

CHAPTER 17   *Solutions to Multiquadrant*
                         Problems   243

                         17.1   Supporting File System Aspects of an
                                Application   **243**

                         17.2   Supporting Lower-Right Quadrant
                                Applications   **247**

                         17.3   Summary   **252**

CHAPTER 18   *Database Design for Object-*
                         Relational DBMSs   253

                         18.1   Relational Database Design   **253**

                         18.2   Reasons for Problems   **257**

                         18.3   Challenges in Object-Relational Database
                                Design   **262**

                         18.4   Summary   **264**

CHAPTER 19   *The Next Great Wave in DBMS*
                         Technology   267

                         19.1   Overview of the Book   **267**

                         19.2   Overview of the Object-Relational
                                Marketplace   **270**

                         19.3   Integration of Object-Relational Features
                                with Database Services   **275**

                         19.4   A Brief Historical Perspective   **276**

                         19.5   Summary   **277**

                         References   279

                         Index   283

Preface

This book explores a new and promising class of database management systems, the object-relational DBMS. The spectrum of application areas covered by the object-relational DBMS ranges from video and graphic asset management in the entertainment industry to time series analysis problems in the financial services market, scientific databases, and geographic information systems (GISs). In addition, the exploding market for multimedia data, often accessed through the World Wide Web, is best served by object-relational technology. Object-relational DBMSs capture the real semantics of traditional business data processing objects such as part numbers, dates, and names. This book explains why object-relational DBMSs will replace relational systems to become the next great wave of database technology.

This book was written primarily for application programmers and information services (IS) managers who want to understand how this new technology fits into their environments. It contains many examples and tables to help you make informed decisions about object-relational systems.

Chapter 1 begins by introducing a two-by-two matrix for classifying all DBMS applications. File systems, relational DBMSs, object-oriented DBMSs, and object-relational DBMSs are each represented by a quadrant of the matrix. Not only is the matrix a handy way to classify DBMS applications, but it also provides a perspective on where object-relational DBMSs fit in the database world.

Chapters 2 through 7 explain the following four main features of an object-relational DBMS:

- Support for base type extension in an SQL context
- Support for complex objects in an SQL context
- Support for inheritance in an SQL context
- Support for a production rule system

The book also describes the specific requirements needed to fully support each of these features.

Chapter 2 discusses base type extension, and Chapter 3 provides several specific examples of the concept. Chapter 4 provides the support requirements for complex objects in an object-relational DBMS. The following type constructors are needed to build complex types:

- Records of objects
- Sets of objects
- References (pointers) to objects

However, there are other plausible type constructors, and some of the more important ones are described in Chapter 5. Chapter 6 continues with a discussion of inheritance and indicates the requirements for an object-relational DBMS to fully support this concept. The last required feature, a rules system, is the subject of Chapter 7.

While the first half of the book discusses the required features of an object-relational DBMS, the second half of the book focuses on the actual mechanisms required to support an object-relational DBMS engine. Chapter 8 covers parser requirements, and Chapters 9 and 10 discuss optimizer requirements. Chapter 9 describes how a traditional relational optimizer operates; Chapter 10 indicates the changes that must be made to turn a traditional optimizer into a good object-relational one. Because most vendors are not forthcoming about the quality of their optimizers, the chapter also includes a collection of tests you can perform to discover the relative merit of the optimizer in any target system. Chapter 11 finishes the implementation discussion with a treatment of rule systems.

As you will discover in Chapters 8 through 11, a relational engine must be largely rewritten to include object-relational functionality. Chapter 12 lists the available technical options for commercial vendors who want to move their engines to the object-relational quadrant and indicates which options some vendors have taken.

Clearly the performance delivered by an object-relational engine depends crucially on having a good optimizer, which is the topic of Chapter 10. However, there are two other issues that have a major performance impact. An object-relational engine must call user-written extensions. Those extensions can be called in the DBMS address space, in another address space, or even supported in middleware outside the engine. Chapter 13 explores the performance consequences of these decisions. Next, Chapter 14 demonstrates that the actual algorithms implemented by user-written extensions can also be a major determiner of performance.

There is much talk in the literature and at trade shows about component models, typically supported in client-level or middleware-level systems. Because object-relational extensions are a component system, Chapter 15 discusses how they relate to other component models.

Chapters 16 and 17 look at a vexing problem that many users of DBMS technology will face in the future—what do you do if you have a "multiquadrant" application, one that exhibits the characteristics of more than one quadrant in Chapter 1's matrix? Two examples of multiquadrant problems are given in Chapter 16. Chapter 17 offers available solution possibilities.

No book on DBMS technology is complete without a discussion of database design. Chapter 18 shows that the challenges of designing for a standard relational database are increased with the more general data model presented by the object-relational DBMS. To conclude, Chapter 19 surveys the current marketplace and looks at how successfully, or unsuccessfully, current products match up to a list of required features for an object-relational DBMS. Because rapid progress is being made in this field, you are advised to check with specific vendors for updated descriptions of products of interest.

This book pays little attention to traditional DBMS services, such as concurrency control, crash recovery, views, protection, replication, parallelism, and distributed DBMS support. These topics are crucially important for any DBMS, regardless of its data model and query language. In fact, many lump this collection of features into a single requirement—that the DBMS must scale to large numbers of users and large amounts of data. Because object-relational DBMSs introduce no new spin on these services, they are not explored in this book in the interest of brevity. Instead, the book focuses exclusively on defining the functionality of an object-relational DBMS.

Throughout the book, there are examples of object-relational features, typically expressed in SQL. The question naturally arises, "Which SQL should I use?" There are draft SQL documents on both SQL-3 from the ANSI X3H2 SQL committee (Melton 1997) and OQL from the Object Data Management Group (ODMG) (Cattell 1998). These standards are evolving rapidly and, as a result, the details change frequently. Alternatively, there are extended SQL systems from a variety of commercial vendors. This book uses the SQL currently implemented by the Informix Dynamic Server with Universal Data Option (IDS-UDO) because it will seemingly have a longer lifetime than the current draft standards.

Three liberties are taken in this book with respect to IDS-UDO. First, for ease of explanation, we have stylized some instances of idiosyncratic syntax. A second liberty we have adopted is to use user-defined operators in this book. Illustra allowed extensibility in the areas of operators and of functions. More recently both SQL-3 and the Informix universal server are moving away from supporting user-defined operators. It looks likely that future SQL systems will probably offer extensibility in one area, but not both. Even through we are "swimming upstream" on this issue, we continue to employ user-defined operators in this book because we believe they often offer a more natural way to express queries. Third, where features are discussed that are not currently in IDS-UDO, we use upwardly compatible SQL syntax, even though it is not currently supported. Because of these liberties, we call the object-relational SQL used throughout this book simply "OR SQL."

To further explore many of the concepts in this book, please contact Informix Software, Inc., 4100 Bohannon Drive, Menlo Park, CA 94025-1032. You can visit Informix's home page at *http://www.informix.com.*

CHAPTER 1   *The DBMS Matrix*

This chapter presents an overview of database management systems (DBMSs) from both technical and marketplace perspectives. To help in classifying applications that require DBMSs, this chapter introduces a matrix; each quadrant in the matrix represents one of four general types of DBMSs. This chapter also examines the types of problems each kind of DBMS solves and where various DBMS products fit in today's marketplace. One size does not fit all in the database world. In other words, there is no single DBMS that solves the requirements of all applications.

1.1   *A DBMS Classification Matrix*

The two-by-two matrix for classifying DBMSs is illustrated in Figure 1.1. In the matrix, the horizontal axis shows simple data on the left and complex data on the right. Of course, in the real world, the complexity of an application's data can vary. However, for the sake of example, assume there are only two possibilities, simple and complex. The vertical axis differentiates whether the application requires a query capability. Again, for simplicity, assume there are only two choices, "query" and "no query."

Depending on its characteristics, an application fits into at least one of the four quadrants in Figure 1.1. Of course, many applications have qualities that place them in more than one quadrant. Multiquadrant problems are discussed in Section 1.6. Until then, assume that an application can be placed into a single quadrant.

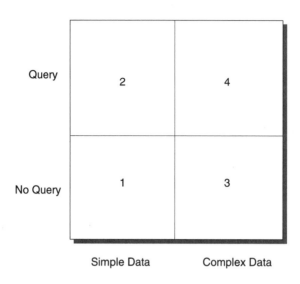

FIGURE 1.1   A Matrix for Classifying DBMS Applications

Quadrant 1, which holds applications having simple data without queries, is examined first.

1.2   *Quadrant 1: Simple Data without Queries*

Consider a standard text processing system such as Word, Framemaker, Word Perfect, vi, or emacs. All enable you to open a file by name, which results in the contents of the file being copied into virtual memory. You can then edit the file and update the virtual memory object. At intervals, the object is saved to disk storage. When you are finished, you can close the file, causing the virtual memory copy to be stored back to the file system.

A text editor qualifies as a "no query" application that does not need or use SQL. (The only "query" made by a text editor is "get file," and the only "update" is "put file.") In addition, a text editor is appropriately served by the data model available in the file system, namely a sequence of characters of arbitrary length. A text editor is a "no query–simple data" application that fits into quadrant 1, the lower-left quadrant of the two-by-two matrix. (In the future, it is quite possible that text editors will move to one of the other matrix quadrants because the data model of text editors is becoming more complex as documents become structured with embedded reports, graphs, and spreadsheets.)

A quick point before proceeding: text editors are being discussed here, not more sophisticated groupware products, such as Lotus Notes. Document management systems, such as Documentum, are also not included in the discussion. Such products have to be independently placed in an appropriate quadrant in the matrix.

The obvious DBMS for applications in the lower-left quadrant of the matrix is the file system provided by the operating system vendor for the hardware in question. In fact, virtually all text editors use this primitive level of DBMS service, and their developers have no plans to move to anything more sophisticated. If you have no need for queries and no need for complex data, then the service provided by the file system is perfectly adequate. Moreover, a file system invariably has higher performance than any more sophisticated system. The bottom line is simple: if you don't need the service, then there is no need to pay for it in terms of lower performance.

A second application in the lower-left quadrant is video-on-demand (VOD). Test beds in this area were prototyped by many of the major telecommunications vendors a couple of years ago. These systems enabled a user to select a movie from a list of about 100 names. The VOD system then delivered 30 frames per second of digitized video plus sound from the disks on a head-end server to an ATM network, to the cable interface in the user's neighborhood, to the set-top box on the user's TV, and finally onto the user's TV screen.

VOD moves bits from disk to network in real time for a large number of connections and requires delivery guarantees. The last thing the application designer wants is a DBMS in the way, and all VOD projects use file system technology.

1.3   *Quadrant 2: Simple Data with Queries*

A well-known database example nicely illustrates the upper-left corner of the matrix. Suppose you want to store the following information about each employee in a hypothetical company: the employee's name, start date, salary, and department. In addition, you require the name, floor number, and budget for each of the departments in the company. You can capture the schema for all of this information with the following standard SQL statements:

```
create table emp (
                name        varchar (30),
                startdate   date,
                salary      float,
                dept        varchar (20));

create table dept (
                dname       varchar (20),
                budget      float,
                floor       int);
```

Notice that the above tables contain a collection of structured records, each with attributes that are simple integers, floats, dates, and character strings—all standard data types found in SQL-92. This data can therefore be classified as "simple."

After you create the schema, you can form the following questions quite naturally in SQL:

1. Find the names of employees with an employment start date after 1980 and who earn more than $40,000.

```
select name
from emp
where startdate > '1980-12-31' and salary > 40000;
```

2. Find the names of employees who work on the first floor.

```
select name
from emp
where dept in
            (select dname
            from dept
            where floor = 1);
```

3. Find the average salary of employees in the marketing department.

```
select avg(salary)
from emp
where dept = 'marketing';
```

Applications with simple data and queries that are easily expressed in standard SQL-92 tend to be identified as "business data processing" applications, and they are a natural fit for the upper-left quadrant of the matrix. Such applications have the following requirements:

Query Language. SQL-89 is a requirement. It is desirable to also have the newer SQL-92 standard.

Client Tools. A tool kit that enables a programmer to set up forms for data entry and display is required. This tool kit must also enable sequencing between forms through control flow logic. Such tool kits are called fourth-generation languages (4GLs). Example 4GLs include PowerBuilder from Sybase, Open Road from Computer Associates, Developer 2000 from Oracle, and products from Easel and Progress. In fact, there are at least 50 4GLs on the market today, all offering similar capabilities. Moreover, it is not a significant stretch to call Lotus Notes a 4GL.

In addition, client tools must include a report writer, a database design tool, a performance monitor, and the ability to call DBMS services from a variety of third-generation languages (for example, C, FORTRAN, COBOL, Visual Basic, and Java).

Performance. Much of the business data processing marketplace entails transaction processing where many simultaneous users submit requests for DBMS services from client terminals or PCs. User interactions tend to be fairly simple SQL statements with many updates. When parallel conflicting updates are processed by a DBMS, then the user requires a predictable outcome. This has led to the notion of two-phase locking, which ensures so-called serializability. (If you are unfamiliar with the concept of two-phase locking, consult a standard textbook on DBMSs, such as Date 1985, Korth and Silberschatz 1986, or Ullman 1980.)

In addition, there is an absolute requirement to never lose the user's data, regardless of what kind of failure might have occurred, including disk crashes as well as operating system failures. Providing recovery from crashes is typically supported through write-ahead log (WAL) technology. (If you are interested in this topic, consult any of the standard textbooks mentioned above.) Together, two-phase locking and a write-ahead log provide transaction management; that is, user queries and updates are grouped into units of work called *transactions*. Each transaction is atomic (it either happens completely or not at all), can be serialized (it appears to have happened before or after all other parallel transactions), and durable (once committed, its effect can never be lost). Transaction management is a sophisticated subject; a definitive reference on the subject is *Transaction Processing: Concepts and Techniques* (Gray and Reuter 1993).

Standard benchmarks that typify this sort of interaction include TPC-A and TPC-C from the Transaction Processing Council. Both are described in *The Benchmark Handbook for Database and Transaction Processing Systems* (Gray 1993).

Besides transaction processing, the second major application area in business data processing is data warehousing. The main purpose of warehousing is to perform enterprise data integration. Data is typically stored in several distinct operational systems, and decision makers wish to access all of it to run decision support queries. The conventional wisdom in warehouse design is as follows:

1. Identify the data to be integrated.
2. Construct an SQL schema for it.
3. Buy a very large machine to hold the warehouse.
4. Write a data pump to periodically copy data from each operational system into the warehouse.
5. Run decision support queries against the data in the warehouse.

The early success stories in warehousing are in the retail area. All major retailers have set up warehouses to capture historical transaction data. Every time an item passes under a wand in a checkout lane of any store in a major retail chain, a record is added to a centralized data warehouse. WalMart, for example, has a data warehouse with approximately two years of retail data. Retail warehouses examine customer buying patterns—what is selling and what is not. The results of such queries are used to rotate stock. Hot sellers are moved to the front of the store, while slow items are sent back to the manufacturer. Most retailers report that a data warehouse pays for itself within six months through better stock management.

Most data warehouses contain numbers and character strings and are a decision-support query environment. High performance in the warehouse space requires a system to run more complex SQL queries efficiently, to load data quickly, and to run complex queries in parallel to achieve better response time. A benchmark that typifies this sort of load is TPC-D, also published by the Transaction Processing Council.

Security/Architecture. Because users put sensitive data, such as salaries, into business data processing databases, DBMSs must be secure. The DBMS must run in a separate address space from the client application with a user ID that is separate from any application. Actual data files utilized in the database are specified as readable and writable only by the DBMS. This client-server architecture, shown in Figure 1.2, is a requirement of upper-left quadrant applications.

The SQL DBMS Market: A Crowded Playing Field

The general checklist of requirements for an SQL DBMS with 4GL client tools optimized for transaction processing and data warehousing is met very well by the many relational DBMS vendors. The main ones are Informix, Oracle, Sybase, and Microsoft. In addition, hardware vendors such as Compaq (Tandem), Hewlett-Packard, and IBM offer relational database products.

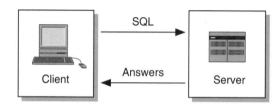

FIGURE 1.2   Standard Client-Server Architecture

These products differ mainly on detailed features; from a distance they all look very similar. To distinguish their products, all vendors engage in considerable marketing hype touting their respective wares. Business data processing is a large and competitive market and vendors have their hands full with the following tasks:

- The DBMS must run well on shared memory multiprocessors.
- The DBMS must interface to every transaction monitor.
- The DBMS must run on every hardware platform.
- The DBMS must provide a gateway to all the other vendors' DBMSs.
- The DBMS must provide parallel execution of user queries.
- The DBMS must solve the "32-bit barrier," that is, run well on very large databases.
- The DBMS must provide "failover" to a backup machine.
- The DBMS must provide "7 times 24" service, that is, never require taking the database offline for maintenance.
- The DBMS must support optimization capabilities appropriate to warehouses and smaller data marts, such as bitmap indexes and snowflake schemas.

Despite the crowded playing field, the relational DBMS vendors are generally very healthy companies. Relational DBMS customers have a seemingly insatiable need for additional licenses, add-on products, and consulting services. Collectively, the relational DBMS market is approximately $10 billion per year and growing at about 20% per year.

The only storm cloud on the horizon is the arrival of Microsoft into this market. They have acquired the Sybase code line for Microsoft Windows NT and have a substantial group in Redmond improving it. The focus is on improving scalability and performance to try to gain parity with products from other vendors. In addition, Microsoft is adding features commonly found in other relational DBMSs, such as row-level locking and parallel query execution.

Microsoft is committed to "PC pricing" for their SQL server and distributes it through the traditional retail "shrink-wrap" channel. However, it is not clear that Fortune 1000 companies will buy mission-critical database systems in this fashion. Such users want high-quality technical support, on-site vendor personnel, and a specific person as an account manager. These characteristics are associated with the distribution model of the relational DBMS vendors and cannot be provided at "shrink-wrap" prices.

Expect all DBMS vendors (including Microsoft) to have multiple distribution models at multiple price points, so that customers can get the services that fit their individual needs at an appropriate price. In effect, this will correspond to "a la carte" pricing, where a consumer can buy only needed services.

1.4   *Quadrant 3: Complex Data without Queries*

The next application fits in the lower-right quadrant of the matrix. In this example, suppose the user is the facilities planner for a company that has an "open floor plan." Nobody gets an office; instead, all the company's employees are arranged into cubicles with partitions separating them. Hewlett-Packard uses an open floor plan. In such a company, departments grow and shrink as employees get hired, are transferred, or quit. Over time, the arrangement of employees on the physical real estate of the building becomes suboptimal, and a global rearrangement of space is warranted. This "garbage collection" of free space and concurrent rearrangement of employees is the target application in this example.

The database for the application can be expressed in the following SQL commands:

```
create table employee (
                    name          varchar (30),
                    space         polygon,
                    adjacency     set-of (employee));

create table floors (
                    number        int,
                    asf           swiss_cheese_polygon);
```

For each employee, the employee's name, current cubicle location (space), and the set of all other employees who share a common cubicle wall with the employee (adjacency) will be recorded.

For each floor, the floor number and the amount of assignable square feet (asf) will be recorded. The asf is the building's outline minus the rest rooms, elevator shafts, and fire exits. It is a polygon with "holes" in it, a "Swiss cheese polygon."

Clearly, this data is much more complex than the emp and dept data discussed in Section 1.3. Because of its complex data, place the floor plan application on the right side of Figure 1.1. The application can be pseudocoded as follows:

```
main ()
{
        read all employees;
        read all floors;
        compact();
        write all employees;
}
```

Here, the program must read all employee records to ascertain current spaces for employees, and it must get the asf for each floor. The program will build some sort of virtual memory structure for the next step of the program. The program's compaction routine then walks the virtual memory structure, perhaps many times, to generate a revised allocation of employees into the asf on each floor. When compaction is complete, each employee record must be rewritten with a new space allocation.

Obviously, this program reads the entirety of both data collections, computes on this collection, and then writes one collection. It is analogous to the text editor that read, computed, and then wrote a single file (page 2). As with the text editor example, there is not a query in sight in this program. Unlike the text editor example, the data involved in this application is rather complex. Thus, this program qualifies as a lower-right quadrant application—one without queries but with complex data.

While the garbage collection/compaction example may seem somewhat artificial, it is, in fact, very representative of most ECAD (electronic computer-aided design) applications. In a typical ECAD application, a chip design is stored on disk as a complex object, read into main memory, compacted by an optimization program, and then written back to persistent storage. Applications that find power consumption or timing faults have a similar structure. The office floor plan application, however, is a simple application that is more easily understood than the details of an ECAD program.

Using a traditional file system for the floor plan application is tedious. The application must manually read the employee and floor information. Converting the data from disk format to main memory format is even more taxing. The adjacency information is a set of employees that can be represented on disk as a set of unique identifiers for employees. These unique identifiers are converted to virtual memory pointers during the load process. Because virtual memory pointers are transient and depend on where the data is actually loaded in memory, they cannot be reused in subsequent executions of the program. Disk pointers are fundamentally different from main memory pointers, and the load process must convert from one to the other. Similarly, when the data is written back to disk, the adjacency information may have been changed by the compaction routine, requiring a reverse conversion from main memory to disk representation.

Loading and converting the data, and then unloading and reconverting it, is a time-consuming effort that must be done by the person developing the compaction routine if the developer is using a file system as a storage engine for the application. A much better solution is to support persistent storage for the programming language (C, C++, Java, Visual Basic, and so forth) in which *compact* is written.

Assuming that this language is C++, *compact* would have a collection of data structures defined for its computation. One such declaration is

```
integer I;
```

In a normal programming language, I is a transient variable. In other words, it has no value until it is initialized by the program, and its value is lost when the program terminates. Suppose persistent variables are utilized in *compact*, declared as follows:

```
persistent integer J;
```

Because J is persistent, its value is automatically saved when the compaction program terminates. This value is also automatically available when the program is restarted the next time. With persistent variables, it becomes the language support system's problem to load and unload data as well as to convert it from disk format to main memory format and back. The person writing the compaction routine need only write the algorithm and is freed from other details.

A persistent programming language offers the best DBMS support for this compaction application. With such a language, you can move away from writing the following code:

```
main ()
{
    read all employees;
    read all floors;
    compact();
    write all employees;
}
```

to merely having to code

```
main ()
{
    compact();
}
```

A persistent programming language is fundamentally very closely integrated with a specific language. Clearly, the persistence system must understand the specific data declarations of the target language. Thus, if someone is developing the *compact* routine in COBOL, then persistent COBOL is required and persistent C++ is completely useless. In short, one persistence system is required for each language.

Notice that our application has the following DBMS requirements:

Query Language. None is required for this application. If one exists, it serves no useful purpose.

Client Tools. The writer of *compact* is presumably using some sort of programming language tool kit such as those from ParcPlace, Microsoft, Symantec, or Java-Soft. Client tools need not be a major focus for a persistent storage company because typically the writer expects to obtain client tools from a programming language productivity company.

Performance. The fundamental performance problem that this application needs to solve is to keep up with a nonpersistent version. For example, if a user runs *compact* on "vanilla" C++ and handles storage management in the program, then the user obtains a certain performance. If the user moves *compact* on top of a persistent language, then the user wishes *compact* to run no more than, say, 10% slower than the nonpersistent case.

Security/Architecture. Keeping up with the execution speed of nonpersistent languages is a fundamental goal in persistent language architecture. As the following discussion illustrates, designers of persistent languages sometimes obtain required performance by giving up security.

If J is nonpersistent, then the following increment statement executes in one microsecond or less:

```
J = J + 1;
```

On the other hand, if J is persistent, then this statement becomes an update. If the storage system runs in a different address space from the user program, then an address space switch must occur to process this command. Because of the address space switch, the command will run perhaps two to three orders of magnitude slower than in the nonpersistent case. Such a performance hit is unacceptable to users, which is why persistent storage systems are designed to execute in the same address space as the user program, as shown in Figure 1.3. Note that the separate functionality shown in Figure 1.2 is collapsed into a single address space in Figure 1.3.

Avoiding an address space change provides much higher performance. However, it has one dramatic side effect. A malicious program can use operating system calls to read and write any data that the storage system is capable of reading or writing. Because read and write calls for both the program and the storage system run in the same address space, the operating system cannot distinguish them from a security perspective. As a result, any user program can read and write the entire database by going around the persistent storage system and dealing directly with the operating system. Clearly, no prudent database administrator ever stores sensitive material such as employee salaries in such an unsecured environment. For many applications that fit in the lower-right quadrant of the matrix, such as ECAD programs, this trade-off of security for speed is acceptable.

Some vendors have generalized the architecture of Figure 1.3 by decomposing the DBMS into two pieces as shown in Figure 1.4. A portion of the DBMS, along with a substantial cache of DBMS data, resides in the client program's address space. The rest of the DBMS deals with long-term data storage and runs as a separate process, perhaps on a separate machine. The cache is updated by communication between the two modules. As long as the client program "hits" the cache, high performance is obtained. On a cache miss, an address space switch occurs to bring needed data into the cache. When data is updated, then cache changes must be propagated back to the other process.

This generalization allows a security system to be implemented in the right-hand module, outside of the client program. However, the added communication between the two pieces of the DBMS can be expensive.

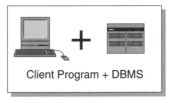

Client Program + DBMS

FIGURE 1.3   The Architecture of Persistent Languages

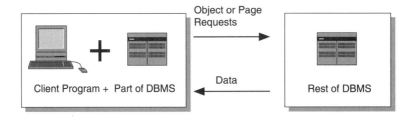

FIGURE 1.4   Generalization of Figure 1.3

Why doesn't this performance versus security discussion apply to relational DBMSs? There is a crucial difference between a persistent language world and a relational DBMS. In the persistent language world, updates are very "lightweight"; that is, they take very small amounts of time. The useful work in the example update

```
J = J + 1;
```

takes at most one microsecond. As a result, an address space switch requires orders of magnitude more time and is therefore prohibitively costly to implement on each update. In the relational world, updates involve locating and then modifying one or more records through a B-tree, which requires a substantial path length. Thus, updates are much "heavier" than in the persistent language world. The following SQL statement is a typical heavyweight update:

```
update emp
set salary = salary * 1.1
where startdate > '1980-12-31';
```

As a result, expressing updates in a low-level language such as C++ is fundamentally different from that in a high-level notation such as SQL. In C++ or any other third-generation programming language, updates are fundamentally lightweight; that is, they modify a single storage location. In this environment, an address space switch per update is prohibitive. In contrast, SQL updates are much heavier, and an address space crossing entailed by the client-server architecture is a less severe penalty.

The Players in the O Vendor Market: Still a Market Niche

Systems that focus on providing tight integration with a programming language and high performance for updates to persistent variables are known as object-oriented DBMSs. Such products are available for C++, Java, and Smalltalk from a collection of object-oriented DBMS vendors, such as Object Design, Objectivity, Versant, Computer Associates, and Ardent. This group is known collectively as the "O vendors."

Because they focus on programming language access to complex data, these systems can be placed in the lower-right quadrant of the matrix. In aggregate, the O vendors are generating about $150 million per year in revenue and are growing at a healthy rate. But this business remains a market niche in the database world and is nearly two orders of magnitude smaller than annual revenues for the relational vendors. Moreover, the market is not large enough to support all the current O vendors. Some will have to go out of business or find something else to do. The repositionings of both Gemstone and Ontos into different markets are examples of this trend.

Your DBMS choices here are quite easy. If you have an application in the lower-right quadrant, choose a vendor of a persistent language for your chosen programming language. That vendor is committed to the performance and features required in this corner of the matrix.

At this point, you might be wondering, "What happens if I have a lower-right quadrant application and I run it on a relational DBMS?" The answer is simple. Instead of being able to state

```
J = J + 1;
```

you have to express this command in SQL to a relational database. Because the C++ type system is much more elaborate than that of SQL, you have to simulate the C++ type system in SQL. This simulation is time-consuming to write and requires you to manually map your C++ variables into SQL on reads and writes. Moreover, you perform a heavyweight client-server address space crossing on most commands. As a result, the application runs very slowly. Put more directly, using a DBMS designed for one kind of application in a very different environment can result in serious problems. Relational systems essentially don't work on lower-right quadrant problems.

The opposite question also bears asking: "What happens if I have an upper-left quadrant problem and I run it on an object-oriented DBMS?" Again, the resulting application is not at all graceful. Some vendors have weak SQL systems and none support the SQL stored procedures in which most transaction processing is specified. So, you have to drop into a third-generation programming language to express your transactions, which results in a great deal more code. In addition, the products of the O vendors are typically not optimized for supporting hundreds, or even thousands, of concurrent updating users, and consequently performance tends to be very poor.

For example, object-oriented DBMSs obtain high performance in a persistent language environment by caching large numbers of objects in the address space of the client program. If there are N clients, then there are N caches. In a multi-user update-intensive environment such as TPC-C, cache coherency is a problem. When an update occurs in one cache, the DBMS must ensure that the data elements are found in all other caches and that they are either updated or invalidated. The conclusion to be made here is that aggressive user space caching is a performance enhancer in the lower-right quadrant, but a performance problem in the upper-left quadrant.

Some of the O vendors have recently focused on improving their transaction processing capabilities. In effect, they are moving their products to provide better multiquadrant support. Also, the relational vendors are moving to addressing persistent language issues in their environments. Therefore, in the future there will likely be better multiquadrant products.

1.5   *Quadrant 4: Complex Data with Queries*

The next application is query-oriented and requires complex data, making it representative of the upper-right quadrant of the matrix. The State of California Department of Water Resources (DWR) manages most of the waterways and irrigation canals in California, as well as a collection of aqueducts, including the massive state water project. To document their facilities, DWR maintains a library of 35-mm slides. Over time this library has grown to 500,000 slides and is accessed many times a day by DWR employees and others.

Typically, a client requests a picture by content. For example, an employee might need a picture of "the big lift," the massive pumping station that lifts northern California water over the Tehachapi Mountains into southern California. Other requests might include San Francisco Bay at sunset; Lake Cachuma, a Santa Barbara County reservoir with a low water level; or an endangered species of waterfowl on the banks of the American River.

DWR has found that it is very difficult to find slides by content. Indexing all the slides according to a predefined collection of concepts is a prohibitively expensive job. Moreover, the concepts in which clients are interested change over time. For example, interest in low reservoir levels grew during California's last drought. More recently, flood conditions in the San Joaquin Valley and elsewhere in the state have focused attention on images depicting high river levels.

DWR has a written caption about each slide, for example, "picture of Auburn Dam taken during scaffold construction." DWR also maintains a fairly primitive system that can identify slides from specified keywords. This keyword system is not operating very well because many concepts of interest are not mentioned in the caption and therefore are difficult to retrieve.

As a result, DWR is scanning the entire slide collection into digital form and is in the process of constructing the following database:

```
create table slides (
                id              int,
                date            date,
                caption         document,
                picture         photo_CD_image);

create table landmarks (
                name            varchar (30),
                location        point);
```

Each slide has an identifier, the date it was taken, a caption, and the digitized bits in Kodak Photo CD format. Photo CD format is a collection of five images ranging from a 128 byte × 192 byte thumbnail to the full 2 KB × 3 KB color image. DWR has digitized about 40,000 images and is well on its way to building a database, which will be around three terabytes in size (Ogle and Stonebraker 1995).

DWR is very interested in classifying their images electronically. As noted above, classifying them by hand is not practical. One of the attributes DWR wishes to capture is the geographic location of each slide. DWR's technique for accomplishing this geo-registration involves a public domain spatial database from the U.S. Geologic Survey. Specifically, they have the names of all landmarks that appear on any topographic map of California, along with the map location of the landmark. This is the table landmarks mentioned above. They propose to examine the caption for each slide to determine whether it contains the name of a landmark. If it does, the location of the landmark is a good guess for the geographic position of the slide.

In addition, DWR is also interested in writing image-understanding programs that will inspect an image and ascertain attributes of the image. For example, you can find a sunset in this particular slide library by looking for orange at the top of the picture. Low water in a reservoir entails looking for a blue object surrounded by a brown ring. Many attributes of a picture in which DWR has an interest can be found using fairly mundane pattern-matching techniques. Of course, some attributes are much more difficult, such as ascertaining whether the picture contains an endangered species. These harder attributes will have to wait for advances in pattern recognition.

The schema mentioned above contains a caption field that is a short document, a picture field that is a Photo CD image, and a location field that is of type geographic point. Because it has complex data, this example belongs on the right side of the matrix on page 2.

Moreover, the clients of DWR's database will submit ad hoc inquiries. One such inquiry is to find a sunset picture taken within 20 miles of Sacramento. Clients want a friendly interface that assists them in stating the following SQL query:

```
select id
from slides P, landmarks L, landmarks S
where sunset (P.picture) and
contains (P.caption, L.name) and
L.location || S.location and
S.name = 'Sacramento';
```

Here are the steps involved in making the query:

1. Find the geographic location of Sacramento (S.location) in the landmarks table.

2. Then, find other landmarks (L.location) that are within 20 miles of S.location. | | is a user-defined operator defined for two operands, each of type point, that returns true if the two points are within 20 miles of each other. This is the set of landmarks that can be used to ascertain if any appear in a caption of a picture.

3. The function *contains* is a user-defined function that accepts two arguments, a document and a keyword, and determines whether the keyword appears in the document. The function *contains* yields the set of pictures that are candidates for the result of the query.

4. Last, *sunset* is a second user-defined function that examines the bits in an image to see whether they have orange at the top. The net result of the query is the one desired by the client.

Obviously, this application entails "query mostly" on complex data. It is an example of an upper-right quadrant application. You might be inclined to think that object-relational applications are multimedia in nature from this example. But in fact, there are a wide variety of upper-right quadrant problems. In Chapter 2, Section 2.1, we present three additional examples that have a decidedly business-oriented flavor.

Here are the basic requirements for upper-right quadrant applications:

Query Language. Notice in the example query about Sacramento sunsets that there are four clauses in the predicate of the query. The first contains a user-defined function, *sunset*, and is thereby not in SQL-92. The second clause has a user-defined function *contains*. The third clause contains a user-defined operator, | |, which is not in SQL-92. Only the last clause is expressible in SQL-92. Upper-right quadrant applications require a query language that allows at least user-defined functions and operators. The first standard version of SQL with these capabilities is SQL-3, now in draft form. Any SQL-2 DBMS is useless on this application because three of the four clauses cannot be expressed in SQL-2.

Client Tools. DWR wants its application to display a map of the state of California. Then, the user can circle with a pointing device the area of the state that is of interest. On output, the user wants to see a map of Sacramento County with a thumbnail of each image positioned at its geographic location. With the ability to "pan" over the county, the user could examine thumbnails of interest. In addition, the user wants the capability to "zoom" into given areas to obtain the higher resolution images stored in Photo CD objects. Such a "pan and zoom" interface is typical of scientific visualization products such as Khoros (Rasure and Young 1992), Data Explorer (Lucas et al. 1992), and AVS (Upson 1989). DWR also wants a visualization system fully integrated with the DBMS. Notice that a standard 4GL is nearly useless on this application; there is not a business form in sight.

Performance. The user requires good performance for queries such as the Sacramento *sunset* query. These are typically decision support queries with significant predicates in them. To perform well in this environment, a collection of optimizations are required. For example, the *sunset* function often consumes 100 million or more instructions. As such, if the query optimizer ever sees a clause of the form

```
where sunset (image) and date < '1985-01-01'
```

it should perform the second clause first, thereby eliminating some of the images. Only if there is nothing else to do should the *sunset* function be evaluated. Being smart about functions that are expensive to compute is a requirement in the upper-right quadrant. Moreover, if many queries use the *sunset* function, then it will be desirable to precompute its value for every image. Therefore, you would execute the function once per image in the database, rather than once per query wanting sunsets. Automatically supporting precomputation on image insertions and updates is a very useful optimization tactic. Last, in order to find the landmarks within 20 miles of Sacramento, an efficient "point in circle" query is needed. Such two-dimensional queries cannot be accelerated by B-tree indexes, which are one-dimensional access methods. Traditional access methods (B-trees and hashing) are worthless on these sorts of clauses. To accelerate such spatial clauses, you need a spatial access method, such as a grid file (Nievergelt et al. 1984), R-tree (Gutman 1984), or K-D-B tree (Robinson 1981). A DBMS capable of handling these kinds of queries must either have such "object-specific access methods" or allow a sufficiently wise user or system integrator to add an access method. Obviously, the best technical answer is both.

Security/Architecture. Because upper-right quadrant applications require security, the DBMS should run in a client-server architecture as noted in Figure 1.2 on page 6. Security is rarely tradable for performance in this environment. Moreover, since this is a complex query world, the commands are very "heavy," and the performance win to relinquishing security is much less dramatic than in the lower-right quadrant.

The Players in the Object-Relational DBMS Market

DBMSs that support a dialect of SQL-3, include nontraditional tools, and optimize for complex SQL-3 queries are called object-relational DBMSs. They are relational because they support SQL; they are object-oriented because they support complex data. In essence they are a marriage of the SQL from the relational world and the modeling primitives from the object world. DBMSs that have these criteria are a fit for the upper-right corner of the matrix.

The early object-relational vendors were start-up companies that included Illustra, Omniscience, and UniSQL. In February 1996, Illustra was acquired by Informix, who immediately announced that the Informix relational DBMS would be combined with the Illustra server to create an object-relational engine. More recently, Oracle, IBM, and Sybase have announced aggressive plans for object-relational capabilities. In addition, some of the object vendors have been aggressively adding SQL engines to their products. Obviously, there is significant latent demand for object-relational capabilities; otherwise, the vendors would not have uniformly embraced the technology.

To explore the reasons for this level of interest, let's examine Illustra in a little more detail. In 1995 there were two market forces facing Illustra: customers wanted a server with object-relational features, but they also wanted it to be scalable with good transaction processing performance for their more standard enterprisewide database applications. Customers loved the Illustra technology for its ability to solve upper-right quadrant problems (complex data with queries). But they also had requirements for upper-left performance (simple data with queries). The result was a desire to deploy Illustra applications in enterprisewide mission-critical applications. However, customers were naturally leery of Illustra's ability to scale to enterprise-level environments (hundreds of users, hundreds of gigabytes, very high availability, etc.) and of its ability to provide good transaction processing performance in a large, high-use setting. Illustra did great on the upper-right quadrant—it could handle complex data with queries well—but it had never been optimized for the large enterprise environment. Thus, the twin considerations of scalability and transaction performance came up in most Illustra sales situations.

To abstract the situation, let's define an application that requires both upper-right and upper-left capabilities as a *universal application*. Customers with universal applications found Illustra's technology appealing but not a complete solution. In contrast, relational vendors also had a piece of the required solution, namely scalability and transaction performance, but lacked Illustra's object-relational features. When Informix approached Illustra in late 1995, it was clear immediately to both companies that they could produce a scalable object-relational engine with good transaction processing performance much more quickly by joining forces than either could by themselves. As a result, the desire to bring a product to market quickly that would support both upper-left and upper-right quadrant universal applications drove the merger of the two companies. A server with both relational and object-relational capabilities is commonly called a *universal server*. Universal applications and servers are illustrated in Figure 1.5.

In the next section we explore several examples of such universal applications.

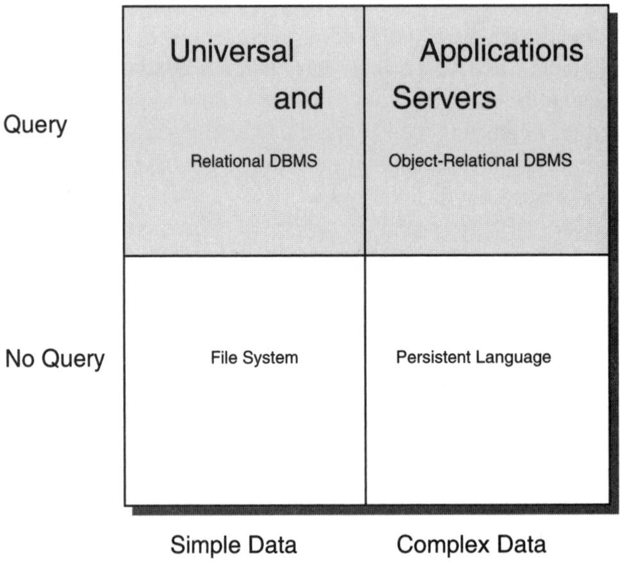

	Universal and	Applications Servers
Query	Relational DBMS	Object-Relational DBMS
No Query	File System	Persistent Language
	Simple Data	Complex Data

FIGURE 1.5   Universal Applications and Servers

1.6   *Universal Applications*

There are many problems that exhibit characteristics of the top two quadrants shown in Figure 1.5. This section discusses four examples.

Risk Assessment and Fraud Detection in the Insurance Industry

Consider a typical insurance company that has a customer database and a claims database, presumably implemented as a traditional business data processing application in a relational DBMS. To this application, the insurance company wants to add a diagram of each accident site, a scanned image of the police report, a picture of the dented car, the latitude and longitude of each accident site, and the latitude and longitude of each customer's home. The company has two goals that drive this extension: obtaining finer granularity risk assessment and fraud detection.

The insurance company wants to set rates for each customer based on the demographics and individual risk level of each customer, as denoted by the number of accidents on roads in the customer's neighborhood. Fraud detection can be implemented by examining the dented cars most like the one in an incoming claim and then computing if the proposed claim is out of line with those recorded for similar accidents.

The insurance application will have two major components:

- An upper-left component consisting of the standard business data processing functions, such as claim submission and customer processing.
- An upper-right component consisting of decision support queries on a mix of simple and complex data. These queries would deal with fraud detection, risk assessment, and other such matters.

This application has characteristics of both the upper-left and the upper-right quadrants.

Modernizing a Traditional Human Resources Application

As a second example, consider a traditional human resources (HR) application. It uses the emp table discussed earlier in Section 1.3. Servicing changes in employee benefits, status, and salaries has been a standard business application so far. However, an HR professional might wish to add the following data elements about each employee:

- The geographic position of the employee's home address, so that car pools can be formed
- The employee's resume, so that queries can be run by managers with open positions to see if there is an employee in the company with the appropriate skill set
- The employee's picture, so that security personnel can access the image of each employee and not have to rely on the thumbnail print typically found on the employee's badge

HR applications can add rich content to what has traditionally been a business data processing application. With the rich content comes the decision support applications such as resume searches and car pool clustering. Again, we see an application that requires both upper-left and upper-right quadrant services.

Multimedia and GIS Data Enhance Travel Reservation Systems

A third example is drawn from the travel industry. Traditionally, travel databases contain flight schedules and fare information and allow a travel agent to book space on a flight appropriate to the customer's requirements. Consider the future requirements of a vacation traveler. During the winter, the traveler wishes to take a one-week vacation in a warm sunny place. The traveler wants to stay in a room with an ocean view in a hotel that has a five-star Italian restaurant and a championship golf course within walking distance. Moreover, the traveler's total vacation budget is X

dollars. To satisfy this customer, the traditional travel database must be augmented with destination hotels, including their amenities, nearby attractions, and geographic position. In addition, the menu of the hotel restaurant and the view from sample hotel rooms must be captured. Again, rich content will be added to a traditional business application. The resulting decision support queries augment a traditional business workload, and the resulting application requires services in both of the upper quadrants.

The three examples discussed so far in this section are ones where rich content is added to a traditional business application, causing the application to move from the upper-left quadrant to become a universal application. The final example in this section illustrates another significant trend.

Removing the Mapping Layer: Tracking Part Numbers

Consider a typical collection of information used by a manufacturer of parts with multiple factories:

- Part number
- Commission schedule
- List of plants that manufacture a part
- Quantity on hand at each plant

In a relational database, this information is recorded as

```
part (part_number, commission)
plant (plant_number, part_number, quantity_on_hand)
```

Generally speaking, part_number is a highly encoded field, as illustrated in Figure 1.6.

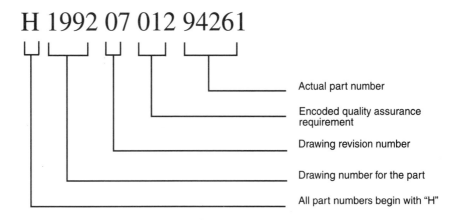

FIGURE 1.6   Example of a Highly Encoded Part Number

Many companies use an object model in their application environment to capture the detailed semantics of their application. A typical application model for parts might be

- Actual part number
- Commission schedule
- Reference to the drawing for the part
- Revision level
- Quality assurance requirement
- Set of references to (plant, quantity_on_hand) pairs

In this situation, the user must transform the application object model to and from the database relational model. This mapping is tedious and often causes performance problems.

It is common to implement such applications in a relational DBMS and to think of them as upper-left quadrant problems. However, in all probability they are really universal applications with a mix of simple and complex data that you access with SQL. Implementing such applications in a relational DBMS means you must write a mapping layer. This is a tedious task that may result in very bad performance. However, by treating the application as a universal application that needs SQL services on a mix of simple and complex data, the need for a simulation layer disappears and high performance is obtained.

In this section, you have seen four examples of universal applications. All resulted from adding complex data to business applications. The first three entailed adding new rich content while the last one became a universal application by removing an object simulation layer. With this backdrop, the next section explores the major forces that we see driving the future DBMS market.

1.7   *Technological Drivers in the DBMS Market*

We see two major forces driving the database market.

Force 1: Business data processing applications will largely become universal applications.

The examples in the previous section all illustrated universal applications either that need rich content, or that had an object model in the application and need to have mapping logic removed. Although, of course, there are business applications that have no need for rich content and do not have an application object model, we expect the majority of the current relational market to become a universal server market over the next decade. The early adopters with the largest needs in this area will lead this transition, followed by successive waves of applications (as explored in Moore 1995).

Force 2: New multimedia applications will drive the market.

Users are computerizing complex data at an astonishing rate. As noted above, the DWR application is scanning data not currently in electronic form. It is estimated that 85% of the world's useful information is not in electronic form. As significant amounts of this data are captured, they will generate a huge market for upper-right quadrant applications. For example, users are placing information on the World Wide Web at an incredible rate. Almost all Web applications have the same flavor as the DWR application (which incidentally is a Web application), namely, the wish to publish digital content using the Web as a transport mechanism. Queries are all ad hoc and typically to multimedia objects. Every Web site has a content creation, content management, and content access problem.

The Web, which was virtually nonexistent just four years ago, is one example of an explosive new market that will be query-oriented on complex data. A second example where rapid growth is occurring is digital film. Over the next decade conventional film may well disappear as a storage medium for data. This will occur at the high end in medical devices, such as X-ray and ultrasound systems, as well as at the low end in home photography. With a digital camera for snapshots, users generate a digital slide collection in computer storage. Then, to browse the collection or form a slide presentation for friends or family, you must run queries against complex data.

Digital slide management is an upper-right quadrant application with tens of millions of potential users.

A third example is the utilization of global positioning systems (GPS). Right now a GPS costs about $100 and is the size of a floppy disk drive. Expect both their footprint and cost to decrease quickly, which will allow GPS technology to be inserted in many information appliances, such as cellular phones. If a cellular phone is simultaneously equipped with a larger display and a programmable CPU, then it will be possible to run queries from a cellular phone. For example, a hungry traveler could use his cellular phone to ask if there is an Italian restaurant within five miles of his current position.

All of these examples are new applications where a user runs decision support queries to a database of content. That is, these are upper-right quadrant applications. Therefore, we see the following DBMS markets unfolding over time:

- A relational market, consisting of the business applications that have not yet moved to universal applications.
- A universal server market, consisting of applications that require both relational and object-relational services, i.e., the upper half of our 2×2 matrix. It will include the relational market that has added rich content or discarded their object-to-relational mapping layer as well as some new applications.
- An object-relational market, consisting of the primarily new applications in the upper-right quadrant.
- A persistent language market, consisting of the market for persistent programming languages.

Our best guess is that the relational market and the persistent language market will continue to be approximately their same relative size. That is, the relational market will remain about two orders of magnitude larger than the persistent language market. We expect there will be explosive growth in the two remaining markets, the object-relational market and the universal server market, as a result of the two market forces discussed in this section. Because both require a scalable object-relational engine, we will, for simplicity, lump them together and call them the object-relational market. As a result of forces 1 and 2, we expect the object-relational market, as just defined, to be bigger than the relational market by the year 2005. Therefore, Figure 1.7 gives our best guess of the relative sizes of the three markets at that time. The reason for the interest in the object-relational DBMSs by the relational vendors is now obvious. The universal server and object-relational markets are the future, and all relational vendors are moving there as quickly as

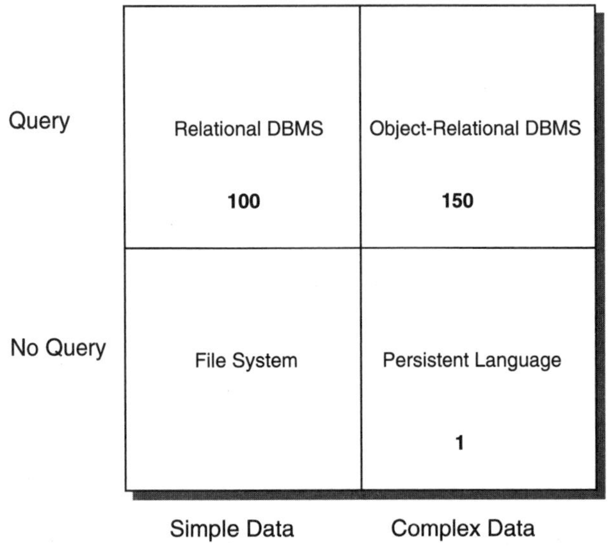

	Simple Data	Complex Data
Query	Relational DBMS **100**	Object-Relational DBMS **150**
No Query	File System	Persistent Language **1**

FIGURE 1.7　Relative Size of DBMS Markets in Year 2005

possible. Moreover, this also explains the recent interest in SQL and transaction support by several O vendors.

1.8　*Summary*

As previously noted, universal servers and object-relational DBMSs will be the largest database market by the year 2005. They will be the next great wave. All the relational DBMS vendors realize exactly this point and are scrambling to include object-relational capabilities. Additionally, several O vendors are also moving in this direction. Informix saw this trend early on and made a tender offer for Illustra. Illustra realized that they had an excellent object-relational engine, but lacked the scalability and high online transaction processing (OLTP) performance required by universal applications. Hence, they had part of the answer, and Informix had the other part. Both companies realized that they could produce the DBMS required by universal applications by joining forces much faster than either company could do on its own.

CHAPTER 2

Characteristic 1: Base Data Type Extension

This chapter discusses extensible base data types, the first of the four fundamental characteristics of an object-relational DBMS listed in the Preface, and explains why extensible base data types are invaluable for solving upper-right quadrant applications. Three simple example applications in this chapter show how problems that are difficult to deal with in SQL-92 can be easily handled using base type extension. This chapter also explores the mechanism for defining new data types, how to define new operations on data types, and the requirements for a system to be considered fully object-relational in terms of base data type extension.

2.1 Need for Base Type Extension

SQL-92 restricts a table column to one of the following data types:

- Integer
- Floating-point number
- Character string, fixed or variable length
- Date, time, datetime, interval
- Numeric and decimal

Additionally, SQL-92 defines a precise (and hard-coded) collection of functions and operators that are available for each data type. For example, the standard arithmetic and comparison operators are available for integers using the conventional notation. However, it is not possible to easily perform other, more interesting operations such as counting the number of zeros in an integer, or determining if an integer is divisible by some number, because these operations are not defined in SQL-92.

Because SQL's set of data types and operations is limited, many real-world problems are extremely difficult to code and, once coded, perform badly. This section presents three such examples.

Example 1: A Calendar for the Bond Market

The first example is a bond market application. It concerns an actual application developed by an Ingres user. At the time, Ingres (now a division of Computer Associates) had recently released a version of its DBMS that supported date and time as a data type. An Ingres user, who had patiently waited for this new functionality, called the Ingres consulting staff in a rage, saying that Ingres had implemented date and time incorrectly.

Here is a simple version of the user's application and the reason for his agitation. Consider the following (simplified) table that holds a portion of a financial portfolio:

```
create table Bond (
                bond_id        integer,
                coupon_rate    float,
                face_value     decimal(10,2),
                bought         date,
                matures        date,
                value          decimal(10,2));
```

This table holds a bond portfolio, giving an ID for each bond, the rate that the bond pays, the bond's face value, the date it was purchased, and the date it matures. The irate Ingres user was required to compute the last field in the table, which is the value of the bond to the current holder. This value is the sum of its face value and the interest that accrues from the purchase date to the bond's maturity date.

The customer ran the following SQL command to find the bond value:

```
update bond
    set value = face_value + coupon_rate * (matures - bought)
```

When he ran this command, the Ingres system implemented date subtraction according to the Gregorian calendar. (Using the Gregorian calendar, March 15th minus February 15th is 28 days. During leap years it is 29 days.) In other words, the exact semantics of the date data type were really Gregorian dates because all the SQL operators on the type utilized this calendar.

Unfortunately, the bond market in the United States does not use the Gregorian calendar! Instead, a bondholder receives the same amount of interest on a financial bond during each month, regardless of how long the month is. In other words, the monthly coupon is a constant and does not vary with the length of the month. This special Wall Street calendar is integral to the U.S. bond market. (However, it is not universal; most foreign bond markets use the Gregorian calendar.)

The reason for the user's anger became apparent soon enough. The above SQL statement does not calculate the correct value because it is operating on the wrong calendar. What the user wanted was a definition of date subtraction that obeyed the calendar used on Wall Street. In fact, according to this calendar, March 15th minus February 15th is always 30 days, and each year is composed of 12 equal-length months, each of 30 days.

From his point of view, Ingres had implemented date incorrectly. More accurately, he wanted bond dates and Ingres had implemented Gregorian dates. Because the date type operated incorrectly, he could not use the SQL command shown above. Instead, he had to write his own date subtraction function. Then, he had to retrieve the two dates and the coupon rate from the database, call his function in user space to perform the correct subtraction, and then put the correct rate back in the database. His lament concerning this solution was twofold:

1. *Unacceptable pain for the developer:* Every time the user required a calculation on dates, he had to do it in user code. This essentially turned every SQL command into a program. Moreover, the client had to manage the library of bond time functions himself.

The irate user's request to Ingres was, "Why can't I replace the Ingres date subtraction routine with my own?" Of course, Ingres at the time was not architected to allow this functionality, and the answer was that it could not be done. Abstracting this example a little, the user was really asking for the ability to create new data types with their corresponding operators and functions within an SQL context. This capability is called "base type extension."

2. *Unacceptable application performance:* The user's application was more than a factor of three slower than the corresponding Gregorian date application. This resulted from the necessity of retrieving data across the client-server boundary and controlling the iteration through the bond table from an application. Chapter 13 uses this situation as an example of the performance problems caused by having to simulate data types in an application or in middleware.

Example 2: Alphabetizing Non-ASCII Characters

Consider a version of the traditional emp table, as follows:

```
create table emp   (
                name            varchar(30),
                startdate       date,
                salary          int);
```

And, suppose you want to run the following command:

```
select name, salary
from emp
where name > 'McT' and name < 'McU'
order by ascending name;
```

The command requests the salaries of a group of employees within a specific alphabetic range. For a U.S. implementor, this command presents no difficulties. Because the collating sequence for ASCII is the same as for U.S. names, the correct employees will be identified and then sorted into the proper order.

Unfortunately, names in other countries do not necessarily sort according to ASCII. For example, in French, names can have acute accents, grave accents, and circumflexes over certain letters. "E" with an acute accent is not in the ASCII character set. Therefore French names cannot be represented directly in ASCII. If you use a nonprinting character for "E" with an acute accent, it will be grouped with the nonprinting characters and not the "E"s. In other words, the above query will not give the correct answer for French names. The same comment applies for German names, Israeli names, names from most Arabic countries, Japanese names, and Chinese names. In fact, ASCII is only appropriate for names from certain English-speaking countries.

To better support international character strings, facilities were added to SQL-92 to define alternate character sets and alternate collating sequences. These capabilities adequately support many European names. However, most Asian and some European character strings remain problematic. A simple illustration of this issue can be seen by opening the pages of the phone book in Edinburgh, Scotland. There, you will find (for example) that the names McTavish, MacTavish, and M'Tavish are all collated together. These are all variations on the same name, and for sorting purposes, the apostrophe character, "c," and "ac" are considered nulls when they follow an initial "M." Thus, all three variations of the clan's name appear in the phone book along with other names beginning with "MT." This important context sensitivity is not addressed by SQL-92. Simulating the data type "Scottish name" is tedious. You must map "M'," "Mc," and "Mac" into three adjacent ASCII characters. This means remapping all characters so that the sort sequence of the resulting simulation is the proper one for Scottish names.

Of even more significance, the SQL command mentioned above will probably use a B-tree lookup to identify the appropriate employees. B-trees will find all employees who are in collating sequence between "McT" and "McU." The query execution engine will only work correctly with B-tree indexes if the user maps both "McT" and "McU" to their simulated values.

Again, writing the simulation is tedious. Moreover, it is slow because every name must be mapped, character by character, when it enters the DBMS and when it leaves the DBMS. We explore the performance of this application in detail in Chapter 13.

Example 3: A Car Pool

The final example concerns geography. Suppose you want to write a program to manage car pool activity for the employees in a company. You have employee data in an SQL-92 database system, which is illustrated by the following table:

```
create table emp(
            name          varchar(30),
            startdate     date,
            salary        int,
            address       varchar(30),
            city          varchar(30),
            state         char(2),
            zipcode       int);
```

Obviously, candidates for car pools are those who live in the same neighborhood and have a desire to share a ride. Each employee's mailing address is available in the table: the street address, city, state, and ZIP code. Using the city field in the table emp, the car pool program can try to match prospective riders who live in the same city. If Sam lives in Fresno, then the car pool candidates for Sam can be found by the following query:

```
select name
from emp
where city = 'Fresno';
```

This will not be a very precise implementation because some cities are very large (for example, Los Angeles) and some are very irregular in shape (for example, New York with its five boroughs).

Alternatively, the program could match riders' ZIP codes. However, ZIP code regions are rather small for a car pool application and are also quite irregular. With substantial extra effort, you can record some sort of adjacency information for ZIP codes that allows the program to search neighboring regions.

But the best solution is to record the geographic position of each employee's home as a (latitude, longitude) point. Then, the car pool program can find neighboring employees as those employees who live within any given distance of each other, where distance is measured "as the crow flies."

With an SQL-92 system, you can add two numbers to the example table as follows:

```
alter table emp add column lat float;
alter table emp add column long float;
```

Here (lat, long) are the coordinates of an employee's home address. Next, suppose you wished to identify prospective car pool candidates for any given employee as those people living close by. ("Close by" will be defined as living within one mile.) The following SQL-92 query identifies the desired car pool candidates for a given employee, Joe:

```
select r.name
from emp j, emp r
where j.name = 'Joe' and
(j.long - r.long) ** 2  + (j.lat - r.lat) ** 2 < 1;
```

There are two (by now very familiar) problems with this SQL-92 statement: unacceptable pain for the developer and unacceptable application performance.

In the unacceptable pain for the developer category, the "close by" calculation is somewhat complex to implement, especially for a novice programmer, and the resulting SQL is not intuitive. As a result, new programmers will take a while to come up to speed on this application.

After the query execution engine finds Joe and returns Joe's longitude and latitude, it must find all employees that satisfy the second clause. This calculation is sufficiently complex that no indexing will be used, and a sequential search of all employees is required. Sequential searching slows performance in almost all cases. Last, performing detailed arithmetic in SQL is much slower than the corresponding calculations in a third-generation programming language, such as C, C++, or Java. These factors lead to unacceptable performance.

The basic problem here is the necessity of simulating the data type "geographic point" in SQL-92. Because it is not an SQL-92 data type, it must be simulated by using two numbers (lat and long). Moreover, an operation is needed to find points that lie within a designated circle. And, because this operation is not in SQL-92, it must be simulated by coding a collection of numeric operations. This simulation is sufficiently complex that the query optimizer cannot execute the resulting query efficiently.

You have just read three examples that share a common theme. They all entail data types and operations that are not in SQL-92. In each of these examples, simulating the required functionality in SQL-92 is painfully difficult to code and results in very poor performance.

The remainder of this chapter discusses extensible base types, a solution to both of these problems. The examples in the rest of the chapter use the OR SQL type extension system as noted in the Preface.

2.2   *A Better Way: Extensible Data Types*

The extensible data types available in an object-relational DBMS eliminate the awkward type simulations that cause efficiency problems. For example, the car pool application described earlier in this chapter can be neatly streamlined with extensible data types, as shown below.

Informix packages a collection of data types, their associated functions and operators, and access methods into *DataBlade modules*, using the metaphor that the DBMS is a razor into which DataBlade modules are inserted. (Oracle uses the term *cartridge* to describe a similar concept, and IBM, the term *extender*.) One of the Informix DataBlade modules supports 2-D geometric objects and contains a 2-D point data type, in addition to lines, polygons, ellipses, circles, and many other 2-D types. (Of course users are also free to construct their own types and functions.) By using the point data type, you can add the following attribute to the car pool application's emp table:

```
alter table emp add column location point;
```

The point data type encodes a 2-D point by recording a pair of floating-point numbers. Included in the 2-D Spatial DataBlade module is a function that determines the distance from one point to another and one that constructs a circle, given a point as the center and a number for the radius. With the types and functions in the Informix universal server 2-D DataBlade module, you can recode the car pool query in OR SQL as follows:

```
select r.name
from emp j, emp r
where j.name = 'Joe' and
distance (j.location, r.location) < 1;
```

This query is more understandable and more accessible to a novice programmer than the SQL-92 statement discussed earlier. Moreover, instead of a B-tree as an access method, the Informix universal server 2-D Spatial DataBlade module uses an R-tree (Gutman 1984), which is much more efficient for this application. All told, query execution for this application is dramatically faster than that for an SQL-92 system. Similar improvements in performance and development time are available in the other two example applications by using extensible base data types.

The next section in this chapter describes how you can create your own base data types. (For query optimization, there are steps a user needs to take when defining a new type. This discussion is deferred until Chapter 10.)

Creation of Base Data Types

In an object-relational DBMS, you create a new base data type by indicating the name of the type and some storage information about the type. Here is an example of the creation of a new base data type, called mytype_t:

```
create type mytype_t (
                    internallength = 8);
);
```

Internallength indicates that eight bytes are to be allocated to store each instance of the type. Then, you can create a table that uses the new mytype_t as follows:

```
create table my_table (
                    name       varchar(30),
                    some_data mytype_t);
```

To use this new type, you must also specify how instances of *literals* are converted to instances of the new type. This is handled with a cast that instructs the server to invoke a user-defined function to make the conversion.

```
create cast (varchar to mytype_t) as myTypeInput;
create cast (mytype_t to varchar) as myTypeOutput;
```

The purpose of these functions can be best illustrated by considering an integer example. Suppose an employee, Jane, is assigned a salary of $10,000 as follows:

```
update emp
set salary = 10000
where name = 'Jane';
```

In this SQL statement, notice that the value 10000 is five ASCII characters (1,0,0,0,0) and is 40 bits long. A traditional SQL engine will automatically call the built-in function, ASCII-to-INT, to convert the 40-bit representation into a 32-bit quantity in integer representation for internal storage. Suppose you run another command from an interactive terminal monitor, for example,

```
select salary
from emp
where name = 'Jane';
```

On disk, Jane's salary is stored as a 32-bit integer consisting of 18 leading zeros and then 10011100010000. To display this value on the user's screen, a traditional SQL system will call another built-in function, INT-to-ASCII, to convert the value to an ASCII representation. SQL-92 data types have hard-wired input and output functions to convert between ASCII and the disk representation of the type. In essence, each type has an external (ASCII) representation and an internal (stored) representation.

In an extensible type system, instead of hard-coded routines to move values between internal and external format, the definer of a new type specifies the conversion routines (cast functions) to be used to move to and from character string representation.

These conversion routines allow wide flexibility on how values are managed. It is possible for the input and output routines to do nothing. If this is the case, the internal and external representations are the same. For example, internal and external representations are the same for the varchar data type, and the conversion routines are not required. It is also possible for conversion routines to perform an arbitrary transformation. For instance, you can define an encoded data type that encrypts each value before it is stored. The encryption algorithm can be implemented in the input routine while the decryption occurs in the output function.

It is also possible to define data types that include constraints. For example, for determining a pool of potential retirees, it might be required that an employee have an employment start date greater than January 1, 1950, so that the data type start-date cannot have legal values outside of this bound. Conversion routines are a natural place to insert such arbitrary checks on values for the data type. In this case, the input conversion routine can easily perform such integrity checks and reject inappropriate start dates.

Last, more exotic transformations are also possible. You can use the input routine to store the actual value external to the DBMS, say, in the file system or on a nontraditional storage medium. Then, you can store some sort of identifier of the actual value in the allocated space in the table. Simple examples of this methodology include "file as a data type" or "moniker as a data type."

At this point, you might be wondering what the relationship is between domains in a relational system and data types in an object-relational system. In an object-relational system, a data type is defined as a stored representation of a particular kind of information together with the appropriate operators and functions for the information. In other words, a data type is both information and operations. In contrast, the relational notion of a domain includes only the stored representation, and there is no behavior associated with a domain.

The flexibility of object-relational type systems makes them an extremely powerful means to model complex database applications. But by themselves, new data types are not very useful unless you can perform operations on instances of the type. The rest of this chapter provides the remaining piece of the extensible data type puzzle—how you can define operations on the type.

2.3   *User-Defined Functions and Operators*

In a traditional SQL system, arithmetic and comparison operators are available for arithmetic data types. For user-defined types, you must be able to add type-specific operations. This requires an extension capability for functions and operators.

In an object-relational DBMS, you can write functions in either OR SQL or a general-purpose third-generation programming language such as C and then register them with the system. Over time, it will be possible to write functions in a variety of languages such as Visual Basic and Java. To register a function, you must indicate the name for the function, its arguments, its return type, and the code to execute for the function. The format of this command is

```
create  function function-name (type_info_1, type_info_2,...,
type_info_k)
returning type-name
as
["External Filename" or "database expression"]
language [routine language];
```

For example, you can specify a very simple *hourly_pay* function that divides an annual salary by the 2000 hours in a year:

```
create function hourly_pay (int Arg1)
returning float
as
select Arg1/2000;
```

Here the function *hourly_pay* accepts an integer argument and returns a float. The actual computation is expressed in SQL as the argument, Arg1, which is presumably the annual salary of an employee, divided by 2000 (the number of hours worked in a year). The function *hourly_pay* can now be freely used in any query, for example,

```
select name
from emp
where hourly_pay(salary) > 12.50;
```

At runtime, an object-relational server substitutes the definition of the function into the query to produce the following query, which is actually executed:

```
select name
from emp
where salary/2000 > 12.50;
```

Thus, functions written in SQL are *unwound* during query execution. Use of such functions simplifies user queries and results in no performance degradation. Here is a slightly more complex function, *salary_diff_Joe*, that returns the difference between a given employee's salary and that of Joe:

```
create function salary_diff_Joe (int Arg1)
returns int
as
select Arg1 - salary
from emp
where name = 'Joe';
```

Again, you can freely use *salary_diff_Joe* in a query, for example:

```
select salary_diff_Joe (e.salary)
from emp e
where e.name = 'Fred';
```

Like all SQL functions, this one is unwound during query execution to

```
select f.salary - e.salary
from emp e, emp f
where e.name = 'Fred' and
f.name = 'Joe';
```

You can also write user-defined functions in C. Here is a more complex function, *vesting*, that determines the percentage of an employee's stock option that has vested. The following pseudocode specifies monthly vesting over five years. (Note that the actual vesting calculation does not kick in until the employee has worked for one year.)

```
float vesting (startdate)
{
compute result = current_date - startdate;
convert result to months;
if result < 12 months return 0;
else return result/60;
}
```

If the above function is compiled and the executable result stored in the file foo, you can then register this function using the following statement:

```
create function vesting (date)
returns float
as external name 'foo'
language C;
```

With this definition in place, you can again use the function in an OR SQL statement:

```
select name
from emp
where vesting(startdate) > 0.6;
```

Execution of user-defined functions written in C differs from the execution of those written in OR SQL. C functions are "opaque" and cannot be unwound by the execution engine. Instead, the C function must be called by the execution engine during query processing. In fact, the Informix universal server dynamically loads the code for the function during execution in the server process. Also, there are other pieces of information specified at function registration time that deal with query processing. Discussion of these is deferred to Chapter 10.

Next, we examine user-defined operators. Notice that traditional SQL supports a considerable collection of operators. For example, the comparison operators { <, <=, =, >=, >, <>} are defined for both integers and floats. Syntactically, an operator is a function with two arguments and the operator name appears in between its arguments. For example, consider the query

```
select name
from emp
where salary > 10000;
```

Here, > takes two integers as arguments and returns a Boolean. The above query is equivalent to

```
select name
from emp
where GreaterThan (salary, 10000);
```

Thus, an operator in SQL is really a special kind of function that has two arguments and uses a different notation. A more complex example dealing with a new data type is now presented. Return now to the car pool example for Joe, first introduced on page 31:

```
select r.name
from emp, emp r
where emp.name = 'Joe' and
distance (emp.location, r.location) < 1;
```

This query can also be expressed as

```
select r.name
from emp, emp r
where emp.name = 'Joe' and
contained (r.location, circle (emp.location, 1));
```

Here, a circle of radius one mile around a center of Joe's location is first constructed. Then, the outer function, *contained*, finds the points that are inside this circle. The outer function takes two arguments, a point and a circle, and returns a Boolean. Notationally, the function is to the left of its arguments, which are delineated using parentheses. Alternatively, the following operator notation could be used:

```
select r.name
from emp, emp r
where emp.name = 'Joe' and
r.location << circle (emp.location, 1);
```

Here, the token << represents the operator notation corresponding to the function *contained*.

Support for User-Defined Operators

Traditional SQL has a fairly rich set of operators as well as a few functions, for example, *sum* and *like*. You saw in the discussion above how to define functions for new data types. How are user-defined operators supported? Recall the GreaterThan example in the previous section. In that example, the object-relational DBMS takes the > operator and calls its internal *GreaterThan* function to perform a compare of two values in a query. To support a new operator, you simply create a new function with appropriate semantics and then bind it to an operator token. The object-relational DBMS will invoke the function when required.

In OR SQL, you use the **create operator** command to register operators, namely,

```
create operator
binding oper-name
to function-name;
```

This section concludes by indicating how functions relate to database procedures in relational systems. Basically, a database procedure is a collection of SQL statements with other statements interspersed in a vendor-proprietary programming language. Database procedures were pioneered by Britton-Lee as a performance enhancement for transaction processing applications and subsequently adopted by all major relational vendors. Using traditional SQL, the TPC-A benchmark is five commands that result in 10 messages between client and server processes (Gray 1993). With a database procedure defined on the server, the user merely executes it and only two messages are required. Thus, a database procedure is merely a function written in a vendor-specific language. Like functions, a database procedure can take arguments and results in code activation on the server. Unlike functions, database procedures can only be executed; they cannot appear in the predicate or target list of a user command. Therefore, they are very restrictive user-defined functions.

User-Defined Aggregates

Besides functions and operators, there is another computation facility in SQL, *aggregates*. In SQL-92, there are five aggregate operators: count, sum, max, min, and avg. By using aggregates, you can find the average employee salary:

```
select avg(salary)
from emp;
```

Unfortunately SQL aggregates are worthless if you want some other calculation over a set of values. Useful possibilities *not* in SQL-92 include

- the median employee salary
- the second largest employee salary
- the standard deviation of employee salaries
- the average employee salary, discarding values that are outliers, that is, more than two standard deviations away from the mean

If you want one of these more general aggregation calculations, you must retrieve the collection of values of interest to a user program and do the computation yourself. This is error prone, in addition to creating a serious performance bottleneck because a large data set must be transmitted over a client-server connection.

A better solution is to support user-defined aggregates inside the DBMS. To show what is required, we will discuss how an SQL-92 system deals with the average employee salary described above. There are three distinct steps:

1. *Initialization:* Before the first salary is examined, the computation must be initialized. This is accomplished by declaring two variables, count and sum, and setting them to zero.
2. *Iteration:* The following calculation must be performed on each salary:
   ```
   count = count + 1;
   sum = sum + current_salary;
   ```
3. *Finalization:* After the last salary is read, the final value of the aggregate must be computed as
   ```
   value = sum/count;
   ```

It should now be clear that in order to support user-defined aggregates, an OR SQL system must allow users to define three functions:

```
intialize ( ) returns state

iterate (value, state) returns state

finalize (state) returns output
```

With these three functions in place, an OR SQL system merely needs to call the *initialize* function before a scan of the collection of values. (Remember the state that is returned.) Then, it calls the *iterate* function for each tuple processed, passing data from the tuple and receiving a new state in return; and last, the system calls the *finalize* function to produce the actual value for the aggregate.

And, with this logic in place, a user can define a new aggregate by defining the three functions required using the **create function** command noted earlier. State, value, and output can be any data types understood by an OR SQL system. Here is a definition of a median aggregate for the integer data type:

```
create aggregate median (integer) returns (integer) as
initialize = my_func_1,
iterate = my_func_2,
finalize - my_func_3;
```

Of course, the most obvious applications for user-defined aggregates are in the fields of decision support systems and data warehousing. Many companies have developed algorithms for analyzing large data sets to produce summaries. At the moment, these algorithms run as client programs that stream data out of the DBMS. Introducing these algorithms into the DBMS as user-defined aggregates would improve the performance of these tools and enhance their flexibility by making all of the ad hoc facilities of SQL available to them.

2.4   *Fully Object-Relational Type Extension*

The previous sections discussed the concepts of user-defined types and their associated functions, operators, and aggregates. This section suggests specific features that a system must support in order to be *fully* object-relational in terms of base type extension.

Feature 1: Dynamic Linking

A good object-relational DBMS dynamically links user-defined functions so that they are not in the DBMS address space until they are needed. The following paragraphs explain why this requirement is so important. In a good object-relational

DBMS, it must be easy for the user to add a new data type, operator, or function. Having to take the system down to install a new type or function means that installation must be scheduled, sometimes days in advance, with a central system administrator. As a result, static linking is highly inconvenient for users.

User-defined functions are often refined over time by the developer. When this occurs, the function must be redefined to the DBMS. If the DBMS performs static linking of functions, then the DBMS must be taken down, relinked, and reinstalled. Taking the system down and rebuilding it is a heavy penalty to pay for an algorithm improvement.

A typical object-relational DBMS installation is expected to have a substantial number of user-defined functions. If they are statically linked in the DBMS address space at the time the DBMS is installed, then the "footprint" of the DBMS is enormous. It is plausible for the size of the DBMS to increase by a factor of 5, or even 10, as a result of static linking of a big library of user-defined functions. This is especially true for pattern recognition and image understanding functions, which are both numerous and large. In most operating systems there is additional operating system overhead and paging activity as the footprint increases. And, if the footprint becomes too large, some operating systems will actually "choke."

Thus, for reasons that range from operating system performance to user convenience, a good object-relational DBMS dynamically links user-defined functions.

Feature 2: Client or Server Activation

A second required feature concerns where the function is activated. An obvious option is to activate a function on the server in the same address space as the DBMS. Consider the function *contained* from the above example (page 39). In this case, it must be called for a collection of possibly qualifying emp records and be passed an instance of a point and a circle. If the function is activated in the same process as the DBMS, then this activation is a local procedure call and there is little overhead to the call.

On the other hand, if the function runs in a different address space or on a different machine, then a remote procedure call (RPC) must be used and the arguments copied to a different address space. The overhead of a remote procedure call is substantial, and performance will degrade significantly in this case. Simply put, if the cost of executing a function and/or copying the arguments is not large when compared with the cost of an RPC, then the RPC will add significant overhead. If the function is called many times, then performance will degrade badly.

In contrast, consider a function that is very expensive to compute, such as the *sunset* function mentioned in Chapter 1. This function may consume 100 million or more CPU cycles per invocation, and the cost of an RPC is lost in the noise relative to function execution. In this case, it is possible to run the function in a separate address space or on a separate machine without disastrous consequences. Moreover, if the server is executing work on behalf of many clients, then it may make sense to activate computationally intensive functions on the user's desktop machine, where large numbers of cycles are readily available. In this case, activation of functions in the address space of the client program is most desirable. There are, however, two additional considerations.

First, there are environments where you might be running a very lightweight client and a very heavyweight server. For example, in video-on-demand applications it is essential to use the cheapest possible computer as a set-top box in order to keep the cost of the box in line for the home customer. Second, the "head-end" machine is a very powerful multiprocessor since it must be able to play multiple video streams simultaneously. In this situation, server-side activation is appropriate for most functions.

The second consideration concerns bandwidth. Return to the *sunset* function introduced in Chapter 1. In this example, the argument to the function may be a 2 KB $\times$ 3 KB color image. Even in compressed form, this may be a megabyte or more in size. If client activation of the *sunset* function is used, then this amount of data will be copied from the server to the client. Depending on the speed and cost of the network connection between the client and the server, this may (or may not) be a serious problem. If the client and server are connected by FDDI or ethernet, then it may be reasonable to pay the cost of a megabyte transmission to move the sunset computation from the server to the client. On the other hand, if the client and server are connected by a lower speed network or even the Internet, then client activation will be very problematic.

In conclusion, both server-side and client-side activation can make sense, depending on the particular application. A good object-relational DBMS supports both options. In addition, it may be desirable to switch back and forth as machine speeds, load, and network connectivity change over the life of an application.

Because the performance consequences of the client or server function activation are so great, we further explore this topic in Chapter 13. There, we present several detailed scenarios and time client and server activation for the Informix universal server.

Feature 3: Integration with Middleware

There has been a great deal of debate at trade conferences regarding thin clients versus thick clients and where to locate business logic in a processing hierarchy. Some believe that logic should be executed on the client desktop (thick client), while others believe it should be executed in a middleware layer between the client and the bottom tier, which is the DBMS (i.e., thin client—or thick middleware). Although the debate is currently heated and there is clearly a trend toward thin clients, we will complicate the picture in this section.

An object-relational DBMS allows business logic to be run inside the DBMS at the bottom tier of the hierarchy. Using DataBlade technology, it is now possible to support a thick database to complement thick client and thick middleware.

A moment's reflection should convince you that there are situations where each one is desirable. Business logic exists that is very "datacentric"; that is, it is optimized if run as close to the data as possible. An extreme example of such a module would be a data-mining algorithm that paws over a great deal of data looking for patterns and then outputs a summary data structure to a user. A second example is a statistical function that reads a great deal of data and then generates a statistical computation. Such logic will be optimized by execution inside the DBMS as a DataBlade module.

Other business logic interacts intensively with the screen and will be optimized if run as close to the client as possible, that is, as thick client. An example of such a function is one that does interactive data cleaning by prompting the user for help. Another example would be a display function that converts an object into a bitmap for presentation on the screen. This latter computation reads a small object and produces a big one; hence it is optimized by placement on the client.

Finally, there are functions that are best deployed in a middle tier. They often have a large footprint or will be shared by a large number of users, or both. In this case, a middleware server, which multithreads the execution of many clients using a single copy of the logic, will be advantageous. Client machines may not be large enough to run the business logic; moreover, a significant number can share a single copy on a shared machine.

Thus, thick client, thick middleware, and thick DBMS all make sense, depending on the circumstances. Moreover, circumstances may change; hence it is essential to be able to move extensions from DBMS to middleware to client and back. And, it must be possible to do this without rewriting the extension. Some tool kits, such as Forte, support transparent movement of logic among the top two levels; this concept must be extended to all three levels.

Specifically, the DBMS must provide a DataBlade developer's kit with the following capability: It must be possible for a user to write business logic once and have the tool compile the logic for thick database as a DataBlade or compile it with an OLE or CORBA wrapper, so that it can be called by popular middleware or client tool kits. With such a tool, seamless movement among all three levels is supported.

Because the topic of middleware is so important, we have dedicated part of Chapter 13 and all of Chapter 15 to it.

Feature 4: Security

With server-side activation there is always the danger that, when users define their own functions, they can accidentally (or intentionally) create a security loophole by reading or writing over database data. It is imperative that a system supporting server-side activation preempt this security risk.

If client-side activation is used, then the function runs in a process with the client's user ID. If server-side activation is used, then the function runs in a process with the DBMS's user ID. Consider a function that is not completely debugged and executes an illegal instruction or makes a jump to a nonexistent address. If client-side activation is in place, then the client process will crash, an annoying but contained event. However, if server-side activation is used, then the DBMS process will crash, perhaps disrupting a whole community of users attached to that system.

And if the client crashes, clearly the problem lies with the user's code. However, if the server crashes, then it is not so obvious whether the problem lies with the DBMS or with a user function. This ambiguity is heightened in the case that the function makes a jump that lands in the DBMS code segment, making it even more difficult to isolate the source of the problem. Because the DBMS is not supposed to have control, it will crash, even though the problem actually lies with the user function.

More ominously, consider the case that the function is malicious. With client-side activation, a function can read (and/or destroy) any data that is readable or writable by the client. This, in itself, is a security problem. However, it is far more serious if server-side activation is used. In this case, the function can read and destroy all the data in the database. The reason for this is that all DBMS data is placed in files that are readable and writable by the DBMS process. With server-side activation the database administrator must trust that user-defined functions are not malicious. In many environments this level of trust is not reasonable.

It is imperative that a system supporting server-side activation be able to plug this security loophole, and four techniques are available. First, server-side functions can be activated in a process separate from the DBMS. In this case, the function can be run in an address space with a user identification different from the DBMS. This solves the security problem, but reintroduces the necessity of a remote procedure call and its associated overhead, meaning that although secure, the functions will be slow.

Alternatively, you can use a technique called *firewalls*. In this case, a program performs the firewalling by examining the object code of the user's function. If the program finds any jumps in the code or any system calls, it modifies the user's program to be safe. The jumps can be runtime checked with extra code inserted into the user program to ensure that they do not go outside the region occupied by the code. System calls can be disallowed by causing them to generate runtime exceptions. Using this technique, the resulting program can be guaranteed to have no security problems. Firewalling offers minimal degradation of performance, providing security at a much lower price than running the function in a separate server address space. Further information on firewalling can be obtained from Wahbe et al. (1993).

The third technique is to write functions in an interpreted language such as Java. Although the performance of interpreted language is worse than that of compiled languages such as C, there are significant benefits, including bounds checking of each address generated during execution. It is hoped that Java virtual machines and just-in-time Java compilation technology will ameliorate this performance problem over time.

The final strategy to achieve safety for user-defined functions is certification by a trusted third party. In point of fact, *no* competent system administrator *ever* adds modules to a production system without testing them exhaustively. User-defined functions added to a production DBMS are no different from such modules. Therefore, it is crucial to test them carefully. Since user-defined functions are often written by a third party who may (or may not) have a strong focus on quality, it is important that a user get assurances that each user defined function meets rigid quality standards. This can be achieved by a certification process by a trusted third party, often the DBMS vendor. This third party will subject the function to exhaustive testing and then certify that it operates as specified. Users can then install certified extensions without fear for their safety.

Certification is the strongest strategy of the choices above. Obviously, an extension that has a severe enough bug will crash when executed. This crash could cause the process in which the extension is running to fail, and the transaction that called the extension would then abort. Moreover, the functionality of the extension will be unavailable until the damage is repaired. The consequences of such a failure are painful, at the very least. Carefully testing software is the only way to avoid these headaches.

Furthermore, as will be seen in Chapter 13, the performance consequences of RPC are often ruinous, representing an order-of-magnitude degradation in end-to-end performance. Therefore, RPC is often not a realistic option. In addition, the DataBlade market is largely a third-party market in which extensions are written by domain experts. Since it is impossible for a single vendor to be an expert in all the areas where extensions are required, the only way to get a substantial number of DataBlade modules is for domain experts to produce them. Usually these Data-Blades are adaptations of existing third-party application logic. Unfortunately, it is not feasible to insist that extensions be written in a specific interpreted language because that would require the domain expert to rewrite his logic, a prohibitive undertaking. Hence, insisting on an interpreted language is often unfeasible.

Last, firewalled execution is an elegant solution; however, it too has a big problem. Firewalling must be performed on the object code of the extension. If you are content to run the extension on a single architecture, say, Wintel, then this process need be done only once. However, a DBMS must run on a variety of hardware platforms, and this requirement will not disappear anytime soon. If there are N architectures, then firewalling must be done N times, and this strategy becomes very expensive.

Certification appears the strongest of the tactics. However, at some point this issue may be best resolved by changes in computer architecture. If a computer architecture supported rings of protection, such as found in Multics (Organick 1972), then the function could be activated in a different ring from the DBMS. With high-speed ring crossing supported by the hardware, security could be achieved at low overhead without the necessity of custom-firewalling software. Unfortunately, this alternative requires the cooperation of hardware designers, which has not been forthcoming to date.

Feature 5: Callback

Consider once more the *sunset* function from Chapter 1. It is perfectly reasonable for the function to maintain a private database of images that are known to be sunsets. Then, it can accept an image as an argument and compare it against its database of known images for similarity. In this way, the function computes its result by comparing its argument against a private database. Supporting this functionality requires that user-defined functions be capable of "callback." That is, it must be permissible for them to run queries inside the function. Specifically, a client program can include arbitrary DBMS commands through a client application program interface (API). A user-defined function must be able to use the same interface to invoke DBMS services. Put differently, a function must operate exactly the same way whether it is linked into an application program or invoked by the DBMS as a result of a user issuing an SQL command containing the function.

Note that the SQL command invoked by a function performing callback may, in turn, have within it a user-defined function also performing callback. This may mean there is an arbitrary nesting of callbacks, and a good object-relational DBMS supports this without getting confused.

Feature 6: User-Defined Access Methods

Return now to the car pool example discussed earlier in this chapter. Suppose you submit the following query:

```
select name
from emp
where contained (location,box (0,0,1,1));
```

which requests the employees who live inside a rectangle bounded by the origin and the point (1, 1).

Current DBMSs have implemented B-trees and perhaps hashing as access methods to accelerate queries. Unfortunately, these access methods are only appropriate for numbers and character strings and are useless in speeding up geographic queries.

A B-tree is an efficient accessing structure for data that has a one-dimensional linear order, such as employee names or salaries. In order to use a B-tree for the geographic point data in the emp table, locations must be put into a one-dimensional order. Consider ordering points in longitude order. With a B-tree built on longitude, then the DBMS can solve the above car pool query by examining all employees within a vertical tube containing the required box, as illustrated in Figure 2.1. Clearly, this may be a substantial fraction of all employees, and this absence of precision makes B-trees an ineffective access structure for geographic points.

There is no shortage of access methods optimized for geographic data. These include quad-trees, K-D-B trees and R-trees. Probably the most promising one is an R-tree, first introduced by Gutman (Gutman 1984). An R-tree generalizes B-trees to work in multiple dimensions.

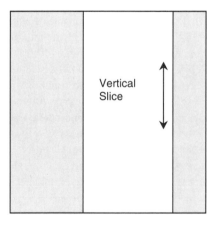

FIGURE 2.1   The Search Region for the Car Pool Query

A B-tree can be built on a field of the emp table, say, salary. It is a secondary storage structure containing the following elements of information for each employee:

- A value for the salary of each employee
- A pointer to the appropriate employee record

These (key, pointer) pairs are stored in sorted order on disk pages that form the leaf levels of a hierarchical structure. Figure 2.2 shows a portion of a B-tree with a single leaf page containing (key, pointer) pairs for Joe, Bill, and Sam.

The high key of each disk page is then stored in the next level of the index, along with a pointer to the correct page. Hence, along the next level of the index are stored pairs of (high key, leaf level page). As before, these are grouped onto disk pages and the structure is recursively built until the root level has only a single page, as noted in Figure 2.2.

The search for the record that matches a given key proceeds by examining the root page for the lowest key greater than the one required. Following the pointer, the search is repeated on the appropriate page at the second level. When the leaf level is reached, the page is searched for an exact match; if found, the pointer is followed to

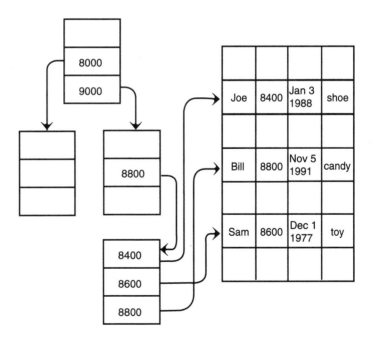

FIGURE 2.2 Example Secondary Index

locate the desired record. In this way highly optimized search is possible for exact match queries. Also note that range queries are similarly optimizable.

The beauty of a B-tree is that insertions and deletions can be done without destroying the balance of the tree. Hence, for arbitrary inserts and deletes, all records remain exactly the same distance form the root of the tree and can be obtained with a fixed number of disk accesses.

R-trees generalize this structure to multiple dimensions. For simplicity, we will concentrate on R-trees with two dimensions and use location in the emp table as an example. As in B-trees, (key, pointer) pairs are stored on leaf pages in a hierarchical structure. However, rather than storing a (high_key, pointer) pair at the next level of the index, an R-tree stores a (rectangle, pointer) pair. This rectangle is constructed to contain all the location points stored in the leaf-level page below it. The structure is built recursively so each level contains rectangles that contain all the rectangles on the page below it. Figure 2.3 shows a portion of this structure for the emp table. Here, a leaf page is shown for Joe, Bill, and Sam with their locations indicated. In the next index level appears a rectangle that bounds the locations of the three employees along with a pointer to the leaf page. This rectangle is represented in Figure 2.3 by two points at the lower-left and upper-right corners. Also shown is a root page with a rectangle containing this intermediate rectangle (and the others on the appropriate page).

Now consider the car pool search indicated above. The root page is searched for those rectangles that intersect the search rectangle in the user's query. For any qualifying rectangle, the search is repeated on the intermediate node pointed to. The process identifies a collection of leaf pages whose records intersect the search rectangle. Each page is searched for qualifying keys, and the appropriate records are then retrieved.

Hence, an R-tree indexes records in multiple dimensions. Moreover, the search may have to descend multiple paths in the hierarchical structure to identify all qualifying records. Using this technique, the search region from Figure 2.1 is drastically reduced, and a more efficient structure is provided. On geographic queries, an R-tree outperforms a B-tree by several orders of magnitude. Thus, an object-relational DBMS that wishes to store geographic data must provide a multidimensional access method.

Since it is impossible for the DBMS vendor to predict all of the access methods that will be required for the various kinds of objects to be stored, clearly a vendor should provide an interface whereby a type designer can add a new access method. Of course, this is a complex operation that must be done by a sophisticated programmer, as Chapter 10 explains.

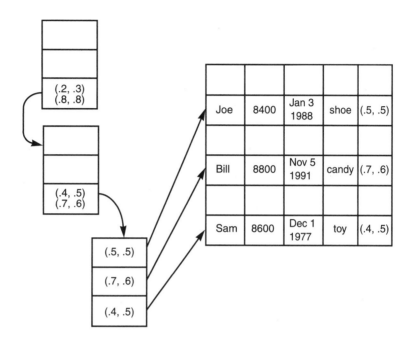

FIGURE 2.3 An R-Tree on the emp Table

Feature 7: Arbitrary-Length Types

The next required feature is to have user-defined data types without length restrictions. Clearly, there are data types that are fixed length and short (such as location in the emp table). However, there are also data types that are fixed length and long, such as an image type. Furthermore, there are data types that are variable length and long, such as a compressed representation of an image. Obviously, a good object-relational DBMS supports any permutation of {long, short} and {fixed, variable} length.

It is sometimes argued that the BLOBs (binary large objects) present in relational systems adequately support fixed- or variable-length data types of arbitrary length. Unfortunately, you can only fetch or store BLOBs. Therefore, because they have no operations available for them, they are not data types.

Feature 8: Open Storage Manager

Earlier, we noted that it might be useful for a type designer to actually store his data outside the DBMS in some other storage system. Moreover, we indicated how the design of our type system allowed this to occur by supporting an internal representation different from an external one and allowing a user to write input and output cast functions. In this way, a type designer could store data in files or on a specialized storage media, such as a video disk system.

Although this option is available to the type designer, it suffers from a major disadvantage. Each type designer must manage his own storage by allocating space for new objects, reclaiming space when objects are deleted, and dealing with the optimal placement for objects on a device. A second type designer wishing to use the same device must redo all this work. Thus, there is no design for reusability of the low-level storage code. Obviously, this is an undesirable characteristic, and we would wish to do better. This leads us to a discussion of Feature 8, an open storage manager.

Traditionally, the internal design of a DBMS has divided the engine into two halves. The top half, the query manager, is responsible for tasks like parsing and optimizing queries, and for scheduling their execution. The lower half of the DBMS is usually called the storage manager. It implements all of the algorithms and data managements tasks used by the SQL engine.

Typically, the DBMS opens a table and then fetches records one by one from a table in the storage manager interface into the execution engine. When a table scan is complete, the table is closed. This interface separates the execution engine from the storage system, which includes the buffer manager and the disk storage system. However, a better, more flexible design is to provide an open storage manager, that is, support an open interface whereby third parties can write storage managers in which records can be stored.

In this way, a vendor with a specialized hardware device can write a storage manager for the device. Then, by making the specialized storage manager accessible to the DBMS's execution engine, any table can be stored on this device and accessed by the DBMS. The type designer does not need to worry about storage, but instead can focus on providing the type and the functions for it. A user who creates a table containing instances of the type merely needs to place the table in a specialized storage manager and thereby enjoys the benefits of optimized performance.

An open storage manager also has an important benefit, not related to object-relational capabilities, but with the integration of legacy systems into modern DBMSs. In any large enterprise, mission-critical data can be found in a variety of places, including at least the following:

- *Operational data stores (ODS):* Includes relational DBMSs and other older DBMSs such as IBM's IMS and Cullinet's IDMS.

- *Legacy systems:* Most companies have proprietary, home-built systems in which mission-critical data can be found. Most companies are aggressively trying to retire such "smokestack" applications; this is an issue of legacy system migration, about which much has been written.
- *Spreadsheets:* One vendor (Microsoft) reports that 85% of all enterprise data is stored in Excel spreadsheets.
- *Web servers:* There has been a headlong rush to bring content up on the Web by installing Web servers. Such content is often documents or images and can be stored in a file system behind a Web server or in an object-relational DBMS.
- *Document management systems:* Many enterprise documents are stored in a document management system, such as Documentum or Saros.
- *File systems:* There is considerable mission-critical data stored in the file system for the operating system in use on specific machines.

It is clearly desirable to allow an SQL engine to access data that is in this plethora of systems. Since many of these systems look very much like the storage managers mentioned above, it is straightforward to write gateways from the DBMS open storage manager interface to many of these systems. Hence, an open storage manager not only facilitates storage of objects in specialized systems but also is a good way to support integration of legacy storage systems. Currently, Informix offers such an interface, called VTI (Virtual Table Interface). Additionally, Microsoft is readying a similar capability as part of OLE DB.

2.5 *Summary*

This chapter describes how an object-relational DBMS enables users to define data types, functions, and operators. Such extensibility extends the functionality of an object-relational DBMS tremendously by eliminating tedious simulation of new data types and functions necessitated in traditional DBMSs. The payoff is high performance that is obtained relatively easily.

CHAPTER 3   *Examples of Base Type Extension*

This chapter examines examples of base type extension from three distinctly different application areas:

- Geographic information systems (GISs), which provide geographic query capability on data defining two-dimensional spatial objects
- Digital libraries, which store several formats of image files in image databases
- The quantity data type for use in applications that manipulate physical units

By following through these examples, the practical importance of base type extension will become clearer. Although each example application manipulates a different kind of data, they all benefit from the power of user-defined base types and customized type libraries.

3.1   *Geographic Information Systems Applications*

GISs are potentially large database systems that store information that is useful for constructing and querying two-dimensional maps. Most governments maintain maps of objects in their jurisdiction. In addition, companies with geographically dispersed assets, such as pipelines and utilities, also maintain a GIS. In order to perform geographic queries, a collection of two-dimensional data types is required. Some of the types you probably need include

- 2-D point, represented as an (X, Y) pair

- 2-D line, represented as a pair of points, corresponding to each end of the line
- 2-D polygon, represented by a sequence of points indicating the vertices of the polygon
- 2-D path, represented by a sequence of points (in other words, a polygon that is not closed)
- circle, represented by a 2-D point as its center and a numeric radius
- 2-D rectangle, represented by a pair of points corresponding to the upper-right and lower-left corners
- 2-D trapezoid, represented by four points, corresponding to corners
- 2-D ellipse, represented by two points, corresponding to its centers, and a single number indicating the distance from any point on the boundary to both centers

In addition, 100 or so functions are appropriate for these data types, including the following:

- *distance(point, point)* returns number.
- *distance(point, line)* returns number.
- *distance(point, polygon)* returns number.
- *distance(line, line)* returns number.
- *distance(line, rectangle)* returns number.

- *contained(point, polygon)* returns Boolean.
- *contained(point, rectangle)* returns Boolean.
- *contained(point, circle)* returns Boolean.

- *overlaps(rectangle, rectangle)* returns Boolean.
- *overlaps(polygon, polygon)* returns Boolean.
- *overlaps(line, polygon)* returns Boolean.
- *overlaps(circle, circle)* returns Boolean.
- *overlaps (circle, polygon)* returns Boolean.

- *make_rect (point, point)* returns rectangle.
- *make_line(point, point)* returns line.
- *make_circle(point, number)* returns circle.
- *make_ellipse (point, number)* returns ellipse.

There are many possible representations for two-dimensional spatial objects, leading to the possibility of a corresponding number of type libraries. To illustrate this point, a second possible representation for 2-D spatial data is discussed next.

Consider storing points as in the above example. Then, instead of representing a line as a pair of points, make it a pair of pointers to points. And similarly, store a polygon as a set of pointers to lines. In this way, points are stored directly, while lines and polygons are stored as collections of pointers. This representation has certain advantages and disadvantages, relative to the first implementation.

The main advantage to storing data using indirection is that if a point is moved, then every line in which it appears is automatically moved. Similarly, every polygon in which these lines appear is automatically adjusted. In other words, automatic data integrity is supported. If, for example, a river changes course, then the polygon on one side of the river will not change unless the one on the other side is also changed. On the other hand, if you store the lines and polygons directly, then each instance of a line containing the point that moves must be found and updated. Moreover, every polygon must be identified and updated. Because this process demands multiple updates, it is error prone.

Obviously, indirection has advantages. However, it also comes with one severe disadvantage, namely performance on queries. For example, to find whether a given point is inside a polygon, the polygon must be constructed out of its lines, which in turn must be constructed from its points. Two levels of pointers must be followed to materialize the polygon so that the correct check can be performed. In contrast, if the polygon is represented directly, then the indirection is not necessary, leading to much better performance.

Thus, representing polygons directly offers higher performance on retrieval in return for the necessity of multiple updates in certain situations. These updates can easily be done automatically using the triggers in modern object-relational DBMSs, as discussed in Chapter 7. As a result, data integrity problems can be easily solved.

In summary, a direct representation provides better retrieval performance than an indirect representation, in exchange for worse update performance. Therefore, expect type libraries for both representations to have marketplace advocates. But remember that either type library requires a user-defined access method such as an R-tree to perform well, as noted in the previous chapter.

3.2   *Image Type Library Applications*

A second example concerns digital images, such as those in a digital image library. A wide variety of formats are available for image data, including tiff, gif, group 3 fax, group 4 fax, Photo CD, and JPEG. All have found acceptance in certain vertical markets, and it is likely that someone would like to store all of them in a DBMS. You could construct a data type for each of the 50 or so popular formats. Alternatively, you can construct a single data type that supports image storage in a variety of formats. The advantage of the latter choice is that a column of a table can store images in more than one format, a desirable feature in "mixed mode" image libraries.

This chapter discusses only a few of the large number of operations required for the image data type. Obviously, you need standard manipulation operations on an image, such as the following:

- *rotate(image, angle)* returns image.
- *transpose(image)* returns image.
- *flip(image)* returns image.
- *crop(image, rectangle)* returns image.

Furthermore, it is often desirable to provide contrast enhancement to an image or make it look as if it were created with a different medium, such as oil paints. More sophisticated operations include

- *enhance(image)* returns image.
- *oil_ painting(image)* returns image.

Operations on pairs of images are also a requirement:

- *plus(image, image)* returns image.
- *minus(image, image)* returns image.
- *multiply(image, image)* returns image.
- *intersection(image, image)* returns image.
- *union(image, image)* returns image.

Last, there are applications where you want to perform content-based retrieval on a collection of images. In general, you want one of two capabilities. First, you might want to find all the images that have a certain semantic characteristic. Chapter 1 has a example of a user who wants to find images that contain sunsets. Second, you might want to find images that are similar to a given image. In this case, you identify an image of interest and then request more images like the indicated one.

In the first case, it could be helpful for the type library to support color analysis by building histograms. The following function is useful for this:

- *histogram(image)* returns relational table.

Other possibly useful functions include edge detection, for example,

- *edge(image)* returns setof (open_polygons).

Using these primitives, you can construct functions to recognize specialized semantic constructs, such as sunsets. In addition, over time, texture and shape information can be included as building blocks.

To find images that are similar to a given image, the following function is required:

- *similarity(image, image)* returns number.

The current technology in this area is to construct a vector of color, shape, edge, and texture characteristics for each image. Then, the *similarity* function finds the distance between pairs of these vectors. Currently, both the vector to be constructed and the distance metric used must be content specific. Therefore, finding similar landscapes is fundamentally different from finding similar portraits or clip art. The performance of commercial products in this area, such as the VIR DataBlade module for the Informix server, and a similar type extension for DB2 6000, is surprisingly good.

3.3   *The Quantity Data Type*

In our final example in this chapter, we consider a data type to store quantities, which may have various unit systems. Example quantities include

- 1.04 acres
- 12.3 inches
- 62 pounds
- 12 fluid ounces

It seems reasonable to store values of the quantity data type as (floating_point _number, units_encoding) pairs. The units_encoding field is a code for all units recognized. In a 16-bit field, all conceivable quantity metrics can be represented.

There are three classes of operations on the quantity data type. The first is to convert a given quantity into a specific unit system. There is a function for each desired unit that converts a quantity into that unit's system, for example:

- *centimeters(quantity)*

When the function is passed the value (12.3 inches) it returns the quantity (31.242 cm). There are also functions to extract the value of a quantity along with its units:

- *value(quantity)* returns float.
- *units(quantity)* returns code.

Last, there are operations on pairs of quantities, such as

- *plus(quantity, quantity)* returns quantity.
- *minus(quantity, quantity)* returns quantity.
- *times(quantity, quantity)* returns quantity.
- *divide(quantity, quantity)* returns quantity.

For example, *plus(12.4 inches, 10.2 inches)* yields 22.6 inches. Similarly, *times (12.4 inches, 10.4 inches)* yields 126.48 square inches. In this way, quantities can be combined in the obvious ways. Of course, some operations make no sense, such as *times(12 gallons, 2.1 inches)* and must be disallowed. Using this scheme, a general quantity data type can be constructed that understands all popular unit systems and frees the programmer from having to worry about what units the quantities are in.

CHAPTER 4

Characteristic 2: Complex Objects

This chapter explores the second basic requirement of object-relational DBMSs, support in SQL for complex objects—objects that are composed of multiple base or user-defined types. The first part of the chapter describes three type constructors: rows, sets, and references. The remainder of the chapter provides extensive examples of the use of each kind of constructor.

4.1   *Type Constructors*

The following three type constructors are basic building blocks for creating complex types in object-relational DBMSs:

- Composites (row types)
- Sets (collection types)
- References

Rows as a Type Constructor

A *row* is a data type consisting of a record of values, as shown by the following two examples:

```
create row type phone_t (
                    area            varchar(3),
                    number          varchar(7),
                    description     varchar(20));

create row type auto_t (
                    name        varchar(12),
                    year        int,
                    license     varchar(7));
```

To construct a row type, indicate the name of the type along with the name and data type of the constituent pieces. It is acceptable for the pieces of a row type to be row types themselves. Stated more formally, if $T_1, \ldots, T_n$ are any data types, then a row (or record) can be constructed as a data type, consisting of an instance of each of the constituent data types.

You can create a table to hold instances of a row type, as shown in the following example:

```
create row type employee_t (
                    name        varchar(30),
                    startdate   date,
                    salary      int,
                    address     varchar(30),
                    city        varchar(30),
                    state       char(2),
                    zipcode     int);
create table emp of type employee_t;
```

The first statement constructs a row type, employee_t, and then the second statement constructs the table emp to hold instances of this type. Think of tables as containers into which you can place instances of a row type. Making a clear distinction between types and tables allows you to have many different tables that hold instances of the same type, rather than just one. The advantages of this possibility are discussed in Chapter 6. Notice that the above statements construct the same emp table defined in Chapter 2.

In addition to placing instances of a row data type into tables, you can also define individual columns of a table as instances of a row data type. For example, the following table associates a job and the employee who fills it:

```
create table jobs    (
                    job_desc  varchar(30),
                    employee  employee_t);
```

Sets as a Type Constructor

Support of various kinds of sets as a type constructor is a useful feature for an object-relational DBMS. In SQL-3 there are proposed type constructors for sets, multisets, and lists. Moreover, as discussed in the next chapter, additional type constructors make sense and may be added over time. SQL-3 uses the word "collection" to stand for the three type constructors, and this is the term we use throughout this book. We use the word "set" for the specific type constructor for sets as well as for the abstract mathematical notion.

Formally stated, if T is any type, then collection(T) must also be a type, where there are several kinds of type constructor (set, list, multiset), each of which imposes slightly different rules on collection membership. It is a requirement to support collections of base types, collections of row types, collections of collections, and collections of references.

References as a Type Constructor

It is also useful to support references (pointers) as a type constructor. Thus, if T is a type, then ref(T) must also be a data type that can be used as the type of any column of any table. As a result, the following data types are required:

- Reference to a row
- Reference to a collection
- Reference to a base data type

(In practice, it is not clear that there is a lot of utility to the last data type, and Informix has chosen not to support it.)

4.2 *Using Type Constructors*

The following sections provide examples of how complex objects can be supported in an object-relational DBMS. Throughout these examples, the following table is used. It contains the name of a department, the floor it is on, the name of its manager, and five other fields that are described later in the chapter:

```
create row type dept_t(
                   dname         varchar(30),
                   floor         int,
                   manager       varchar(30),
                   phone         phone_t,
                   autos         set(auto_t ),
                   manager_ref   ref(employee_t)
                                 references (emp),
```

```
            colors          set(varchar(30)),
            workers         set(ref(employee_t)
                            references (emp)));

create table dept of type dept_t;
```

Manipulating Row Types

In the dept table above, phone contains the phone number of the department, which is a row type. In order to manipulate row types, some extensions to standard SQL are required:

1. User-defined functions can take arguments or return a result of a row type.

2. Functions returning a row type can appear in the from clause of an SQL query.

3. The "cascaded dot notation" references attributes of a row object.

User-Defined Functions. It is permissible to write functions that take arguments or return results that are composites. For example, you can define a function *bonus* where employee's bonus is equal to 10% of the employee's salary:

```
create function bonus ( employee_t, Arg1  )
returning int;
as select  Arg1.salary * 0.1;
end function;
```

Like any other function, *bonus* can be used in any syntactically legal place in an SQL expression. For example, the following SQL finds the bonus for employee Mike:

```
select bonus(e)
from emp e
where e.name = 'Mike';
```

It is also possible to ask which employees receive a bonus of over $1000, as follows:

```
select e.name
from emp e
where bonus(e) > 1000;
```

Functions in the From Clause. In traditional SQL, the from clause contains the name of a table, which is a set of rows. Because a row is a singleton set, it is possible to place a function that returns a row type in the from clause of an SQL command.

Suppose a function is registered that constructs the phone number of the shoe department, as follows:

```
create function shoe_phone ()
returning (phone_t)
as select phone
from dept
where dname = 'shoe';
```

The *shoe_phone* function can then be used in an SQL from clause:

```
select number
from table(shoe_phone())
where area = '510';
```

This query uses the phone information returned from the function *shoe_phone*, and then returns the seven-digit phone number if it is in the 510 area code.

Because functions can be written in SQL, it will come as no surprise that you can put a select query instead of a function name into the from clause. Here is an alternative way to solve the above query:

```
select number
from table( select phone
        from dept
        where dept = 'shoe' )
where area = '510';
```

In this case, the scope of the from clause is a query that returns a row. The select and where clause of the outer query are then applied to the row.

Cascaded Dot Notation. The third notation that is useful in the manipulation of rows is the cascaded dot notation (called "path expressions" by some researchers). Consider traditional SQL, which allows attributes of a table to be referenced as

```
table_name.column_name
```

The dot notation references the columns of a table. Similarly, the dot notation can be used to reference the columns in a row type. So, to find the seven-digit shoe department phone number, you can write

```
select phone.number
from dept
where dname = 'shoe';
```

This query addresses the dept table, retrieving the phone column. Because the phone column is itself a row type, you can use cascaded dot notation to indicate that you wish to examine only the number subfield within the phone column.

The cascaded dot notation can also appear in the qualification. To find the names of departments that have a number in the 510 area code, you can type

```
select dname
from dept
where phone.area = '510';
```

There is another interpretation of the cascaded dot notation. As indicated above, you can think of a row as having a collection of attributes, addressed as

```
row_name.attribute_name
```

You can also think of a row as having a collection of functions, one per attribute. The name of the function is simply the name of the attribute. Typically, you use standard function notation to utilize functions in a query, for example,

```
attribute_name (row_name)
```

Using this notation, the above query becomes

```
select dname
from dept
where area(phone) = '510';
```

As you can see, the combination of cascaded dot notation, generalization of the from clause, and user-defined functions referencing rows provides an extremely powerful mechanism to manipulate rows in SQL.

Manipulating Collections of Rows

Not surprisingly, the same SQL extensions that applied to rows can also be used for collections of rows, for example, the autos attribute of dept.

User-Defined Functions. You must be able to register functions that accept arguments and return results that are collections of rows. For example, suppose a function is written that returns a Boolean if a department has a 1985 automobile. This function, *has85*, can be used in SQL queries, for example,

```
select dname
from dept
where has85(autos);
```

Functions in the From Clause. Suppose a function is registered that constructs the autos in a company's transportation department, as follows:

```
create function transport_autos ()
returns set( auto_t);
as select autos
from dept
where dname = 'transportation';
```

The *transport_autos* function can then be used in an SQL from clause:

```
select name
from table(transport_autos())
where year = 1989;
```

This query uses the year information returned from the function *transport_autos* and then returns a car's name if the car is a 1989 model.

Cascaded Dot Notation. Consider the following query:

```
select dname
from dept
where 1985 in autos.year;
```

This query uses the cascaded dot notation to find the departments that have a 1985 automobile. Specifically, autos.year determines a set, and the predicate is true if 1985 occurs in the set. Now consider a more complex query:

```
select dname
from dept
where 1985 in autos.year and
'Ford' in autos.name;
```

This query returns the departments that have a 1985 car and that also have a Ford of any model year.

If you want to find the departments that have a 1985 Ford, you must run a different query:

```
select dname
from dept
where exists  ( select 1
               from dept.autos
               where year = 1985
               and name = 'Ford');
```

A more succinct notation to accomplish the same thing might be something like

```
select dname
from dept
where autos.(year = 1985 and name = 'Ford');
```

In summary, the combination of user-defined functions, cascaded dot notation, and generalized from clauses provides you with the same power for manipulating sets that is available for rows.

Of course, you should realize that whenever you store a row or collection of rows, there may be multiple copies of the same object. For example, if there is a company phone list table, then each phone number appears once in the dept table and once in the phone directory table, causing an integrity problem in maintaining the list in both locations. Specifically, to update a department's phone number, you must change it in every location. Therefore, rows and collections of rows are only appropriate for data that

- rarely changes or
- appears only once

In other cases, use references, the subject of the next section.

Using References

References are a natural substitute for a primary key–foreign key relationship found in traditional SQL systems. In the dept table, the manager column is a foreign key and records the name of the employee who is the manager of the given department. In contrast, manager_ref is another field in the dept table that serves exactly the same purpose, that is, to identify the employee who manages the department. This section explores both implementations in some detail.

Using the foreign key implementation, if you want to find the start date of the shoe department manager, then a join must be performed:

```
select e.startdate
from emp e, dept d
where e.name = d.manager and d.dname = 'shoe';
```

This query is difficult to understand because of the presence of the join. Also, joins are heavyweight operations, and most vendors optimize their join algorithms for large data sets.

In addition, you have a foreign key (manager) in the dept table, which must match a primary key (name) in the emp table. Referential integrity in SQL-92 is required to indicate which actions to take to guarantee that the foreign key values in the dept table all appear as primary keys in the emp table. Some action must be taken when

- a department is created with a nonexistent manager
- a manager of a department is deleted

In SQL-92 you can specify the following actions to be taken on the insertion:

- Refuse the insertion.
- Allow the insertion but change the manager value to a default value.

- Allow the insertion but change the manager value to null.
- Allow the insertion and in addition create a new employee with the name of the manager.

Similarly, on a deletion, the following actions are possible:

- Refuse the deletion.
- Allow the deletion but change the manager field to a default value.
- Allow the deletion but change the manager field to null.
- Allow the deletion and in addition delete the department.

In an object-relational DBMS you could use the above implementation, which is the only one available in a traditional SQL-92 system. However, there is a second option available, using references, which is discussed next.

An object-relational DBMS allows a column in a table to contain a reference to an instance of a row type stored in another table in the database. Conceptually, this data type is a pointer to a row of a specific type in a table. In the dept table, manager_ref is a pointer to a row of type employee_t.

With this information in mind, note that the actual value stored in the manager_ref field in each row of dept is an OID. In this application, the OID is the one for the manager of this department.

The extensions to SQL required to support references are the following:

1. A specific *deref* function that returns the actual row, given a reference to it
2. More generally, support for functions that take arguments or return results of type reference

Obviously, you can run traditional SQL queries on the dept table, for example,

```
select manager_ref
from dept
where dname = 'shoe';
```

This query returns a reference to an employee, which is the OID of the employee who is the manager of the shoe department. To dereference the pointer in the manager_ref field, the object-relational DBMS provides a *deref* function that takes a reference as an argument and returns a row of the type pointed to. You can use this construct to find the manager of the shoe department:

```
select deref(manager_ref)
from dept
where dname = 'shoe';
```

Deref is an example of a function provided for all reference data types. If you choose to, you can write additional functions. Consider the function *get_mgr,* defined as follows:

```
create function get_mgr ( varchar(30), Arg1 )
returning employee_t;
as select deref(manager_ref)
from dept
where dept = Arg1);
```

With this notation, the query can be simplified to

```
select get_mgr ('shoe');
```

You might ask if there is a *ref* function performing the inverse of the *deref* function. Of course, the answer is yes. To get back the OID of the manager, you can code the following statement:

```
select ref(deref(manager_ref))
from dept
where dname = 'shoe';
```

The function *ref* takes an argument that is an instance of the type employee_t and returns a reference (OID) to the instance. A perhaps more realistic use of the *ref* function is to assign a new manager to the shoe department. Using the traditional implementation, you can give the shoe department a new manager named Mark in the following manner:

```
update dept
set manager = 'Mark'
where dname = 'shoe';
```

Using the *ref* function, the same update is coded as follows:

```
update dept
set manager_ref =
    (select ref ( emp )
    from emp
    where name = 'Mark' );
```

Here, *manager_ref* will be assigned a new OID for the shoe department. This OID is constructed by identifying the employee named Mark and then using the *ref* function to find his OID.

The result of the *deref(manager_ref)* function is a row. You can utilize the cascaded dot notation explored in the previous section to find the birth date of the manager of the shoe department as follows:

```
select deref(manager_ref).birthdate
from dept
where dname = 'shoe';
```

To find both the start date and salary of the manager, type

```
select deref(manager_ref).startdate, deref(manager_ref).salary
from dept
where dname = 'shoe';
```

These examples illustrate the use of primary key–foreign key relationships as well as a pointer implementation to support representing the manager of a department. You can use a character string (the name of the manager) as a logical pointer, or you can use an OID (reference) as the pointer. Generally, it is somewhat safer to use the reference implementation because an OID is guaranteed to be unique and never change, while an employee's name is not necessarily time invariant.

On the other hand, unlike a character string, OIDs have a format that people cannot easily read. For example, dumping the contents of the manager field in the implementation with an OID pointer reveals data that you cannot quickly decipher.

In short, there are both advantages and disadvantages to using references, and there is no exact answer to the question of when to use references instead of some other construct.

Using Collections of References

As you read earlier in this chapter, references are pointers to a record of a specific type in a table. If an object-relational DBMS has the notion of collections, it is also appropriate for it to support collections of references. For example, the dept table, defined on page 63, contains a column recording the workers in each department. Because each reference is an OID, it is not surprising that the field workers contains an arbitrarily large collection of OIDs that reference employees who work in the given department. Use *set(ref(employee_t))* if the field can contain more than one reference. If only one object will be referenced, use *ref(employee_t)*.

Clearly, you can use all the capabilities of set manipulation to deal with collections of references. For example, to find the workers in the shoe department, type

```
select workers
from dept
where dname = 'shoe';
```

This command returns a collection of OIDs, which is probably not what you had in mind. To further manipulate the collection, you can put it in a from clause:

```
select deref(*)
from table(select workers
        from dept
        where dname = 'shoe');
```

Here, you dereference the members of the collection to get their actual records. The last step is to indicate you only want employee start dates, as follows:

```
select deref(*).startdate
from table(select workers
        from dept
        where dname = 'shoe');
```

As you can see, the SQL notation to deal with collections and references can be combined in a straightforward way.

Using Collections of Base Types

The favorite colors for each department appear in the example dept table and are a collection of base types (page 64). As with all collections of objects, you must remember that there will be an integrity problem whenever member data is changed. For example, if you decide that magenta is no longer a color and you want it to be called purple, then you have to find all instances of magenta and change them to purple.

How should collections be stored? There are several plausible approaches. Obviously, the number of elements can become arbitrarily large. To keep the data manageable, one approach is to store the members of the collection in disk records separate from the record in which they logically appear. A reference to the extra record is stored in the actual data record. Alternatively, you might create an entirely separate "backing" table to contain the collection data and references back to the actual data record. Both of these approaches have the advantage that they can reuse the DBMS's other facilities, indices, and so on.

The disadvantage is that reconstructing the collection requires a join. An alternative approach, suitable for small collections, is to keep the collection data together with the rest of the row data. This approach to managing collection data does not require the join to reconstruct the collection. However, it presents another problem. Conventional indexing schemes call for every row in the table to have exactly one entry in the index. Index structures that store a data row multiple times in different places in the index are called "inverted" indices. To efficiently support queries that involve collections that are stored "in line," an object-relational database needs to support inverted indexing structures.

4.3   *Collections and Client-Server Communication*

Another use for collections is to reduce the amount of data passed between the object-relational DBMS and a client program. Consider the traditional way to express the query, "Show me all of the employees in the shoe department, and their salaries":

```
select d.dname,  e.name, e.salary
from emp e, dept d
where e.dname = e.dname and
d.name = 'shoe';
```

This produces a set of rows of the following form with one row for every employee:

```
(dname,  name, salary)
```

Notice that dname is repeated for every row. The client program must iterate over the result rows, stripping off the dname value from the first row, and then the employee details from all rows. This is excessively complex for the client program, and, as a side effect, a large amount of redundant information is passed between the DBMS and the client program.

In an object-relational database, you can use collections to eliminate this redundant data. The query above can be rewritten as

```
select d.dname, set(e.ename, e.salary)
from dept d, emp e
where e.dname = d.dname and
d.dname = 'shoe'
group by d.dname;
```

This query returns exactly one row. The second element of this row is a set of values, one for each employee. Using this technique, you can improve the performance of certain applications by reducing the amount of data that must be passed between the object-relational DBMS and the client program.

4.4   *Base Types and Complex Objects*

As you have seen, a good object-relational DBMS enables you to extend the system by

1. defining new base data types and functions

2. defining new complex objects and functions, through the type constructors collection, ref, and row

Naturally, you are probably wondering why these two mechanisms exist. There are four reasons why a good object-relational DBMS supports two type systems, one consisting of extensible base types and one consisting of complex data types. The reasons revolve around

- naturalness

- encapsulation

- OIDs

- data conversion and ordering

Naturalness

The first reason to support both type systems concerns what is natural for a user to understand. The types phone_t, dept_t, and employee_t are naturally rows, with visible attributes of various types. Moreover, the rows of a table are naturally instances of a row type. Many types, however, are naturally single quantities, such as Scottish names, positive integers, and images. These are naturally viewed as base types, and it requires some contortion of thought to view them as rows consisting of a single field of one of the SQL-92 types.

In the last decade three new base types have been added to most commercial relational DBMSs: date, money, and kanji character string. These additions clearly demonstrate the need for base type extension. As a result, both complex objects and base type extension are very natural constructs in specific situations. Thus, it is desirable to support both possibilities.

Encapsulation

A second reason for both kinds of types concerns encapsulation. Base types are completely encapsulated. The only way to manipulate a base type is to retrieve it or execute a function that takes its type as an argument. In contrast, row objects are completely transparent. You can see all the fields, and they are readily available in the query language. Of course, an intermediate position is to allow some fields of a row object to be public (visible) and the remainder to be private (encapsulated). This is the approach used by C++.

Obviously, you can change the internal representation of a base type at will. You need only redefine the input and output functions to store the bits in a different way. Programs that utilize the type will continue to run correctly. This ability to change the internal parts of a type is a good argument in favor of encapsulation. In contrast, visible fields in a complex object cannot be redefined, or all programs that use the type will stop working. In general, base types are appropriate for encapsulated data, while complex objects are appropriate for unencapsulated data.

OIDs

In general, complex objects have a system-allocated OID assigned to them, while base types do not. Therefore, there is a space penalty for using complex types. As noted earlier, a reference is an OID, and a base type does not have one. Thus, references are available only for complex types.

Data Conversion and Ordering

Return to the Scottish character string example introduced in Chapter 2. Using base type extension, you can construct a base data type, Scottish character string, and then define a collection of comparison operators for the new type. Values can be stored in a B-tree in ascending order according to the user-defined notion of < (less than), as will be explained in Chapter 10. A user query such as

```
select salary
from emp
where name > 'Ly' and name < 'Me';
```

is processed directly by using the B-tree index with the predefined comparison operators.

Although Scottish names do not require different external and internal formats, there are many data types, including integers, that do. The input and output cast functions available for base types naturally support format conversion. As a result, format conversion and user-defined ordering are powerful features of base types.

If base type extension is not supported in a DBMS, then some other mechanism must be available to provide this functionality. The alternate character sets and collating sequences available in SQL-92 are an inferior solution particularized to a specific kind of data. Therefore, specification of type semantics in the underlying language is not attractive.

Alternatively, it is plausible to define input and output functions as well as operators for complex objects. Then, you could cast a Scottish name to a complex object to get the required functionality. This seems much less natural than supporting base type extension. Format conversion, indexing, and user-defined operators seem best handled at the base type level.

4.5   *Summary*

You have seen several reasons why a good object-relational DBMS must support both base types and complex objects. To conclude the chapter, this section presents the features that a system needs to support in order to be considered fully object-relational in terms of complex types.

Feature 1: A rich collection of complex types must be supported.

At a minimum, the type constructors collection, row, and reference must be supported. Without these three mechanisms, there will be problems that will be very difficult to express. For example, if a DBMS does not support collections of base types, then the colors column in the dept table (defined on page 63) cannot be expressed as

```
colors     set(varchar(30) ),
```

Instead, you have to create a row type, color_t, containing a record with one column, color, as follows:

```
create row type color_t (
                  color   varchar(30));
```

Then, colors can be contained in the dept table through the following, rather unnatural, construct:

```
colors        set(color_t),
```

Also, depending on the implementation of sets of rows, the second implementation may have worse performance than the first one. The best solution is to support all the needed collections and references.

Feature 2: Functions must be available for all complex types and have the required properties of functions mentioned in Chapter 2.

Clearly, you cannot do much with complex types unless there are user-defined functions available. And in order to be useful, these must include the *ref* and *deref* functions, explored in this chapter. The same reasons for having required properties for functions on base types hold for complex types.

Feature 3: There can be no limit on the size of complex types.

Obviously, collections can be unbounded in size. Any restriction on the number of members of a collection or on the amount of space they can consume will be an obvious hardship.

Feature 4: SQL support for complex types is required.

For rows, the cascaded dot notation is required to reference the member attributes of the row. In addition, functions that return a collection, including ones written in SQL, must be able to appear in SQL anywhere that a table can appear in an SQL query.

CHAPTER 5

Other Type Constructors?

Chapter 4 discussed the various collection type constructors supported by an object-relational DBMS. You will learn in this chapter about two other plausible type constructors:

- Time series data
- Multidimensional data

We will also discuss how they should be implemented.

Compared with the collection constructors discussed in Chapter 4, these constructors have more limited utility. However, in specific applications, they can be very useful. Although most object-relational vendors have focused their initial attention on the type constructors discussed in the previous chapter, it is likely that they will expand their offerings over time. To show why additional type constructors enhance the functionality of an object-relational DBMS, this chapter explores the utility of time series data. This discussion is based on Informix's Timeseries DataBlade module. Following this discussion, we point out the utility of a specific array type constructor.

5.1   *A Time Series Example*

Time series data is common in financial or scientific applications where data values are gathered regularly at set time intervals. For example, on Wall Street trading companies want to track the prices of various financial instruments over time. For a large number of stocks, bonds, and derivatives, they want to store trading price and volume information. A common requirement is to record the trading volume and trading price every 20 seconds, which is called the *tick interval*. Over time, a tremendous amount of this data is accumulated by an application.

Typical questions using tick data that traders are interested in answering are as follows:

- Show me stocks where the 30-day trading range is outside the 5-day range.
- Show me stocks with a net price change for the week of October 1993 that exceeded 12%.
- Show me today's momentum (price change times volume) for IBM.

Answering these kinds of queries requires using tabular data and time series data together.

The conventional way to handle time series data, which is the approach taken by other database companies seeking to support time series, is to create a table that contains, in each row, the stock, the volume, the price, and a timestamp for the measurement interval. This results in a table that looks like this:

```
create table stockprices(
                    stock        char(5) ,
                    timestamp    datetime,
                    price        decimal(10,2),
                    volume       int     );
```

Thus, each tick interval for each security becomes a row in the stockprices table. If there are 3000 stocks, each with a 20-second tick granularity, then there are 4,320,000 rows in the stockprices table per day (assuming an eight-hour trading day) and 86,400,000 rows in a typical month. The first two queries noted above clearly read a vast number of rows. Only the final query, which has a scope of a single day, can be executed efficiently.

In general, relational DBMSs have been unable to deliver the kind of functionality or performance demanded by Wall Street time series applications. Therefore, at this time the market for time series data management products is dominated by several domain-specific tools.

The only way that a general-purpose DBMS can adequately support time series applications is to change the core engine by adding a time series type constructor.

Time Series Data in an Object-Relational DBMS

Rather than managing tick data as a row in a table, a more efficient approach is to take advantage of the nature of time series data. For example, consider the following schema:

```
create row type stocktick(
                    price   decimal(10,2),
                    volume  integer );

create table stockprices(
                    stock   char(5),
                    trades  timeseries(stocktick, '20 secs',
                                        starttime) );
```

The type constructor timeseries concatenates an indefinite number of stock ticks (one every 20 seconds, starting at the indicated time). This data is stored in one contiguous block, so when a user asks for the stock value at a specific time, the ORDBMS can compute the offset for this data within the time series object. Further, because the data is stored in order, operations to calculate aggregates that are time dependent can simply stream over the time series data.

This approach, which is basically the same one taken by the specialized time series tools, is far more efficient than the "tick-per-row" approach. In fact, Informix Timeseries DataBlade module users indicate that it is two to three orders of magnitude faster than the tick-per-row method on common operations.

In addition, because an object-relational database can be extended by developers to understand new functions, aggregate functions like "weighted moving average" can be written in C and added to the object-relational database. Then, queries, like the ones introduced earlier in this chapter, can be stated in SQL and do not require a user program. Last, it must be possible to support a time series with elements that are any data type. Thus, the time series must be a type constructor and not merely a new user-defined base type.

5.2   *An Array Example*

Consider the following sample application, which uses sales data for a hypothetical company. This company distributes several kinds of products and maintains sales data for each one. Sales data is available by sales region on a monthly basis for the last several years. The company has several different channels by which it distributes its product. Its sales data can readily be organized into the following four-dimensional array:

```
sales (product, time_period, channel, region_number)
```

Naturally enough the company president wishes to browse this sales data. On a two-dimensional computer screen, it is difficult to visualize a four-dimensional array. To assist in her analysis of sales, the president wants to see various combinations of the data displayed. For example, she might want to see

```
sales (product, time_period)
```

with sales aggregated for channel and region. Or, she might wish to see

```
sales (channel, region_number)
```

aggregated for product and time. Other users might want to see this aggregated data for subsets of the array. A sales rep might want to see

```
sales (channel, region_number)
```

only for the eastern portion of the United States. To meet the needs of such applications, a variety of online analytical processing (OLAP) companies provide efficient storage for array data and high-speed aggregation operations.

Optimizing Array Storage for Aggregation

This section briefly explores why array storage must be optimized for aggregation operations. The naive way to organize a large multidimensional array is "FORTRAN style," with the indices of the array ordered from 1 to n. Then, values of the array are ordered in storage, with the nth index varying most rapidly and the first index least rapidly. This organization is illustrated in Figure 5.1, which depicts a two-dimensional array, A. Figure 5.1 also shows that FORTRAN-style arrays result in one matrix row being stored on each disk page (assuming that a disk page holds exactly n array elements). If you are going to read the whole array or if the array is present in main memory, then this is a reasonable representation.

However, if you are going to read a "cube" of data from the array that is specified in an ad hoc manner, then FORTRAN representation will not perform well. Because the unit of transfer from disk to main memory is in units of whole pages, not only will the cube be read, but also a lot of extra data that is outside the scope of your query, as shown in Figure 5.2.

To avoid reading extra data with each query, the array should be "chunked," as illustrated in Figure 5.3. Using this methodology, a "stride" is specified for each index of the array, and the array is stored on disk in chunks specified as a single stride in each of the indexes. With this organization, it is likely that reading a chunk will entail much less wasted I/O. In the example, the extra data can be seen to be a much smaller set. Several studies (for example, Sarawagi and Stonebraker 1994) have shown that this tactic is generally a very good idea.

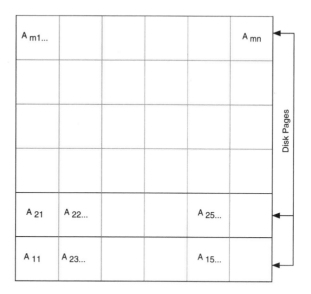

FIGURE 5.1 FORTRAN Representation

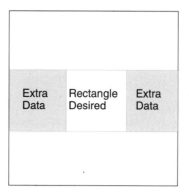

FIGURE 5.2 A Performance Problem

Current products implement such functionality in specialized engines. As a result, data must be loaded into such systems, typically by capturing historical data from a transaction processing system. Often the production system uses relational DBMS technology, which leads many users into the architecture indicated in Figure 5.4. Notice that the user must copy data from a relational engine into the second system. In other words, you need two systems, and a clever application program to transfer data from one system to the other.

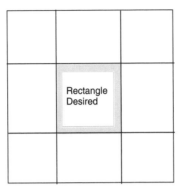

FIGURE 5.3 Chunked Representation

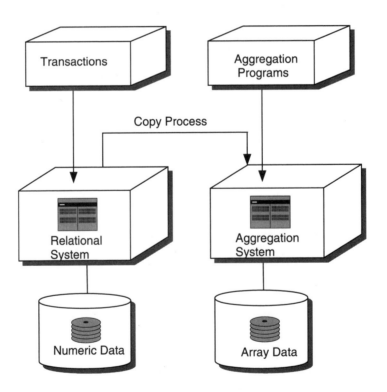

FIGURE 5.4 Traditional Aggregation Operation

In contrast, suppose an object-relational DBMS added the following features to its engine:

1. An array type constructor
2. The appropriate functions and operators on arrays
3. Optimized storage for arrays through chunking

With these extensions, an object-relational DBMS becomes a natural aggregation engine, and the architecture of Figure 5.4 is simplified to that of Figure 5.5. First, the user benefits from using an object-relational DBMS for an aggregation application. Specifically, you can put all of your data in a single DBMS, as shown in Figure 5.5. Moreover, if you wish, for performance reasons, to have array data also appear in a different format for transactional access, then it is straightforward to implement a rule in an object-relational engine that will correctly update the replicated information. (Rules are discussed in Chapter 7.)

The user also gets additional functionality. Specifically, an object-relational engine can support arrays of any data type, not just numeric arrays—a limitation that commonly straightjackets specialized systems.

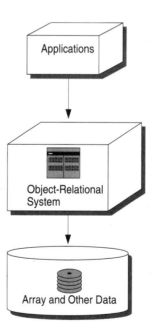

FIGURE 5.5 Object-Relational Support for Aggregation

As a result, expect object-relational DBMSs to add additional type constructors over time to provide needed functionality for specific vertical markets. Although time series and arrays were used as the examples in this chapter, it is highly likely that the same basic argument can be applied to a variety of other type constructors as well.

5.3   *Summary*

A rich set of type constructors along with a mechanism for user-defined functions is a powerful combination. On Wall Street, this allows high-performance access to historical tick data through time series calculations. Arrays plus optimized storage allow an object-relational DBMS to easily integrate OLAP functionality. This integration not only provides you with a more powerful system, but it simplifies administration and eliminates the need to run two systems.

CHAPTER 6 — *Characteristic 3: Inheritance*

The third major characteristic of a good object-relational DBMS is support for inheritance of various characteristics from supertype to subtype. The first section of this chapter concentrates on data inheritance. The next section focuses on function inheritance.

Like base type extension and complex objects, inheritance allows you to define new data types. All three facilities should be carefully used to create schemas that closely model the user's actual problem. Uncontrolled use of any of the facilities can create an explosion of types that may be very difficult to manage.

6.1   *Data Inheritance*

Data inheritance applies only to composite types. Suppose you construct the person_t data type with a single attribute, name:

```
create type person_t(
                name         varchar(30));
```

You can now construct two additional data types, employee_t and student_t:

```
create type employee_t (
                        salary    int,
                        startdate date,
                        address   varchar(30),
                        city      varchar(30),
                        state     varchar(30),
                        zipcode   int)
under    person_t;

create type student_t(
                    gpa     float)
under    person_t;
```

These statements each create a subtype under the supertype person_t. Each of the subtypes inherits all of the data fields from its supertype. The type employee_t inherits name from person_t and then specifies a collection of six additional attributes. Similarly, student_t inherits the same attribute from person_t and then adds a single additional attribute of its own.

A good object-relational DBMS supports multiple inheritance, which means a subtype can inherit data elements from multiple supertypes. And, an inheritance hierarchy can be multiple levels deep. For example, you can construct a student_emp_t data type as follows:

```
create type student_emp_t (
                            percent float)
under employee_t, student_t;
```

This statement indicates that the type student_emp_t inherits data elements from both student_t and employee_t. Specifically, it inherits the seven elements from employee_t and the two from student_t. Because name appears in both student_t and employee_t, then student_emp_t ends up with a total of nine fields as follows:

- name inherited from person_t
- salary, startdate, address, city, state, zipcode inherited from employee_t
- gpa inherited from student_t
- percent, specified in the type declaration

Data inheritance allows you to group composite types into an inheritance hierarchy; the complete type hierarchy for our example is illustrated in Figure 6.1. Types near the bottom of the hierarchy inherit many of their fields from supertypes. This is a good idea because it encourages modularity and consistent reuse of schema components. In addition, inheritance automatically adds all appropriate fields, making it impossible to leave any out. In a system without inheritance, you could inadvertently make mistakes, causing data element inconsistencies.

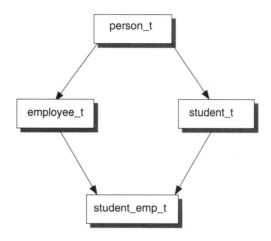

FIGURE 6.1 Example Inheritance Hierarchy

When a data type can inherit its fields from multiple supertypes, there is the possibility of ambiguity. For example, suppose you added the field address to student_t, but assigned it a different meaning than was present in employee_t. Specifically, suppose address in student_t was the complete student address, recorded as a varchar(60). In contrast, the same information is recorded in four fields in employee_t. In this case, student_emp_t has an ambiguity, in that both supertypes have an address field with different meanings.

To deal with this situation, consider taking the simplest possible approach, to disallow the definition of the student_emp_t, which caused the ambiguity to occur. Because of the ambiguity, you must redefine one of the address fields in one of the supertypes before proceeding with the definition of student_emp_t. The alternative is to have ambiguity resolution rules defined by a database administrator. These are invariably complex and difficult for users to understand.

Inheritance only applies to data types. If a table is constructed that is not of a named type, then this table will be of an anonymous type and cannot utilize inheritance. Therefore, you are encouraged to construct types and then assign them to tables rather than merely creating tables. In the former case, you can leverage inheritance; in the latter case, you cannot.

Clearly note that there is no storage associated with types, and tables must be constructed to hold instances of types. For example, you can construct the following four tables:

```
create table person of type person_t;

create table emp of type employee_t
under person;

create table student of type student_t
under person;

create table student_emp of type student_emp_t
under student, emp;
```

These four tables are constructed with specified types. More importantly, they illustrate the construction of a so-called table hierarchy, shown in Figure 6.2. Because the four types appear in the inheritance hierarchy of Figure 6.1, you would naturally expect to construct applications in which instances of each of the four types would be present. Moreover, the opportunity to have the scope of SQL commands be all persons (including those that are employees, students, and student_emps) is important. More generally, it should be possible to reference any table in the table hierarchy of Figure 6.2 and have the scope of the command be the table plus all tables underneath it.

For example, consider the following SQL statement:

```
select name
from emp
where salary = 10000;
```

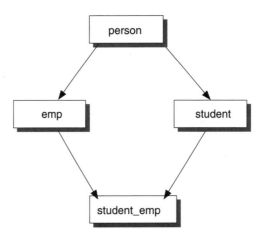

FIGURE 6.2   Example Table Hierarchy

This statement examines the table emp for employees who earn $10,000; however, it additionally examines all tables under emp in the table hierarchy for other qualifying instances. Thus, the scope of the "from emp" clause is automatically assumed to be the emp table and all tables that are underneath it in the table hierarchy. If you wish to only examine the emp table, then you would use the following syntax:

```
select name
from only (emp)
where salary = 10000;
```

In this case, only instances from the emp table and not descendent tables are returned.

Consider just the person and emp tables and suppose there are P instances in the person table and E instances in the emp table. In this case, the natural implementation is shown in Figure 6.3, namely, two containers, one with P records and one with E records.

Alternatively, you can store P + E records in the person container, one for each person and employee giving values for their name, and then E records in the emp container giving the additional fields for employees. This possibility is shown in Figure 6.4. Notice that some mechanism is required to join records in emp to their corresponding records in person, so that all fields of employees can be accessed. For this purpose, you could use a reference to a person record in the emp table. This latter implementation is advantageous for queries such as the following:

```
select name
from person
```

FIGURE 6.3   Informix Universal Server Representation

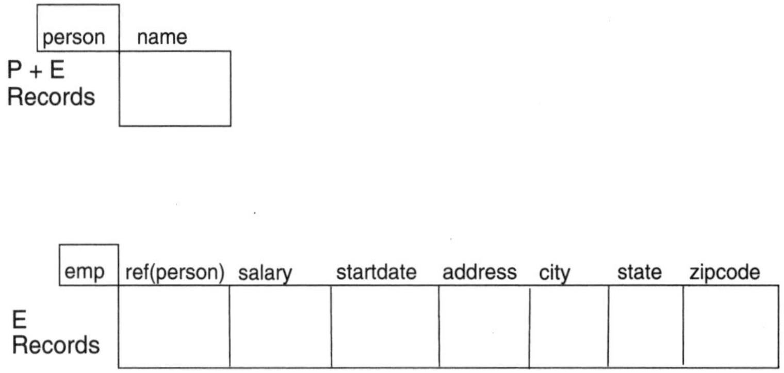

FIGURE 6.4   Alternative Representation

Here, an execution engine must access the single container person to solve the query; the natural implementation described earlier requires accesses to two containers. In contrast, however, consider the following query:

```
select salary
from only(emp)
where name = 'Joe';
```

In this case, fields in Joe's record appear in both containers, so accesses to both will be required if the alternative implementation is chosen. The natural implementation, however, requires only accesses to the emp container.

A final design is to put all instances in a single large container. This has the disadvantage that indexes are required to find the instances of any given table. A "table per container" model does not require such indexes.

As a result, different implementations of inheritance have different performance properties. You need to understand which option has been selected by the object-relational DBMS you are using, and then try to design databases that are the fastest for that implementation.

Inheritance on types allows a subtype to inherit data elements from supertypes in the inheritance hierarchy. In addition, table hierarchies allow you to scope SQL commands to return results from a table and its descendent tables in a single command.

There is one final point to be explained before leaving this topic. Consider the following query:

```
select *
from emp
where salary = 1000;
```

This query retrieves instances from both emp and student_emp, which have different collections of attributes. It is natural to retrieve only those columns that exist in emp from both tables.

In contrast, you should also be able to retrieve all attributes from both tables, resulting in a "jagged return." This can be accomplished with the following query:

```
select e
from emp e;
```

This feature gives you great power; however, the client program must be prepared to deal with the complexity of a jagged return.

6.2 *Inheritance of Functions*

The inheritance behavior of a user-defined function is determined by its arguments. Specifically, think of attaching to each node in the inheritance hierarchy the names of all functions that have this data type as an argument. Consider, for example, the addition of a new function, *overpaid:*

```
create function overpaid (employee_t, Arg1)
returns Boolean
as select Arg1.salary > (select salary from emp where name = 'Joe');
```

This function takes an instance of the type employee_t as an argument and returns a Boolean to indicate whether the employee is overpaid. In this example, *overpaid* returns true if the instance of employee_t makes a greater salary than that of Joe in the emp table. Figure 6.5 is Figure 6.1 with the addition of the function *overpaid*, which is attached to the employee_t node.

Now consider the following query:

```
select e.name
from only (emp) e
where overpaid (e);
```

This query evaluates in the obvious way, using the *overpaid* function just defined. However, consider the query with "only" removed:

```
select e.name
from emp e
where overpaid (e);
```

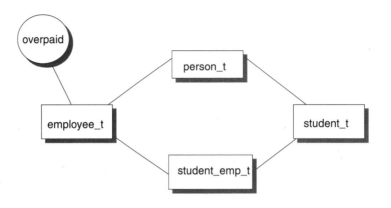

FIGURE 6.5 A Modified Type Hierarchy

Here, the scope of the command is the emp table plus the student_emp table. Clearly *overpaid* can be evaluated on the emp table as above. However, suppose there is no function *overpaid* defined on the type student_emp_t. Here, a good object-relational DBMS automatically inherits the function from a supertype. In this case, there is a supertype employee_t, and the *overpaid* function from that data type is used.

If an object-relational DBMS is asked to evaluate a function, and there is no function with the correct name and arguments, then the system searches the type hierarchy for a supertype on which the function is defined with the proper arguments. If one is found, then the system uses this function. In effect, student_emp_t inherits the function *overpaid* from employee_t.

It is permissible to have as many *overpaid* function definitions as are required to implement the user's application. This means if there is a different meaning for student employees being overpaid, then you can add a second *overpaid* function, for example,

```
create function overpaid (student_emp_t, Arg1)
returns Boolean
as select Arg1.salary >
        (select salary from student_emp where name = 'Bill');
```

This function returns true for those student employees who earn a salary greater than Bill's in the student_emp table. With the addition of this function, the inheritance hierarchy becomes the one shown in Figure 6.6.

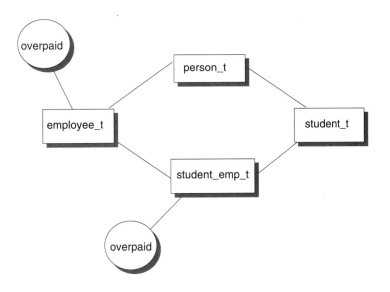

FIGURE 6.6 A Further Modified Type Hierarchy

Now if you run the query

```
select e.name
from emp e
where overpaid (e);
```

an object-relational DBMS uses one *overpaid* on the emp table and the second *overpaid* on the student_emp table. The answer will be the same as if the user had typed the following two queries:

```
select e.name
from only (emp) e
where overpaid (e);

select s.name
from only (student_emp) s
where overpaid (s);
```

This example illustrates that it is permissible to overload the name *overpaid* with two different definitions, applying to different data types. At runtime, an object-relational DBMS must utilize the correct function definition. Moreover, there will be queries, such as the one above, for which multiple functions will have to be used in the same query. This concept is also called *polymorphism*, because the function *overpaid* can be applied with different meanings to multiple types.

Consider the deletion of the *overpaid* function on student_emp_t and the definition of a new function *overpaid* for the data type student_t. This results in the inheritance hierarchy of Figure 6.7.

Next, consider the query

```
select s.name
from student_emp s
where overpaid (s);
```

In this case, there is no function *overpaid* defined for the data type student_emp_t. Moreover, there are two possible *overpaid* functions that could be inherited from supertypes, namely the ones for employee_t and student_t. In other words, there is an ambiguity concerning which one to use.

Again, we recommend issuing an error to indicate the ambiguity. It is then your responsibility to resolve the ambiguity by renaming one of the two functions to remove the problem or to write another *overpaid* function that addresses the special case of student employees. Other object-oriented languages address the problem of ambiguity in various ways, all with considerable additional complexity.

In many object-oriented languages user-defined functions are called *methods*. Conceptually, user-defined functions and methods are exactly the same thing. Therefore, we favor the term *function*.

The following is an alternate explanation of function inheritance in terms of data inheritance. Consider the function *overpaid*, which takes an instance of employee_t as an argument and returns a Boolean. This function can be thought of in either of two ways.

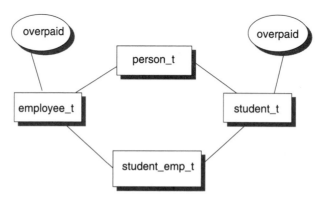

FIGURE 6.7   A Different Modification of the Type Hierarchy

First, it can be thought of as a function, whose argument is of type employee_t as above. As such, it can be used in queries, for example,

```
select e.name
from emp e
where overpaid(e);
```

This is the interpretation used in this chapter, so far. However, there is a second interpretation of *overpaid*. Specifically, it produces a value for any instance of employee_t. As such, it can be thought of as an additional *virtual* constituent attribute in the employee_t data type. Normal fields in an instance of a composite object are referenced as emp.name, emp.salary, and so on. Using this interpretation, *overpaid* can be referenced like any other attribute, for example,

```
select e.name
from emp e
where e.overpaid;
```

These two queries produce the same answer because you can define *overpaid* either as a virtual attribute or as a function. Put differently, you can place the function first in the query and put its argument in parentheses, or you can put the argument first and use the dot notation.

Using the second interpretation, *overpaid* is an attribute of employee_t and therefore can be inherited by descendent nodes in the inheritance hierarchy. As a result, you can think of functions as decorating the inheritance hierarchy and being inherited from supertypes if needed. You can also think of functions as virtual data elements in a type that are inherited from supertypes using standard data inheritance. In the first interpretation function notation is appropriate. In the second, data notation is preferred.The only difference is whether the function precedes its arguments and uses parentheses, or whether the argument comes first and the dot notation is used.

So far, we have seen how inheritance works with composite types. Inheritance with base types is also a good idea. A sensible approach is to allow developers to create new base types under existing base types, and then to specialize these subtypes by adding new functions that operate over them. For example,

```
create type positive_integer
under integer;

create function positive_integer_input ( string )
returning integer
as external name '$INFORMIXDIR/extend/positive_integer.bld'
language C;

create cast ( string to positive_integer)
as positive_integer_input;
```

This SQL creates a new data type called positive_integer that inherits all of the features of the integer base type: size, behavior, indexing, query management facilities, and so on. Then, the new *positive_integer_input* function converts the string to a positive_integer type. Note that within the same field size the new positive_integer can store a positive value twice as large as the value that a normal integer can store.

Unfortunately, the draft SQL-3 standard is at this time committed to a quite different approach to base type inheritance, using the notion of distinct types. To create a new SQL-3 base data type that inherits the properties of another base data type, you would use the following syntax;

```
create distinct type positive_integer
as integer;
```

Coupled with the definition of a cast function, this syntax has exactly the same effect as the "create type under" syntax. This leads to the unfortunate situation that there will be two syntaxes in SQL-3 for inheritance, one applying to base types and one applying to complex types.

6.3   *Summary*

This chapter discusses the third major characteristic of an object-relational DBMS: support of data and function inheritance. The features required for this support are as follows.

Feature 1: Both data and function inheritance must be supported.

In general, data inheritance by itself is not very useful. The real power comes from inheritance of functions.

Feature 2: Overloading must be supported.

It is highly desirable to be able to specialize the definition of a function to subtypes. This requires the possibility of multiple implementations of functions with the same name.

Feature 3: Types and tables must be separate concepts.

This chapter assumes a type hierarchy with separately defined containers (tables) to hold instances. In this case, you can have multiple tables of a specific type, for example, eastern_emp and western_emp. Each automatically has the inheritance properties described in this chapter. In contrast, some systems make the table hierarchy the same thing as the type hierarchy. Here, there can only be one table for a specific type, and considerable flexibility is forfeited.

Feature 4: Multiple inheritance must be supported.

In many applications, such as the example illustrated in this chapter, a given type must inherit from two different supertypes. Only support for multiple inheritance allows this to happen.

CHAPTER 7

Characteristic 4: Rules

The last feature in a good object-relational DBMS is a powerful, general-purpose rule system. Rules are exceptionally valuable in most DBMS applications because they protect the integrity of the data, make maintenance simpler, and are useful to model application work flow. Although relational systems provide some support for rules through the use of triggers, object-relational DBMSs demand a much more flexible system.

The paradigm for rules in DBMSs is a production system, popularized in the 1980s by the artificial intelligence community. The general form of a rule is

on <event>

where <condition>

do <action>

Thus, rules semantics require the DBMS to watch for the occurrence of some event, and if the condition is true, then the DBMS executes the desired action. Rule systems must include the capacity of executing the action before or after the event is processed, typically defaulting to just after execution.

This chapter discusses the following four variations of the basic rules paradigm:

- Update-update rules
- Query-update rules

- Update-query rules
- Query-query rules

7.1   *Update-Update Rules*

The first kind of rule is one where the event is an update and the action is another update. Consider the following rule, which watches for an update to Mike's salary and then propagates the change on to Jane:

```
create rule Mike_Jane_salary_synch
on update to emp.salary
    where current.name = 'Mike'
do update emp
    set salary = new.salary
    where name  = 'Jane';
```

Suppose that Mike's salary is $52,000 and his coworker Jane's salary is $45,000. When Mike's salary is updated, Jane's is also, according to the update-update rule. For example, the following update

```
update emp
set salary = '52500'
where name = 'Mike';
```

will, as a side effect, adjust Jane's salary to $52,500.

This update-update rule watches for the event that updates Mike's salary. When this event occurs, an action is automatically performed, namely to propagate the salary adjustment on to the employee Jane. The action is any legal SQL statement, augmented by the keyword **new**. New.salary refers to the field in the updated record at the time the event occurs, and it is used to provide a data value to the action.

Of course, at the same time, Mike's old salary can also be propagated on to Emma's salary:

```
create rule  Mike_Emma_salary_synch
on update to emp.salary
    where current.name = 'Mike'
(do update emp)
    set salary = current.salary
    where name = 'Emma';
```

When Mike receives a salary adjustment, coworker Emma's salary is set to Mike's old salary, while Jane receives Mike's new salary. Thus, as a result of side effects from the following update,

```
update emp
set salary = '56000'
where name = 'Mike';
```

Emma's salary will be set to $52,500 and Jane's to $56,000.

It is possible to have very general rules, for example,

```
create rule bonus_for_senior_staff
on update to emp.salary
    where current.startdate < '01/01/1980'
(do update emp)
    set salary = new.salary + 500
    where emp.name = current.name;
```

In this example, whenever an employee who started before 1980 receives a salary adjustment, the employee gets an additional $500 raise.

In other database systems update-update rules are often called "triggers." They are very useful in supporting data integrity in a database. When an event occurs that causes an integrity violation, then the corresponding corrective action can be performed as the action part of an update-update rule. In fact, in the Illustra server, referential integrity was supported by converting each referential integrity declaration into an update-update rule that was enforced by the Illustra engine.

7.2 *Query-Update Rules*

The second kind of rule is a query-update rule. With this rule the event is a query and the action that is taken is an update. An example of this second kind of rule is

```
create rule audit_salary_review
on select to emp.salary
    where current.name = 'Mike'
do insert into audit
    values
    ( current.salary, user, current_datetime );
```

Here, the rule watches for an event, which in this case is to retrieve Mike's salary. If this event occurs, then an insert is made into an audit table indicating who made the request (user), the value received (salary), and the time of the request (current_datetime). The audit table uses this information to maintain a complete record of accesses to Mike's salary. Such audit trails are usually very difficult to code in the trigger systems offered by many vendors because they do not support query-update rules.

7.3   *Update-Query Rules*

The third kind of rule is an update-query rule. Here, the event is an update and the action is to generate a response to a user. In other contexts, update-query rules are commonly called "alerters." For example, the Illustra server supported a very powerful alerting system that is specified using two statements:

```
create alert alert_Mike_on_salary_review
(mechanism = 'callback');

create rule alert_Mike_on_salary_change
on update to emp
   where  current.Name = 'Mike'
do raise alert alert_Mike_on_salary_review;
```

The second statement defines an update-query rule that watches for an update to Mike's salary and takes an action to notify an alerter, in this case alert_Mike_on_salary_review. This alerter is created in the first statement, which also indicates how clients will receive notification of this alert (by callback).

It is also possible to specify that clients will poll the server to receive notification of alerts that have occurred since the last time they polled. A client indicates interest in an alert by using the **listen** statement:

```
listen [alert_Mike_on_salary_review]
```

Any number of clients can listen for the same alert, and a client can listen for multiple alerts. A client listening on one or more alerts then goes about the business of doing queries and running transactions.

Some subset of the alerts have a poll mechanism rather than a callback mechanism. For those alerts, the client must periodically poll the server to receive notification of the alerts that have fired since the last time the client polled. The syntax is

```
poll [alert_name]
```

The remaining alerters are specified as "callback." In this case, the Illustra server signaled the application asynchronously that the event had occurred.

Callback is especially relevant for applications that have the sole task of listening for alerters that correspond to, say, abnormal events and then take appropriate corrective action. Industrial plant monitoring systems are often of this form. In such systems, the client wishes to listen for a collection of alerters and idles pending notification of the first one.

7.4 *Query-Query Rules*

The fourth kind of rule is a query-query rule. In this situation, the event is a retrieval and the action to be taken is also a retrieval. In the example on page 102, Mike's salary was propagated on to Jane using an update-update rule. The exact rule was

```
create rule Mike_Jane_salary_synch
on update to emp.salary
   where current.name = 'Mike'
do update emp
   set salary = new.salary
   where name  = 'Jane';
```

Using this scheme an update-update rule enforced that two employees had identical salaries. However, there is another way to accomplish the same goal with a query-query rule:

```
create rule Jane_Mike_salary_synch
on select to emp.salary
   where current.name = 'Jane'
do instead
   select salary
   from emp
   where name = 'Mike';
```

This rule watches for an event that retrieves Jane's salary. When this event occurs, an action is performed. In this example, the action is to retrieve Mike's salary. In addition, the keyword **instead** indicates that the action is to be performed instead of the event that caused the rule to fire. As a result, the following query returns Mike's salary rather than Jane's:

```
select salary
from emp
where name = 'Jane';
```

Thus, Jane's salary is never actually selected and is a *virtual* data element. Mike's salary is physically stored and returned whenever either Jane's or Mike's salary is requested. This is another way to ensure that Jane and Mike make the same salary, namely to store only one salary and then return it as a result of two different queries. Of course, it is possible to update Jane's salary, for example,

```
update emp
set salary = 100000
where name = 'Jane';
```

This statement will store the value 100,000 in Jane's salary attribute. However, the query-query rule will take precedence and always return Mike's salary instead.

Another use of query-query rules is to specify more elaborate protection systems than are possible with normal SQL systems. Specifically, traditional SQL systems have a grant/revoke security system that authorizes users to access tables and views, but only gives them data if they are authorized. Unfortunately, a persistent user can often glean information from such a security system. Suppose, for example, a particular user, Mark, is authorized to read employee salaries below $10,000. This can be accomplished by giving Mark access to the following view:

```
create view mark_emp
as select name as name,
salary as salary
from emp
where salary < 10000;
```

Suppose Mark then runs the query

```
select name, salary
from mark_emp
where name = 'Emma';
```

A null return means that Emma earns more than $10,000, and Mark has received some privileged information about Emma. As you can see, it is possible for SQL security systems to leak some information.

A more dramatic protection scheme now follows. Suppose the following query-query rule is defined:

```
create rule mark_emp_view
on select to emp.salary
   where current.salary >= 10000
do instead return rand_salary();
```

In this case, if Mark asks for Emma's salary, he will receive a random number from which he can derive no useful information. Other users who are properly authorized will receive the correct answer; thus, a query-query rule system can be made to *lie* to unauthorized users instead of giving them nothing.

You can put any collection of SQL statements into the action part of a rule and create composite rules that combine aspects of the four basic kinds of rules—update-update, update-query, query-update, and query-query. For example, the following rule is perfectly legal:

```
create rule emp_audited_view
on select to emp.salary
   where current.name = 'Jane'
do instead
begin
    insert into audit
    values
    (current.salary, user, current_datetime)
    select unique salary from emp where name = 'Mike';
end
```

As a result of a query to Jane's salary, the object-relational engine is asked to take two actions: one is an update to log the access in an audit trail, and the second is a query to return Mike's salary as the answer.

A rule system such as the one described above is a very powerful vehicle for supporting sophisticated DBMS applications. Not only can you trigger extra actions as a result of user updates, but you can also construct tailored audit trails, sophisticated alerting systems, virtual data elements, and elaborate protection. No doubt, as more experience is gained with rule systems, additional uses for these constructs will emerge.

Unfortunately, there is a dark side to rules; as you will see in the following section, they pose certain semantic difficulties.

7.5 *Semantics: The Dark Side of Rules*

It is possible to create some fairly weird (and undesirable) effects with certain kinds of rules. This section describes four potential semantic traps to be wary of:

- Multiple rules firing the same event sometimes cause unpredictable results.
- Chain rules can initiate infinite loops.
- Terminating a transaction also aborts the action part of a rule.
- Timing of rule activation can make a difference in the ultimate state of the database.

Multiple Rules Fired by the Same Event

The first thing to notice is that you can define an arbitrary number of rules. As a result, multiple rules can be fired as a result of the same event. Consider, for example, the following two rules:

```
create rule ambiguous_rule_one
on update to emp.salary
   where current.name = 'Mike'
do update emp
   set salary = new.salary
   where name = 'Jane';

create rule ambiguous_rule_two
on update to emp.salary
   where current.name = 'Mike'
do update emp
   set salary = 2 * new.salary
   where name = 'Jane';
```

In this case, two rules are fired as a result of an update to Mike's salary. The first rule sets Jane's salary to Mike's new salary, and the second sets it to twice that amount. Notice that a single data element (Jane's salary) is set to two different values by the two rules. It is important to note that rules that are fired by the same event are executed in a system-determined order. There is no way for a user to control the order of execution of the action parts of multiple rules. As a result, Jane's ultimate salary will depend on the execution order of the above rules.

If Mike's salary is set to $57,000 by the following SQL command,

```
update emp
set salary = 57000
where name = 'Mike';
```

then we cannot know whether Jane's salary will be $57,000 or $114,000.

This situation is analogous to the case of two users each running a transaction that adjusts Jane's salary at nearly the same time. In this case, Jane's ultimate salary will depend on which transaction committed first, something that is not controllable by the users.

To summarize, avoid constructing multiple rules with conflicting actions that can be fired by the same event. The result of such rules is not predictable.

Chain Rules Can Cause Infinite Loops

Chains of rules can be constructed where the action part of one rule makes the event part of the next rule true. Consider the following two rules:

```
create rule chain_one  as
on update to emp.salary
   where current.name = 'Mike'
do update emp
   set salary = new.salary
   where name = 'Jane';

create rule chain_two as
on update to emp.salary
   where current.name = 'Jane'
do update emp
   set salary = new.salary
   where name = 'Sam';
```

Suppose we update Mike's salary:

```
update emp
set salary = 58000
where name = 'Mike';
```

This update to Mike's salary fires "chain_one," which will propagate the new salary on to Jane's salary, which will cause "chain_two" to fire, further propagating the update on to Sam.

Unfortunately, it is also possible to construct chains of rules that are ill-formed. Consider the following two rules:

```
create rule circular_chain_rule_one
on update to emp.salary
   where current.name = 'Mike'
do update emp
   set salary = new.salary * 2
   where name = 'Jane';

create rule circular_chain_rule_two
on update to emp.salary
   where current.name = 'Jane'
do update emp
   set salary = new.salary * 2
   where name = 'Mike';
```

An update to either Jane's or Mike's salary circularly fires these two rules, leading a system into an infinite loop. A good object-relational DBMS must notice this condition and do something reasonable—for example, execute the loop exactly once. Clearly, you should avoid constructing rules such as these.

Aborting the Action Part of a Rule Terminates the Whole Transaction

Another issue that concerns the semantics of rules deals with the transaction in which the action part of a rule executes. Normally, the action is executed in the same transaction that caused the rule to fire. Note that the action part of the rule will abort if you abort your transaction. In most cases this sequence is desirable. For example, return to the update-update rule dealing with Mike and Jane:

```
create rule Mike_Jane_salary_synch
on update to emp.salary
    where current.name = 'Mike'
do update emp
    set salary = new.salary
    where name  = 'Jane';
```

If you update Mike's salary and then abort the transaction, then the triggered update to Jane's salary should also be aborted.

However, there are situations where this is not the desired effect. Return to the query-update rule from the previous section:

```
create rule audit_salary_review
on select to emp.salary
    where current.name = 'Mike'
do insert into audit
    values
    ( current.salary, user, current_datetime );
```

In this case, if you retrieve Mike's salary and then abort the transaction, the insert to the audit trail is aborted. Obviously, the purpose of the audit trail is to log salary accesses, and aborting a read transaction can circumvent the intent of the rule.

To do the right thing, the action part of the rule must run in a separate transaction from the user's statement. This other transaction always commits, regardless of the outcome of the user's transaction. It is desirable to be able to specify whether the action will run as a separate transaction or as part of the user's transaction. Currently, there are no known mainstream commercial DBMS rule systems with this flexibility.

Knowing When Rules Fire Is Important

A last issue is the time at which the action runs. In most current systems, rules are fired either just before or just after the event is processed. This corresponds to *immediate* execution of rules. In certain applications, you would like rules to fire only when the transaction that activates them actually commits. Currently, such *deferred* execution is not supported in any commercial DBMS that we are aware of.

Both kinds of behavior are desirable. To illustrate the requirement for deferred execution, consider the following rule:

```
create rule cascade_delete
on delete to emp
do after delete department
    where manager = current.name;
```

This rule indicates that when an employee is deleted, the department the employee manages must also be deleted. Now consider the following transaction:

```
begin work;
delete emp
where name = 'John';
update dept
set manager = 'Joe'
where manager = 'John';
commit work;
```

This transaction deletes John and then makes Joe the manager of John's department. If the rule fires at the time of the first update, then John's department is removed. However, at the end of the transaction, there is no department that John manages because the second statement made Joe the manager of any such department; thus, deferred execution of the rule has no effect. In this case, deferred execution is probably what you want to use.

Note that the time the rule is activated can make a difference in the ultimate state of the database at the end of the transaction. Some rules must be run immediately, for example, query-query rules; some can be run either immediately or at the end of the transaction. Ideally, you should be able to specify the timing you want.

7.6   *Summary*

In order for a system to be fully object-relational, it must support a rule system with the following features.

Feature 1: A rule system must support events and actions that are both retrieves and updates.

A system that supports only triggers gives users only a subset of needed capabilities.

Feature 2: The rule system must be integrated with other object-relational capabilities.

For example, the event and action part of a rule must be allowed to be any SQL statement. User-defined functions must be allowed to appear in a rule. In addition, if the object-relational system supports inheritance, then it is crucial that rules be inherited.

Chapter 6 describes an inheritance hierarchy dealing with persons, employees, students, and student employees. In this chapter, numerous rules dealt with the emp table. Because student_emp inherits its behavior from emp, then rules on emp will be inherited by student_emp. Clearly, a rule system requires automatic rule inheritance; you should not have to enter the same rule multiple times, once for each table in a table hierarchy.

Feature 3: A rule system supports {immediate, deferred} and {same transaction, different transaction} execution semantics.

All options are needed to generate the desired semantics for assorted important cases.

Feature 4: The rule system must not loop.

Obviously, the rule system cannot go into an infinite loop. An object-relational engine must have some strategy to recover gracefully from the execution of a circular rule set.

Notice clearly that determining whether a rule set is circular is very difficult. Consider the following slight modification of the rules on page 109:

```
create rule bad_1
on update to emp.salary where current.name = 'Mike'
do update emp
    set salary = 2 * new.salary
    where name = 'Jane';

create rule bad_2
on update to emp.salary where current.name = 'Jane'
    and current.salary <600000
do update emp
   set salary = 2 * new.salary
   where name = 'Mike';
```

Whenever Mike or Jane receives a salary adjustment, the two rules will circularly fire. However, the looping behavior ends when Jane's salary is adjusted above $600,000. Therefore, these two rules terminate while the ones on page 109 do not. It is very tough to tell the difference.

CHAPTER 8

Object-Relational
Parsing

This chapter provides a high-level look at an object-relational parser's design. A parser is responsible for processing the input textual representation of a query into an internal format, and for ensuring that the query is legal with respect to existing database objects. In a relational environment, the SQL dialect accepted is the same for each installation. However, in an object-relational world, the types, functions, and operators vary from database to database.

To discover what SQL is legal on the current machine, an object-relational parser must be completely table-driven from a large database of table, type, and function information. This information is stored in the system catalogs, which are updated as you declare additional tables, types, or functions. Thus, an object-relational parser differs greatly from traditional relational parsers, which are static and hard-coded with (and limited to) the SQL-92 data types and operations on those types.

8.1 *How an Object-Relational Parser Works*

Consider the following table:

```
create row type employee_t(
                        id          employee_id,
                        name        varchar(30),
                        salary      int,
                        startdate   date,
                        location    point,
                        picture     image);

create table emp of type employee_t;
```

Here, id, name, salary, and startdate have the obvious interpretation. Location is a point corresponding to the employee's home address, and picture is an image of the employee.

The following query selects from the emp table:

```
select name
from emp
where salary > 50000 and
vesting(startdate) > 0.6 and
contained(location, circle ('0,0', 1)) and
beard(picture) = 'gray';
```

This query finds all employees whose salary is above $50,000, who are more than 60% vested, whose residence is within a specific circle, and who have a gray beard. The first clause is a comparison of an integer against a constant and is defined in SQL-92. The second clause utilizes a user-defined function on a standard data type. In contrast, the third clause contains a pair of user-defined functions on a nonstandard data type. The fourth clause contains a user-defined pattern recognition function, *beard*, that looks at an image and determines whether the person in the image has a beard.

This query presents a challenge to the parser, which must correctly parse a command with user-defined types and functions. To translate SQL queries, the parser uses the following system catalog tables:

- *Tables:* Contains a row for every table in the database, giving the name of the table, the number of columns, and so forth.
- *Columns:* Contains a row for every column of every table in the database, giving the name of the column, its data type, and other information.
- *Types:* Contains a row for every data type known to the current database with the name of the type, its length, and so forth.
- *Functions:* Contains a row for every function registered in the database, giving the name of the function, the number and types of its arguments, the type of its return, the location of the code for the function, and so forth.

- *Operators:* Contains a row for every operator registered in the database, giving the identity of the function that implements that operator.

There are additional tables in the system catalogs that deal with inheritance, access methods, and rules. These tables are not discussed in this chapter.

The system catalog tables are dynamic; they expand to accommodate new tables, data types, functions, and operators as you define them. When you create a table, the system makes appropriate entries in Tables and Columns. When you create a data type, an entry is made in Types, and similarly, registration of a function causes an insert into Functions. You can think of these tables as metadata, because they contain data about the data in the database. In a relational DBMS, there are metadata only for tables and attributes; types and functions are hard-wired to the SQL-92 definitions.

When an object-relational parser encounters

```
from emp
```

in an SQL command, it looks up emp in Tables to ensure it exists; if emp exists, the parser looks up all the columns of emp in the Columns table. The parser then inserts a descriptor containing this information in a main memory data structure, so that subsequent queries to the same table will not have to pay the overhead of fetching system catalog metadata from disk again.

Much of the query can be parsed based on this information. The way that an object-relational parser handles functions is particularly interesting. Functions are differentiated by the combination of the function's name and the vector of argument types. This allows an object-relational database to have several functions sharing a name that are distinguished from each other by their parameters. For example, an object-relational database can contain two functions called *contained*, as follows:

```
contained(point, circle)
contained(point, box)
```

This combination of a function's name and its argument list is called the function's *signature*.

When an object-relational parser encounters a function expression in a query, it first searches for a function that matches the signature. But it is possible that your query can contain a function with a type mismatch. For example, suppose there is no function *vesting* that takes the date data type as its only argument. When it fails to identify a function that is a perfect match, the object-relational DBMS will evaluate the rest of the type system to find a matching function that uses a supertype, or another type for which a casting rule exists.

Because of the semantics of the SQL language, certain built-in types can be substituted for others. The server retains a "precedence list" of built-in types and tries to find a matching function signature by substituting for other types in a built-in type's precedence list.

Finally, the object-relational database supports the definition of a special function called a *cast*. The following command creates a cast from the date data type to the workday data type:

```
create cast (date to workday)
as date_converter;
```

If the parser fails to find a *vesting* function for date, it looks for a *vesting* function on a different data type where a cast exists between the two. If it finds one, it automatically casts the argument in your query to the new type and then continues parsing using the *vesting* function that exists for this type. Of course, if there are multiple new types to which the argument can be cast, then an ambiguity exists. Chapter 6 describes how an object-relational server generates an error when inheritance ambiguity is encountered, rather than making an arbitrary choice. The same choice is made here. If a casting ambiguity exists, an error is generated.

8.2　*Summary*

You can now see why a redesign is required to convert a conventional relational parser to an object-relational one. You must remove all the hard-coded type, operator, and function information, replace it with a table-driven scheme, and then add support for complex objects and inheritance.

CHAPTER 9

Traditional Relational Optimizers

This chapter shows how traditional relational optimizers work. It is a prelude to Chapter 10, which discusses the extensions that must be made to support object-relational optimization.

9.1　*How Relational Optimizers Work*

All relational optimizers work roughly the same way and employ variations on the techniques implemented in *System R* by Pat Selinger et al. (1979). Given the traditional example relational tables

```
create table emp_R (
                name            varchar(30),
                salary          int,
                startdate       date
                dname           varchar(30));


create table dept_R (
                dname           varchar(30),
                floor           int);
```

and given a query such as the following:

```
select e.name
from emp_R e, dept_R d
where e.dname = d.dname and
d.floor = 1 and
e.startdate < '01/01/1980' and
e.salary > 10000;
```

the optimizer will generate a heuristic subset of all possible ways of performing this query. For each such plan evaluated, the optimizer computes the following cost function in a way to be explained in this chapter:

cost = expected number of records examined   +
                     (fudge-factor * (expected number of pages read))

The cost function estimates total resource usage for the query. In effect, the first term is a surrogate for the expected use of CPU resources by the query. The second term guesses the I/O resources and then multiplies them by a fudge factor, indicating for this installation how important CPU resources are relative to I/O resources. The optimizer computes this cost function for a large collection of possible plans and selects the one for execution that has the lowest expected cost.

For the example query, there are restrictions on both the emp_R and dept_R tables and then a join between them. The optimizer assumes that joins are more expensive than restrictions, and therefore examines plans of the form shown in Figure 9.1.

This is one of the optimizer's built-in heuristics to minimize the number of plans explored.

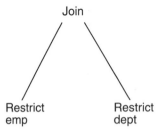

FIGURE 9.1   Join between emp_R and dept_R Tables

9.2   *Performing the Restriction on the Table emp_R*

To perform the restriction on emp_R, there are three possible options to be evaluated:

1. A sequential scan of emp_R
2. An index scan of emp_R using a B-tree index on salary
3. An index scan using a B-tree index on startdate

Sequential Scan of emp_R. Each record of emp_R is evaluated in turn and rejected if the qualification is not true. If there are n-emp records in the table and they occur on N-emp pages, then the cost of this operation is

cost = n-emp + fudge-factor * N-emp

Index Scan of emp_R Using a B-Tree Index on Salary. Most systems employ secondary indexes, where the leaf nodes of a B-tree index contain a collection of records of the form

(indexed-value, pointer-to-a-data-record-with-this-value)

These records are kept in sort order by the B-tree insertion and deletion routines. Figure 9.2 shows a few of the emp_R records and their corresponding leaf B-tree index entries.

In addition, a B-tree has a collection of interior nodes containing records of the form

(value, pointer-to-a-descendent-page)

Typically, the value in any interior record is the highest value found on the descendent page to which the record points. An indexed value can be located by searching the root page for the smallest value that is still greater than the one for which the search is being conducted. Interior pages are searched iteratively until the leaf level is reached, where the value sought can be located. Following the pointer in this leaf record locates the actual data desired. Figure 9.2 (reprinted here from Chapter 2) shows example entries in the nonleaf portions of the B-tree.

Range searches can be performed in an analogous way; the above algorithm can be used to find the start of a scan of the leaf-level records in the index. This scan can terminate when an index record is found that is outside the desired range.

Consequently, if a B-tree index for the startdate attribute exists, then an index scan can be performed by using the following clause:

```
salary > 10000
```

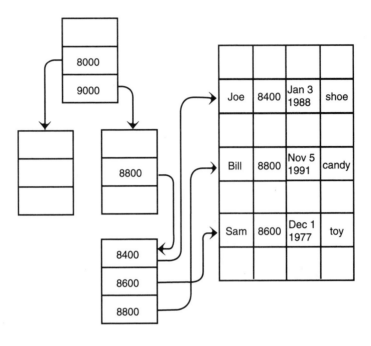

FIGURE 9.2   Example Secondary Index

For each qualifying index entry, the system must fetch the actual data record for this index record and then evaluate the remaining predicate, namely,

```
startdate < '1980-01-01'
```

To evaluate the expected cost of an index scan, the optimizer must estimate the number of records that satisfy the qualification

```
salary > 10000
```

because this is the number of data records that will be examined. This guess is based on statistical evidence.

Specifically, traditional relational systems allow a database administrator to build a histogram for the salary values in emp_R. For example, the values of salary can be quantized into 10 buckets, 0–2000, 2000–4000, . . . ,18,000–20,000, and then the number of emp records that fall within each bucket are computed. This histogram is accurate at the time it is computed and then gradually decreases in accuracy as the emp_R table is updated. Periodically the database administrator must specify that the statistics are to be refreshed.

The optimizer can guess the number of records, K, with salary > 10,000 as the sum of the last five buckets in the histogram. If there are no statistics for the salary attribute, then the optimizer must make an arbitrary guess for K. In the Selinger paper (1979), this guess is

K =   (1/3) * n-emp

Obviously, such a guess is fairly arbitrary.

The I/O cost of an index scan depends on whether the B-tree index is *clustered* or *unclustered*. If the relational engine attempts to keep the data records in approximately the same order as they appear in the index; i.e., the data records are approximately sorted on salary, then the salary index can be called a clustered index. Otherwise, the salary index will be unclustered, and the data records are either in random order or approximately ordered on some other attribute. Figure 9.2 showed an unclustered salary index, while Figure 9.3 depicts a clustered version of the same index.

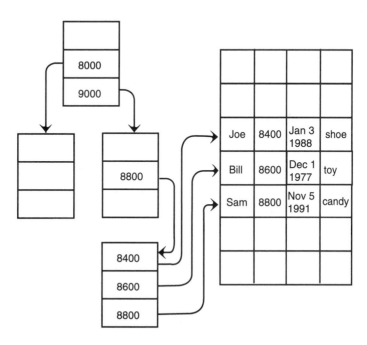

FIGURE 9.3   Example Clustered Secondary Index

If the salary index is unclustered, then the number of I/Os will be approximately equal to the expected number of records examined, a quantity that has already been estimated. The reason for this formula is that each index record contains a pointer to a data record. In an unclustered index, each such record will likely be on a different data page, and one data page must therefore be read per index entry. The cost of an index scan of an unclustered index is

cost = K + fudge-factor * K

In contrast, if the index is clustered, then a different calculation must be made. Specifically, the expected number of employee records per data page is

emps-per-page = n-emp / N-emp

Because the optimizer has already estimated K, the number of records that satisfy the qualification

```
salary > 10000
```

then it will estimate that

total-pages = K / emps-per-page

pages must be examined. The reason for this calculation is that employee records are clustered together in the data set in approximately salary order. As the index is scanned, the next record pointer will probably point to the same page as the previous one, and all employees with salaries greater than 10,000 will be clustered together on as few pages as possible. The complete cost for an index scan of a clustered index is

cost = K + fudge-factor * (K / emps-per-page)

The optimizer now has an estimated cost for an index scan of the emp_R table using the salary index for the two possible organizations of the index.

Index Scan Using a B-Tree Index on Startdate. The optimizer can use methods similar to those just described to determine whether there is a B-tree index on the startdate attribute and compute the expected cost of an index scan using this index.

Some systems implement an additional way to perform the restriction on emp_R. Specifically, it is possible to build an execution plan that uses both indexes. You can scan the startdate index for pointers to employees that satisfy the qualification

```
startdate < '1980-01-01'
```

and then scan the salary index for pointers to employees that satisfy

```
salary > 10000
```

Then, the two lists of pointers are intersected to find the collection of pointers that satisfies both predicates. As a last step the plan accesses the relevant emp_R records to obtain needed data fields. In certain cases, performing list operations on multiple indexes is an excellent query processing option and should also be considered by an ORDBMS.

At this point, the optimizer has an expected cost for all possible ways of performing the appropriate restriction on emp_R. In a similar fashion, it can compute the expected cost of the restriction on dept_R, utilizing all possible ways to perform the restriction.

There are two additional steps performed by all optimizers. The first concerns processing predicates containing the negation operation. If the optimizer ever sees a clause of the form

```
where not some-predicate
```

then it can only solve this query using a sequential scan. Thus, when a "not" appears in a predicate, it is impossible to perform an index scan, and the high-performance way of running the query is not available.

Therefore, optimizers attempt to remove "not" operators from the predicate, by using semantic knowledge of SQL operators. Specifically, the optimizer knows that > is the negation of <=. If the optimizer sees a predicate of the form

```
where not (salary > 10000)
```

it can transform the predicate to

```
where salary <= 10000
```

The operation **not** can be removed from the predicate if the operator inside the predicate is replaced by its negator operator. For all SQL comparison operators {<, <=, =, >, >=, !=}, the optimizer knows the appropriate negator operator and performs the transformation to remove the **not**.

The second modification of a predicate is for bookkeeping convenience. A clause might be written as

```
where  10000  > salary
```

Here, the constant appears on the left-hand side of the operator, and the variable is on the right. Alternatively, the clause might have been written with the constant on the right, for example,

```
where salary < 10000
```

Rather than require the execution engine to understand both forms of clauses, SQL optimizers convert the predicate to *canonical form* by transforming each clause in the predicate to have the constant on the right-hand side. This requires optimizers to have knowledge of the commutator operator for each comparison operator. With the knowledge that > is the commutator for <, the optimizer can convert the first representation into the second one. This processing step allows the engine to only deal with predicates in canonical form and simplifies internal bookkeeping.

9.3   *Methods for Processing the Join*

Next, this chapter discusses ways to process the join that remains after the restrictions have been evaluated and two temporary tables, T1 and T2, have been constructed. This join is

```
select T1.name
from T1, T2
where T1.dname = T2.dname;
```

There are three possible techniques that the optimizer must evaluate:

- Nested loop join
- Merge join
- Hash join

All of these techniques require estimates for the number of records and number of pages in both of the tables to be joined. These tables result from restriction operations earlier in the plan. In the example query, the restrictions are

```
select name, dname
from emp_R
where startdate < '01/01/1980' and
salary > 10000;

select dname
from dept_R
where floor = 1;
```

At optimization time these tables do not exist, so the optimizer must guess their resulting size.

In the case of dept_R, the optimizer has previously guessed the selectivity of the clause

```
floor = 1
```

The optimizer can simply multiply this number by n-dept to estimate the number of records in one argument to the join. Similarly, it can multiply this estimate by the width of the dname field to estimate the number of pages in the argument.

However, the corresponding estimates for the restriction on emp_R are more problematic. Estimates for the selectivity of each of the two clauses have been previously computed. Most optimizers simply multiply them together to arrive at a combined selectivity. Of course, this makes the assumption that the clauses are statistically independent, an assumption rarely justified in practice. This independence assumption introduces errors in the size estimates for temporary arguments, which in turn propagate through the rest of the query plan.

The Nested Loop Join Technique. The first technique, nested loops, can be applied by choosing either T1 or T2 as the "outer" table, and then iterating over this table. If T1 is chosen, then each record in T1 is iteratively retrieved, yielding a value for T1.name and T1.dept. These values are substituted into the query, producing

```
select value-1
from T2
where value-2 = T2.dname;
```

If there are n-T1 records in T1 occupying N-T1 pages, then the cost of this join strategy is

n-T1 + fudge-factor * N-T1

+

n-T1 (expected cost of the resulting query on T2)

The nested loops technique constructs a collection of queries on the table T2, which the optimizer then guesses the cost of, using the techniques described earlier. As a result, there are two computations for iterative substitution, namely, (1) choose T1 as the outer table and (2) choose T2 as the outer table.

The Merge-Join Method. The second alternative is to perform merge-join. Here, both T1 and T2 are sorted on the join field, if they are not already in sort order. After one or two sorts, the two tables are correctly ordered on the same attribute and the two tables can be merged by stepping through both tables in an orderly fashion to produce the joined result. The cost of merge-join is

cost (sort T1) + cost (sort T2) + cost (merge)

The cost of a sort is determined by the algorithm employed. However, most vendors choose a polyphase sort algorithm. Using this algorithm, the CPU cost of the sort is

constant-1 * n * log n

where n is the number of records being sorted. In addition, the number of pages examined is also

constant-2 * N * log N

where N is the number of pages being sorted. For details on the composition of the two constants as well as the base of the logarithm in the calculation, consult a text on sorting, such as Knuth (1973). Merge-joins are clearly an attractive option when one or both arguments are already sorted, such as when the argument is contructed using an index scan.

The cost of the merge operation is simply

n-T1 + n-T2 + fudge-factor * (N-T1 + N-T2)

Adding the three costs together gives the ultimate cost of merge-join as a join strategy.

The Hash-Join Algorithm. The last alternative is the hash-join algorithm. Here, one table is selected and hashed on the join field into a collection of H hash buckets. If there is enough main memory to hold all H buckets, then the algorithm proceeds by sequentially reading the second table for each record hashing on the join field to produce a hash bucket. Then the appropriate hash bucket is searched to see whether a matching record or records is found. In this case, the CPU cost of a hash-join is

n-T1 + n-T2 * (number of records in a hash bucket)

This latter quantity is simply

n-T1 / H

Similarly, the I/O cost is merely the total sizes of both of the tables:

N-T1 + N-T2

Hash-join has I/O that is linear in the number of pages but a CPU cost that is proportional to

(N-T1 * N-T2)/ H

It may be more or less attractive than merge-join, depending on the value assigned to the fudge factor. Last, if there is not enough space in main memory to hold all of one table, then the above algorithm must be modified to utilize less memory. For the details of these modifications, consult a paper on the subject such as Dewitt et al. (1990).

Notice that both hash-join and merge-join are only possible if the join is an equality join, such as in our example. If the join clause does not use equality, then only a nested loop join is possible.

Furthermore, if there are multiple join clauses that connect two tables, then the optimizer must evaluate each one according to the above computations. The other join predicates then become restrictions on the table that is produced as a result of the join.

If you specify a three-way join, then the optimizer must evaluate all possible ways of performing the first join. The result of the first join must then be joined with the remaining table. To compute the cost of this final operation, the optimizer must generate an estimate for the size of the result of the first join. The optimizer has available the expected sizes of the two tables that are to be joined together; however, it must construct an estimate for the size of the answer. Obviously, the number of records in a join can vary from none (i.e., no records from one table join with any records in the other one) to n-T1 * n-T2 (i.e., every record in the first table joins to every record in the second table).

Of course, the latter outcome only happens in rare circumstances. For example, if only one value for the join field is present in each table and they match, then the resulting join will have n-T1 * n-T2 records.

To construct an estimate for the size of the join, the optimizer requires an estimate for the join selectivity, S(T1, T2). With this estimate, it can compute the expected size of the answer as

S(T1, T2) * n-T1 * n-T2

The above calculation is notoriously imprecise. Generally, n-T1 and n-T2 are the expected size tables that resulted from earlier computations in the query plan, so you would expect them to be rather imprecise. In addition, most optimizers utilize crude measures for S(T1, T2). For example, if both of the join fields are unique keys in their tables (i.e., every value is assuredly different), then S(T1, T2) is estimated to be

min (n-T1, n-T2) / (n-T1 * n-T2)

Here, the optimizer is guessing that the size of the join is the same as the smaller of the two tables. Clearly if both join fields are keys, it can be no larger than this number; however, it can, in reality, be much smaller. As you can see, join selectivities are not an exact science.

When a four- or more way join is computed, the optimizer has additional choices to make. It can restrict its search to *left-only* trees—query plans of the form shown in Figure 9.4. In this case, the query plan looks like a tree that goes from lower left to upper right. In addition, only the left-hand side of the join is allowed to be something that results from a previous join, and hence the name "left-only tree."

Alternatively, the optimizer can also evaluate so-called *bushy* trees—query plans that have the form shown in Figure 9.5.

Some optimizers evaluate only left-only trees as a heuristic simplification to cut down on the size of the optimizer search space. Others evaluate all possible plans.

Optimizers differ widely in the quality of plans that they produce. Generally speaking, most vendors' version 1.0 optimizers are fairly dumb. After a number of release cycles and an infusion of significant development resources, an optimizer becomes smarter. Also, some vendors care more about the quality of their optimizer than others. Unfortunately, the only way to determine who these vendors are is to test each company's optimizer with the kinds of queries that you expect to run.

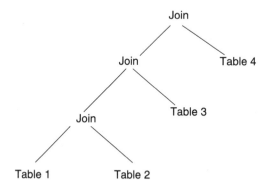

FIGURE 9.4   A Left-Only Tree

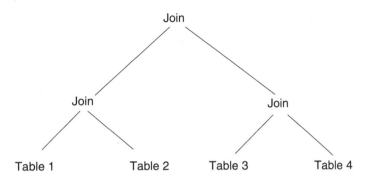

FIGURE 9.5   A Bushy Tree

CHAPTER 10

Object-Relational Optimizers

This chapter examines 16 specific extensions that should be made to a traditional relational optimizer so that it will work well in an object-relational environment. This chapter also offers several test queries to help you ascertain if a particular vendor's optimizer has the necessary object-relational extensions.

The 16 necessary extensions are

1. operator and function notation (page 132)
2. generic B-trees (page 133)
3. user-defined comparison operators (page 133)
4. user-defined selectivity functions (page 135)
5. user-defined negators (page 136)
6. user-defined commutators (page 136)
7. access methods on a function of the data (page 137)
8. smart ordering of the clauses in a predicate (page 138)
9. optimization of expensive functions (page 140)
10. user-defined access methods (page 142)
11. "flattening" complex object queries (page 144)
12. "in-line" sets (page 145)
13. indexes on attributes of sets (page 146)
14. optimization of scans of inheritance hierarchies (page 147)

15. optimization of joins over inheritance hierarchies (page 147)

16. support for user-defined aggregates (page 148)

The examples in this chapter use the emp table from Chapter 8:

```
create row type employee_t(
                        id          employee_id,
                        name        varchar(30),
                        salary      int,
                        startdate   date,
                        location    point,
                        picture     image);

create table emp of type employee_t;
```

The examples also use a B-tree index defined on the salary attribute as follows:

```
create index salary_index
on emp(salary) using B-tree
```

The relational DBMS vendors' track record for providing straight answers on the quality of their optimizers is poor. For many years one major relational vendor processed join queries in the order that the user constructed the clauses in the predicate. This meant that the order in which the user submitted the joins in the predicate determined the order in which the system processed the joins. This required each user of the system to hand-optimize each query by putting the predicates in the correct order. Another major relational vendor has not implemented merge-join or hash-join but relies exclusively on nested-loop joins. Therefore, this chapter provides some test queries that you can run to determine whether a particular optimizer does indeed build in each of the necessary extensions.

10.1   *Extension 1: Operator and Function Notation*

Consider a query such as

```
select name
from emp
where salary > 10000;
```

Clearly, the optimizer can utilize either a sequential scan or an indexed scan using salary_index to solve this query. However, in an object-relational DBMS, you can code the salary query in operator notation as above, or you can use the following function notation:

```
select name
from emp
where GreaterThan (salary, 10000);
```

Because these two queries are syntactically different forms of the same query, you should be able to use the notation that you are most comfortable with. Therefore, the optimizer should be able to deal with either notation.

Test for Extension 1. The two representations for the above query are both allowed, and they should generate the same query plan and run at exactly the same speed.

10.2   *Extensions 2 and 3: B-Trees and User-Defined Comparison Operators*

This section discusses the importance of generic B-tree support as well as user-defined comparison operators in an object-relational DBMS. Consider the following query:

```
select name
from emp
where location N_equator_equals point('500, 0');
```

Here, you are requesting the employees who live at the same distance from the equator as the point (500, 0), that is, those employees who live exactly 500 miles north of the equator. The user-defined operator, N_equator_equals, expresses this request.

Obviously, the optimizer can utilize a sequential scan of emp to solve this query. However, a B-tree index scan is generally faster for this query. After all, employees can be sorted on distance north of the equator and then a B-tree can be built on "northness." With such a B-tree, the above predicate can be used to perform an indexed scan, and a more efficient query plan is likely to result.

In order for this query to be able to use an index scan, the following two extensions to an object-relational system are necessary:

- B-tree code must be made generic.
- User-defined comparison operators are required.

In current relational systems, the B-tree code hard-wires numeric date and character string data types. You can build a B-tree only on these specific types. In an object-relational DBMS, the B-tree system must be generic; it must be possible to build a B-tree on any data type, and not just on alphanumeric types. For example, it must be possible to build a B-tree on instances of the point data type.

Moreover, when presented with an equality search such as the one above, the current relational B-tree search logic begins at the root page of the B-tree and searches for the (value, pointer) pair that has the smallest value greater than or equal to the constant in your query. When this (value, pointer) is identified, the B-tree logic retrieves the page identified by the pointer and repeats the procedure. The process concludes when the leaf level is reached and specific pointers to data records are identified. To perform this search, the logic in current B-trees has a hard-wired notion of the definition of "greater than or equal" for each of the alphanumeric types supported.

To solve the above query using an index scan, it must be possible to build a B-tree with user-defined operators instead of the standard alphanumeric comparison operators. A B-tree can support index scans for the operators {<, <=, =, >, >=}. For user-defined types, such as point, a human must be able to specify the definition of these operators. For example, the following set of comparison operators could be used for the point data type:

- N_equator_greater_than
- N_equator_greater_than_equals
- N_equator_equals
- N_equator_less_than
- N_equator_less_than_equals

There are numerous possible collections of comparison operators for new data types. For example, you can utilize the following possibilities for the point data type:

- Northness, as described in the above example
- Westness, which involves the same general computation as the above example
- Distance away from a specific point, say, company headquarters

It is possible to build a B-tree to support any one of these classes of operators. For example, one syntax to construct the appropriate B-tree index is

```
create index north-index
on emp(location)
using B-tree (northness-class);
```

Here northness-class defines the collection of five comparison operators mentioned above and instructs the B-tree index to be built using them. All insertions to the B-tree are done using the comparison operator "N_equator_greater_than_equals." The optimizer understands that any query containing one of these five operators is a candidate for an index scan solution.

With generic B-trees and user-defined operator classes, it is possible to build a B-tree index that supports index scans on a wide variety of user-defined data types and operators.

Tests for Extensions 2 and 3. The test for extension 2 is simple: it must be possible to build B-tree indexes on user-defined types with user-defined operators. To test for user-defined comparison operator support, run a query such as the one requesting employees 500 miles north of the equator. Can the query use an index scan with a response time of a second or two for a large employee collection?

10.3   *Extension 4: User-Defined Selectivity Functions*

In a relational DBMS, selectivity functions are hard-coded into the optimizer, as discussed in Chapter 9. Clearly, when a new data type and appropriate comparison operators are defined, the optimizer has no possible knowledge of the selectivity of these operators for the new data type. This means there must be a way for you to specify how the optimizer computes selectivities.

In a universal server, a B-tree index uses a specific operator class, such as the northness operators discussed above. Each operator in this class is associated with a specific binary function when the operator is created. For example, the following command binds N_equator_equals to the function *Northness_equal*:

```
create operator
binding N_equator_equals
to Northness_equal;
```

When you define a new function to the DBMS, you can optionally define a second function associated with it, called a *selectivity function*. This feature enables you to tell the optimizer how to compute the selectivities it must have to properly evaluate plans. The following definition of *Northness_equal* illustrates this construct:

```
create function Northness_equal (point, point)
returns Boolean
with selfunc = selectivity_comp
as external name '/usr/Northness_equal'
language C;
```

When the optimizer sees a query such as

```
select name
from emp
where location N_equator_equals point ('500, 0');
```

it will call the function *selectivity_comp* to return a floating-point number between 0 and 1. Then it will multiply this returned value by the size of the emp table to generate an estimate for the number of index records that will be evaluated. The *selectivity_comp* function may construct its value based on statistics, or through some other technique.

Test for Extension 4. It must be possible to specify user-defined selectivity functions to an object-relational DBMS optimizer.

10.4   *Extension 5: User-Defined Negators*

The following example query helps to illustrate user-defined negators:

```
select name
from emp
where not (location N_equator_greater_than point ('500, 0'));
```

Ideally, the optimizer can transform this query to

```
select name
from emp
where location N_equator_less_than_equals point ('500, 0');
```

The second expression can be evaluated for use of an index scan, while the first cannot. More formally stated, the following transformation occurs:

not (attribute operator value) → attribute operator-2 value

To make this transformation, the optimizer must be told the negator (operator-2 in the above example) for each user-defined operator.

In a universal server, when the function *Northness_greater_than* is constructed, the function creator can optionally specify the negator for the function. For example,

```
create function Northness_greater_than (point, point)
returns Boolean
with negator = Northness_less_than_equals
as external name '/usr/Northness_greater_than'
language C;
```

The following test determines whether a given system supports the optimization of **not.**

Test for Extension 5. Can the two versions of the query discussed above execute at the same performance, and can they both utilize an index scan?

10.5   *Extension 6: User-Defined Commutators*

This section describes user-defined commutators as a necessary extension for an object-relational optimizer. Consider the following query:

```
select name
from emp
where 500 N_equator_greater_than location;
```

Clearly, this can use an index scan and is equal to

```
select name
from emp
where location N_equator_less_than_equals 500;
```

Obviously, both queries should run at exactly the same performance. In a universal server, this is assured by allowing the definer of a function to specify the commutator for the function as follows:

```
create function Northness_greater_than (point, point)
returns Boolean
with commutator = Northness_less_than_equals
as external name '/usr/Northness_greater_than'
language C;
```

Test for Extension 6. Can the above two specifications of the query run at the same speed, and can both utilize an index scan?

10.6   *Extension 7: Access Methods on a Function of the Data*

Consider the following query:

```
select name
from emp
where redness (picture) < 0.1;
```

This query contains a user-defined function that computes how red an employee's picture is and returns a floating-point number between 0 and 1. It would be desirable to support the possibility of building a B-tree index on the result of the function *redness*. If this index is constructed, then an indexed scan can be utilized to perform the above query.

Traditional relational systems support only B-tree indexes on the value of an attribute. However, there are a variety of data types, including images, where it is never relevant to build an index on the actual attribute. For example, a B-tree index on image data keeps the index in sorted order on the bytes in the image. This index is not relevant to any user queries. Thus, the only plausible indexes are on a function of the image data.

In an object-relational DBMS, function indexes are allowed and specified as follows:

```
create index picture_index
on emp using B-tree (redness (picture));
```

This command tells the system to build an index on the *redness* function, which returns a floating-point number. Comparison operators are those that are appropriate for floats. Moreover, whenever a new employee is added, the system must compute the *redness* function for the employee's picture and then index the answer. Similarly, when an employee is deleted, the *redness* function must again be computed to find the appropriate index record and remove it. In the unlikely event that an image is updated for an employee, the *redness* function for both the old image and the new image must be computed, so that the index can be appropriately modified.

Notice that the *redness* function is being "eagerly" computed; that is, it is evaluated at the time an employee is added to the database. In contrast, it would also be possible to evaluate the function at the time it was used in a query, that is, using "lazy" evaluation. If an Informix universal server function is indexed, then it is converted from lazy to eager evaluation. As a result, a query using the function receives much better response time, because the computation need not be performed at runtime. Moreover, the result of the function is indexed, possibly allowing the optimizer to construct a better plan for the query. As a result, function indexing is a very valuable optimization technique.

It is possible in some systems to define a collection of triggers that compute *redness* in the action part and store the result in a new column in the table. Indexing can then be performed on the stored data. The disadvantage of this scheme is the necessity of storing the extra column. In addition, if the index is no longer needed, it can be tedious to remove the added attribute. Indexes on functions are a much more elegant solution.

Test for Extension 7. It must be possible to construct an index on the *redness* function, and the optimizer must automatically use the index when appropriate. Your query must be specified the same way whether the index is present or not.

10.7   *Extension 8: Smart Ordering of the Clauses in a Predicate*

Consider the following modification to the previous query:

```
select name
from emp
where redness (picture) < 0.1
and salary > 10000;
```

and assume for the moment that there are no indexes on the emp table. In this case, a sequential scan must be utilized.

A relational DBMS will perform a sequential scan and evaluate the predicate for each retrieved record. However, it will evaluate the clauses in the predicate from left to right. In traditional SQL, this is a reasonable strategy, since all clauses are generally quite simple and do not involve significant CPU time. Unfortunately, this assumption is not true in an object-relational DBMS, as the above query demonstrates. Specifically, the clause

```
salary > 10000
```

requires perhaps 100 CPU instructions to evaluate, while the clause

```
redness (picture) < 0.1
```

requires perhaps $100 * 10^6$ instructions. The reason for this computational intensity is that *redness* must perform a color analysis of a large image, which requires significant CPU resources.

If a query plan evaluates clauses from left to right, then *redness* will be evaluated for all employees. In contrast, if the clauses are evaluated from right to left, then *redness* will only be evaluated for the employees who are highly compensated, a much smaller set. Careful attention to the computational requirements of individual clauses can make an enormous difference in the running time of the above query. The traditional relational cost model discussed in the previous chapter,

cost = expected number of records examined +
            (fudge-factor * (expected number of pages read))

is too primitive to capture the computational requirements of individual clauses.

Specifically, the expected number of records examined is too primitive a measure of CPU usage because it cannot discriminate between different orderings of the clauses in a predicate. In addition, a traditional optimizer assumes that each record is read in its entirety when computing the expected number of pages read. Again, this assumption is not justified when a function is I/O intensive. For example, it is possible that images are stored with a color histogram at a specific location in the representation. If so, the *redness* function need read only the histogram and not the entire image. In effect, the function's I/O requirement will drop from perhaps one megabyte to tens of kilobytes. Obviously, the optimizer must take this fact into consideration when constructing a query plan.

To keep track of the demands of functions that are expensive in CPU and/or I/O resource utilization, a universal server's optimizer must use a more elaborate cost function. And some additional information must be provided when a function is defined. This information is

A = percall-cpu: specifies the per-call CPU cost for the function

B = byte-percentage: specifies the expected percentage of the bytes in the
    argument that the function will read

C = per byte-cpu: specifies the CPU cost per byte read

The CPU cost of a function invocation is

A + C * (B * expected size of argument)

Similarly, the I/O cost is

B * expected size of argument

When presented with a query, a universal server optimizer computes the more detailed cost for each permutation of the clauses in a predicate. The test for extension 8 can easily demonstrate whether an optimizer will deal wisely with expensive functions.

Test for Extension 8. Do the following two queries run at the same speed?

```
select name
from emp
where salary > 10000 and
redness (picture) < 0.1;

select name
from emp
where redness (picture) < 0.1 and
salary > 10000;
```

10.8   *Extension 9: Optimization of Expensive Functions*

An extension of the optimization of expensive functions is their correct placement in a query plan. Consider the following somewhat artificial query:

```
select e.name, f.name
from emp e, emp f
where e.salary = f.salary
and redness (e.picture) < 0.1
and redness (f.picture) < 0.1;
```

This query finds the pairs of employees who earn the same salary and have low redness images. In a traditional optimizer, the restrictions will always be performed

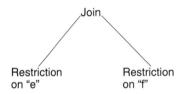

FIGURE 10.1   Restriction, Then Join

first, leading to the structure shown in Figure 10.1 for the query plans that are evaluated.

This strategy is appropriate when all clauses are inexpensive to compute, as is the case for SQL-92. However, when expensive clauses appear in queries, this strategy may be undesirable. Specifically, it will compute redness for all possible employees. Moreover, unless the optimizer is very smart and caches the result of the first collection of redness computations, it will probably compute redness twice, once to evaluate the restriction on "e" and once for "f." The resulting low redness employees will then be joined on salary.

In contrast, it is probably preferable to perform the join first to find pairs of employees who have the same salary. Subsequently, you can evaluate each pair for redness. The resulting query plan is shown in Figure 10.2.

If there are few pairs of employees with the same salary, then the latter strategy is preferable. In this case, push the restriction clauses up the query plan through the join, so they are done last. Depending on the complexity of the restriction and the size of the join, this *predicate migration* may or may not be a good idea. A formal presentation of predicate migration appears in Hellerstein and Stonebraker (1993), and a good object-relational DBMS uses this technique when appropriate.

FIGURE 10.2   Join, Then Restriction

Test for Extension 9. In the case that few employees have the same salary, the above query executes by processing the join first. That is, it executes quickly for a large employee collection.

10.9   *Extension 10: User-Defined Access Methods*

Suppose you submit the following query, which finds employees who live inside a rectangle bounded by the origin and the point (1, 1):

```
select name
from emp
where location contained box ('0,0,1,1');
```

This is a two-dimensional search. Because B-trees are a one-dimensional access method, they are essentially useless in accelerating this query. A multidimensional access method is needed, such as an R-tree, grid file, quad-tree, or K-D-B tree. Similarly, many image applications in the medical and law enforcement fields, such as fingerprint recognition and face matching, require finding an image that is close to a given image. In these vertical markets, there are specialized access methods that accelerate such searches. Sophisticated keyword indexing systems for textual documents usually support proximity searching, where users request pairs of words in a document within a user-specified distance of each other. Again, specialized access methods are used to accelerate proximity searches.

In other words, an access method is needed that is appropriate to the data type, point. Because there can be a variety of new data types defined to an object-relational DBMS and several may need a customized access method, a good object-relational DBMS must allow type definers to add a new access method.

An access method is merely a collection of functions that are called by the execution engine at appropriate places in the execution of a query plan. These functions perform operations such as the following:

1. Open a scan of an index.
2. Get next record in a scan.
3. Insert record.
4. Delete record.
5. Replace record.
6. Close scan.

In the Informix universal server, there are a total of 12 such functions. Because an object-relational DBMS supports user-defined functions and can call them where appropriate, it is straightforward to call user-defined access method functions.

Of course, it is not easy to write an access method. The following tasks must be performed inside access method code:

Locking. Appropriate locks must be set and released on index objects. This requires interacting with the lock management code of the DBMS.

Recovery. Access method code must ensure that the data structures they manage are recovered in the event of a crash. This is accomplished by a combination of logging of index events and/or careful coding. If logging is used, then the access method code must interact with the log manager.

Page Management. Access method code must interact with the DBMS buffer manager when it requires a disk page. To avoid copying pages to a separate location, a good access method will use buffer pool pages in place. This demands careful pinning and unpinning of pages, so that the buffer manager does not inadvertently write an index page out to disk before the access method is through with it.

Another important aspect of a user-defined access method is the mechanism for teaching the optimizer about its characteristics. The basic idea is to generalize the indexing interface using B-trees and hashing as a "template." Specifically, a hash access method supports a single kind of query efficiently:

attribute = value

In contrast, a B-tree supports five operators:

attribute < value

attribute <= value

attribute = value

attribute > value

attribute >= value

Earlier in this chapter the concept of an operator class for a B-tree, which described the actual operators used in a specific index, was discussed. In a similar way, an operator class for a hash access method can also be described, consisting of a single operator defining the notion of equality used in a particular index.

To add a new kind of access method, you need merely specify a template for the operator class that the access method supports. For example, R-trees have the following template:

attribute = object

attribute overlaps object

attribute contains object

attribute contained_in object

Then you indicate which instantiation of the template you are using in a specific index. With this information, the optimizer can get to work.

Test for Extension 10. It must be possible for a (sufficiently skilled) user to add a new access method to a good object-relational DBMS.

10.10   *Extension 11: "Flattening" Complex Object Queries*

Consider a function that returns a set of employees such as

```
create function highly paid()
returns set(employee_t)
as external name '$INFORMIXDIR/extend/salry.bld(highlypaid)'
language C;
```

This function is written in C and identifies (somehow) a set of highly paid employees.

As explained in Chapter 4, you can use such a function anywhere a table is allowed in an SQL query. Therefore, the following query is perfectly legal:

```
select name
from table (high_salary ())
where startdate > '1990/01/01';
```

In this case, the optimizer has no choice but to materialize the result of the function in the from clause. After that it can evaluate the predicate using a scan of the materialized object and compute the target list for qualifying records. Note that C functions are *opaque*. Since the optimizer cannot look inside them, little optimization is possible.

In contrast, the optimizer understands the definition of functions that are written in SQL. Therefore, the optimizer can *flatten* queries with SQL functions wherever possible. Consider the following query:

```
select name
```

```
from table (SQL-function ('01/01/1990'))
where salary >18000;
```

where *SQL-function* is defined by

```
create function SQL-function (date Arg1)
returns set(employee_t)
as select *
from emp
where startdate > Arg1;
```

This query can be unwound to

```
select name
from emp
where startdate > '01/01/1990' and
salary = 18000;
```

If a B-tree index exists for the salary attribute, the optimizer should solve this resulting query using an indexed scan over salary index. Without flattening this query, a poorer strategy will be selected. Therefore, a good object-relational DBMS flattens queries dealing with complex objects wherever possible. This leads to test 11.

Test for Extension 11. The following query executes in one second or less if a B-tree index for salary exists:

```
select name
from table (SQL-function ('01/01/1990'))
where salary = 18000;
```

10.11   *Extension 12: "In-Line" Sets*

Return to the dept table discussed in Chapter 4, namely,

```
create row type dept_t (
                dname           varchar(30),
                floor           int,
                manager         varchar(30),
                phone           phone_t,
                autos           set(auto_t ),
                manager_ref     ref(employee_t)
                                references (emp),
                colors          set(varchar(30)),
                workers         set(ref(employee_t)
                                references (emp)));
```

```
create table dept of type dept_t;
```

and consider the following query:

```
select autos.name, autos.year
from dept
where floor = 1;
```

In this case, the query is looking for the name and year of all autos owned by a department on the first floor. If there is a B-tree index on floor, then the qualifying departments can be quickly located. After that, the autos for each such department must be found. If autos are stored in the same record with their owning department (an "in-line" representation of sets), then this lookup is very fast. If sets are stored in a separate record and then accessed using a level of indirection, then finding the qualifying autos is much slower.

Obviously, a system that uses in-line storage for sets and then overflows to a separate location only when the set becomes very large will dramatically outperform a system that blindly stores sets in a separate place. This leads to test 12.

Test for Extension 12. A good object-relational DBMS must store "small" sets using an in-line representation.

10.12   *Extension 13: Indexes on Attributes of Sets*

Return again to the dept table mentioned above and consider the following query:

```
select name
from dept
where 1982 in autos.year;
```

This query will identify those departments that possess a 1982 automobile. Although it is certainly possible to perform a sequential scan of dept to solve this query, a good object-relational DBMS allows the user to build a B-tree index on the year attribute for all auto instances in any set in the dept table. In other words, the system should support building an index on an attribute of a set. With such an index, the above query will use an index scan and a sequential scan will be avoided.

Test for Extension 13. A good object-relational DBMS must support building indexes on attributes of sets.

10.13   *Extension 14: Optimization of Scans of Inheritance Hierarchies*

The next two optimizations deal with efficiently processing queries whose scope is an inheritance hierarchy. Extension 14 deals with index and table scans. Consider the following two queries:

```
select name
from only (emp)
where salary = 10000
and startdate <'01/01/1990';
```

```
select name
from emp
where salary = 10000
and startdate <'01/01/1990';
```

The first query requests only employees with the correct salary, while the second requests the table hierarchy be "exploded."

It is clearly reasonable for a system to decompose the second query into two actual queries and then run them separately. In this case, the cost of the second query is about twice the cost of the first one. Alternatively, it would be much faster to use one query plan with a scope of two tables. With a "union table" node in the plan tree, the bookkeeping associated with the extra queries can be avoided. Of course, if some of the tables have an index on salary and some don't, then a single plan is inappropriate. This discussion leads to the test for extension 14.

Text for Extension 14. It must be possible to index tables in an inheritance hierarchy so that both of the above queries run in a few seconds. Moreover, the cost of the second query should be less than two times the cost of the first one, assuming each table has the same number of instances.

10.14   *Extension 15: Optimization of Joins over Inheritance Hierarchies*

Return to the person/emp/student/student_emp hierarchy illustrated in Figure 6.2 on page 90 and consider the following join query:

```
select e.name
from emp e, dept d
where e.dept = d.dname and d.floor = 1;
```

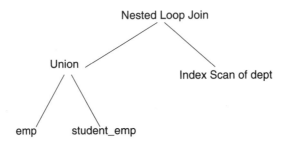

FIGURE 10.3   Using a Union Table

This query finds all employees and student employees who work on the first floor. The naive way to process this query is to replace it with two actual queries:

```
select e.name
from only (emp) e, dept d
where e.dept = d.dname and d.floor = 1;

select s.name
from only (student_emp), dept d
where s.dept = d.dname and d.floor = 1;
```

These two join queries can be subsequently executed on their associated tables. It is possible that the optimizer will perform an indexed scan of dept followed by a nested loop join on the result to emp and student_emp, respectively. Notice that the same index scan of dept is being performed twice. Performing duplicate work is obviously a bad idea. Moreover, as the inheritance hierarchy gets deeper, the number of repetitions done by the naive strategy increases dramatically.

A better solution is to strategically put a "union table" node into the plan tree below the join, as shown in Figure 10.3. With this optimization, the duplication of work noted above is removed. This leads to the test for extension 15.

Test for Extension 15. The above example join query over the inheritance hierarchy should run faster than the two table-specific queries, which have the same functionality.

10.15   *Extension 16: Support for User-Defined Aggregates*

Consider the median aggregate introduced in Chapter 2 in the query

```
select median(salary)
from emp;
```

To allow users to add this kind of functionality, the object-relational DBMS needs to support a **create aggregate** command, which supports the specification of initialization, iteration, and finalization, as noted in Chapter 2. More generally, an ORDBMS needs to be able to support a query like the following correctly:

```
select dname, median(salary)
from emp, dept
where emp.dept = dept.dname
group by dname;
```

Also, processing aggregations can benefit tremendously from parallelism. However, performing these algorithms in parallel complicates them. For example, consider the case where the emp table is distributed over several disks. Ideally, you would want to scan each of these disks in parallel, and merge the results of each of these scans in a single operation. However, the median of a set of subset medians does not equal the median of the whole set. Therefore, parallelizing aggregates requires considerable care.

Test for Extension 16. A good object-relational DBMS must support a create aggregate command, and it must be capable of performing the queries shown above efficiently.

10.16 *Summary*

Sixteen extensions are needed to turn a traditional relational optimizer into a good object-relational optimizer. To make such a conversion, all of the relational DBMS's hard-coded knowledge about fixed data types must be replaced with a table-driven system that can support user definition of types, functions, selectivity functions, operator classes, negators, commutators, and access methods. Complex objects and inheritance must also be efficiently treated by the optimizer. I/O- or CPU-intensive functions must be optimized by extending the cost function evaluated by the optimizer to include more information, and by removing search space reduction tactics, such as always performing restrictions before joins. Just as with parsers, discussed in Chapter 8, the transformation of an optimizer from relational to object-relational requires a major rewrite effort.

CHAPTER 11 · *Implementation of Rule Systems*

This chapter discusses the implementation of rule systems for object-relational systems. It begins with the specific case of triggers. Triggers are update-update rules, one of the four cases discussed in Chapter 7. Triggers are widely implemented by relational DBMSs; the general form is

> **on <event>**
>
> **where <condition>**
>
> **do <action>**

Later in the chapter the more general case is discussed where the condition and action can be either retrieves or updates.

11.1 *Support for Triggers*

There are two common ways to support triggers: with low-level hooks in the executor, and with a procedure called *query modification*. This chapter explains only the simple case where execution of a trigger does not cause other triggers to be activated. Dealing with cascading triggers is more complicated.

Modifying the Executor

Consider the following update-update rule introduced in Chapter 7, which propagates Mike's salary on to Jane:

```
create rule Mike_Jane_salary_synch
on update to emp.salary
    where current.name = 'Mike'
do update emp
    set salary = new.salary
    where name   = 'Jane';
```

When specified to the DBMS, this rule is compiled into an internal form and stored in a table (or tables) in the system catalogs. An identifier for this rule is inserted into the Table table of the system catalogs and is placed in the row that corresponds to the emp table. This makes it easy to ascertain which rules apply to any given table in the database.

When an update occurs, for example,

```
update emp
     set salary = 58000
     where name = 'Mike';
```

the query engine can note that one or more triggers are relevant to the emp table and might be fired during the execution of the command. Therefore, it retrieves the data structure for the appropriate triggers. The optimizer receives the parse tree and develops a query plan for the command, as discussed in Chapters 9 and 10. In this example, it might be an index scan for a B-tree index on the name attribute of emp. As a last step in plan construction, each of the possibly relevant triggers is grafted onto the plan. The predicate in the update condition, in this case,

```
where name = 'Mike'
```

is inserted into the query plan, so that two predicates are checked while executing the plan, as noted in Figure 11.1. One is the real one from the user's query; the second is the condition from the possibly relevant trigger. Whenever the real predicate evaluates to true, then the appropriate update is performed, and the old and new instances of the record are readily available in the executor. These are made available to the grafted predicate, which is then evaluated. If it is true, then the action part of the trigger is processed by the executor before continuing with the index scan of the emp table. Thus, triggers are readily supported by grafting possibly relevant triggers onto the query plan for the user's query.

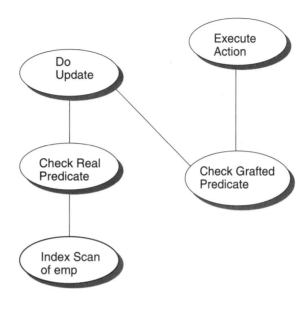

FIGURE 11.1   A Query Plan after Grafting

Notice that this implementation supports *immediate* execution of triggers, which was one of the semantics described in Chapter 7. The reason for immediate execution is because the action part of the rule is executed as soon as a relevant record is identified during execution. To support *deferred* execution, substantial additional work must be performed; namely, the above processing must be done to identify triggers that may have to fire at transaction commit time. Rather than executing the action part of each trigger, it is simply saved in a list in the executor. Moreover, the before value and after value of each updated record must be saved so that the action part of the rule can be executed at commit time, if the condition part of the rule is still valid. Because these values must be saved in the log for crash recovery purposes anyway, it is possible to obtain these values at commit time by reading the log. Alternatively, they can be saved in a form more amenable to commit time processing.

Then, at commit time, the condition part of each trigger in the list must be checked for each before and after image previously identified to ascertain that the condition of the trigger is still true. Because it is possible that a subsequent update in the same transaction made database modifications so that the condition is no longer true, it is necessary to recheck the condition at commit time. If the condition is still true, then the action part of the trigger is executed.

This is a high-level look at deferred execution of triggers. For more extensive treatment of this topic, consult Widom and Ceri (1995). There currently are no commercial relational DBMSs that we are aware of that implement deferred execution of triggers at commit time, although several systems allow actions to be deferred until the end of the current SQL command.

Query Modification

The second implementation choice for triggers is a process called *query modification.* To understand this concept, consider the same rule used above:

```
create rule Mike_Jane_salary_synch
on update to emp.salary
   where current.name = 'Mike'
do update emp
   set salary = new.salary
   where name   = 'Jane';
```

as well as the same user command:

```
update emp
set salary = 58000
where name = 'Mike';
```

In this case, the same marking is placed in the system catalogs as was done in the first implementation option, so that the parser can recognize the potentially relevant rules for each arriving user query.

For each such rule, query modification is performed to replace the user's statement with a different collection of statements. In the case that the command is an update and the action part of the rule is also an update, query modification is straightforward. Specifically, the user's original statement is run, along with a second command that implements the correct effect of the trigger. In this example, the two commands that are executed are

```
update emp
    set salary = 58000
    where name = 'Mike';
```

```
update emp j
set salary = 58000
where j.name = 'Jane' and
exists (select *
    from emp m
    where m.name = 'Mike');
```

The first statement is simply the unmodified user's statement. The second statement is constructed by substituting the user's statement into the action part of the rule. Intuitively, the second statement gives the correct salary adjustment to Jane, but only if there exists a Mike in the emp table. If Mike does not exist, then the user's command has no effect and the trigger also has no effect. On the other hand, if Mike exists, then his new salary should be propagated to Jane. Thus, the second command performs the correct update to the database.

With either implementation of rules, be aware that the overhead is proportional to the number of potentially relevant rules. If there are R rules on the emp table, then the first implementation will graft R predicates onto the user's query. In the second implementation, a total of R + 1 commands will actually be run. To a first approximation, rules introduce an overhead for a command to a table that is proportional to the number of rules defined for that table.

The two implementations have somewhat different performance envelopes. In the example used above, the first implementation offers lower overhead. After all, only one query plan is executed, and the low-level grafting should not slow down execution dramatically. In contrast, the second implementation requires two commands to be run.

However, there are cases where the second implementation is faster, as the next example illustrates. Consider the following rule:

```
create rule update_update as
on update to emp.salary where current.name > 'm'
do   update emp
     set salary = 10000
     where name = 'Jane';
```

and the command

```
update emp
set salary = 20000
where startdate >=  '1980-01-01';
```

If there are M employees with start dates after 1979 whose last names begin with letters that are in the second half of the alphabet, then the rule will be fired in the first implementation M times, and each time the same additional update is performed. Thus, there will be dramatic overhead added to the execution of the user's command. In contrast, the second implementation will perform the following two commands:

```
update emp
set salary = 10000
where startdate >= '1980-01-01';
```

```
update emp
set salary = 20000
where name = 'Jane'
and exists (select name
            from emp
            where name > 'm'
            and startdate >= '1980-01-01');
```

In this case, the second command will ascertain that there exists an employee whose last name begins with a letter from the second half of the alphabet and who has an appropriate start date. If so, the update to Jane will be performed exactly once. As a result, the second implementation will be noticeably faster.

Clearly, both implementations will be preferred in different circumstances, and there is no clear performance winner. Most relational DBMSs use some variation of the first implementation. Moreover, some vendors have even implemented special case code for referential integrity, rather than simply turning referential integrity syntax into the appropriate triggers to be implemented by the standard trigger system. The reason for a special case implementation is to achieve higher performance.

However, neither implementation scales to a large number of triggers. In either implementation, the execution overhead is proportional to the number of rules; in other words, do not try a system with either implementation on a large rule base. In Section 11.3, we return to this scalability issue.

11.2   *Extension to More General Rules*

To support a more general rule system, there are extensions that are required to either of the two implementations above. Consider a query-query rule, such as the one from Chapter 7:

```
create rule Jane_Mike_salary_synch
on select to emp.salary
   where current.name = 'Jane'
do instead
   select salary
   from emp
   where name = 'Mike';
```

In this case, it is fairly straightforward to extend either implementation to behave correctly. The actions that must be taken to support rule execution are local to the scope of the current user's command, and grafting or query modification must merely be extended to cover additional cases. However, there are other cases where this locality is not present. For example, consider the following example from Chapter 7:

```
create alert alert_Mike_on_salary_review
(mechanism = 'callback');

create rule alert_Mike_on_salary_change
on update to emp
    where  current.Name = 'Mike'
do raise alert alert_Mike_on_salary_review;
```

and suppose a second user process indicates interest in the alert by

```
listen my_alert;
```

In this case, there are several additional difficulties that must be dealt with. First, the application program interface (API) must be extended with a listen command. Moreover, the structure of the current API must be changed. Specifically, in current systems the application submits a command and then controls the way processing of the command is accomplished through cursor commands. The DBMS is *passive* and expects instructions from the application concerning how to proceed. In contrast, when alerters are present, the DBMS must be *active* and be able to communicate asynchronously to the client application. This requires some reworking of the libraries that support the API.

Last, a DBMS that supports alerters must be extended with a communication path between the updating user, who gives Mike a salary adjustment, and the listening user, who wants to be notified. This requires the first DBMS task to notify the second one, which can then deliver the alert to the user.

11.3 *Scalability*

In this section we first present an example where a large number of rules is desirable. Then, we indicate the implementation considerations for a rules system that must scale.

Consider a simple piece of an airline reservation system as follows:

```
create table flights(
                number = int,
                date = date_time,
                time = date_time,
                from = varchar(30),
                to = varchar(30),
                lowest_price = int,
                seats_available = int);
```

When a reservation is made, seats_available is decremented by one. When this number reaches zero, then no more reservations can be accepted. Many airlines are very serious about tracking this sort of information. Airlines follow seat availability closely, so that they can vary the price of a seat depending on the number of available seats and the time remaining until departure. Such "seat mining" applications require the implementation of a complex set of rules.

With the advent of the Internet, several airlines want to take this concept to a new level. Specifically, they want to assemble the travel preferences of the millions of potential travelers who can be reached through the Internet.

For example, a customer in Boston might have travel flexibility, yet wishes to take a vacation in Miami. With three hour's notice, the customer would be willing to get to the airport and board a flight to Miami. However, the traveler wants to pay no more than $25 for a ticket, a deep discount to compensate for the inconvenience of traveling at short notice. With six hour's notice, the traveler would pay as much as $50 for a ticket; with 24 hour's notice, the traveler would pay up to $100 for a ticket.

It is easy to imagine that the 100 million customers on the Internet could collectively specify hundreds of millions of travel preferences. To accomplish sophisticated seat mining, an airline could specify these travel preferences as database rules, for example:

```
on update to flights
where from = 'Boston'
and to = 'Miami'
and lowest_pice = $25.00
and date = today
and now-time >= 3 hours
do raise alert notify_me;
```

With this collection of alerts in place, an airline can gradually lower the lowest_price on each flight in an attempt to fill all available seats before the flight departs.

The implementation problem that arises is the support of millions of travel preferences as rules; that is, the rule system implementation must scale! In case you think this is an isolated example, note that the same alerting problem exists with the stock market, where customers wish to be alerted if particular stocks move to specific prices. Also, you can imagine a retail environment where a retailer discounts merchandise gradually until it all sells. In both cases there are a large number of rules to be supported. Neither of the previous implementations is appropriate in such an environment. We now present a third option with better scalability characteristics.

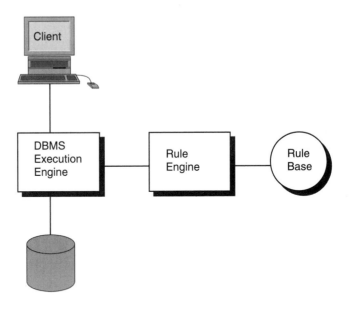

FIGURE 11.2 Architecture of a Scalable Rule System

Consider the architecture in Figure 11.2. Next to the DBMS execution engine is a rule engine to which all updates are passed. This rule engine receives each DBMS update and passes it through a highly optimized data structure that encodes all active rules. Of course, this rule base will be modified as rules are added and deleted.

In the travel database three such rules might be

```
on   update to flights
     where from = 'Boston'
     and to = 'Miami'
     and lowest_price = $50.00
     and date = today
     and now-time > 6 hours
do raise alert notify_cust1;

on   update to flights
     where from = 'Boston'
     and to = 'Miami'
     and lowest_price = $25.00
     and date = today
     and now-time > 3hours
do raise alert notify_cust1;
```

```
on   update to flights
     where from = 'Boston'
     and to = 'Houston'
     and lowest_price = $35.00
     and date = today
     and now-time > 4 hours
do raise alert notify_cust2;
```

We can factor this set of rules into the data structure shown in Figure 11.3. By factoring the rules, we notice that any fare change that is not for one of today's flights

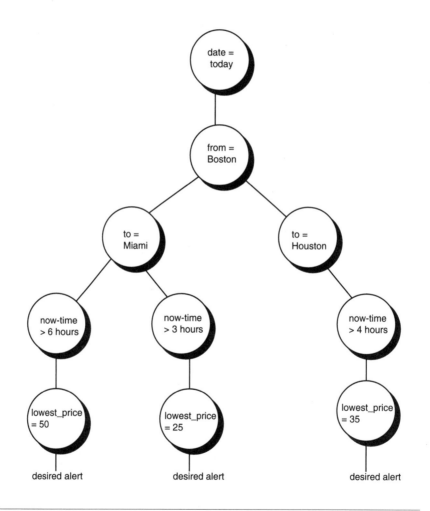

FIGURE 11.3 Rules Data Structure

will not alert any of the three rules, and we can ascertain this fact by examining only the root node. In this way, the vast majority of rules that are not affected by an update can be quickly found and eliminated. The structure of Figure 11.3 is often called a *discrimination network* because it quickly discriminates between the rules that apply to an update and those that don't.

If a DBMS is going to manage a large rule base, then the implementation must be along the lines of the system discussed in this section. Until then, systems will only be able to support a modest number of rules.

11.4   *Summary*

Moving beyond a trigger system to a general-purpose rule system is a fair amount of work. Both deferred execution of rules and retrieve rules cause this implementation complexity. Scalability presents an additional challenge, as we discussed in the airline seating example.

CHAPTER 12 *Architectural Options for Commercial Vendors*

The main players in the object-relational arena are the relational vendors, including Informix, IBM, and Oracle. In addition, some O vendors have added rich SQL systems to their engines to offer object-relational capabilities. Last, at least one start-up company (Cloudscape) markets an object-relational engine. Of course, start-ups get to write object-relational engines from scratch, designed specifically to solve problems that appear in the upper-right quadrant of the two-by-two matrix introduced in Chapter 1. In contrast, the relational vendors must convert their engines from relational to object-relational, which entails at least the following steps:

1. Rework the parser to be table-driven.
2. Rework the optimizer to be table-driven and include expensive function optimization and support for inheritance and complex objects.
3. Rework the executor to support secure, dynamically linked user-defined functions.
4. Rework the access method interface to be open to new implementations.
5. Rework the B-tree code to be generic.
6. Rework storage management to support large data types.
7. Rework the client API so that more general queries can be run and their results returned.

Because the modifications required to a relational engine are so dramatic, amounting to a near-complete rewrite, there are several architectural options available to the relational vendors. Each option offers different performance characteristics, time to market, and risk.

The strategies are the following:

1. Do nothing.
2. Rewrite the engine from scratch.
3. Sell two systems.
4. Implement an object-relational top on a relational storage manager.
5. Incrementally evolve the current engine to add new functionality.
6. Write a "wrapper" on top of a relational engine.
7. Implement a gateway from an object-relational engine to a relational one.

Several object-oriented DBMS vendors have also built products that address the upper-right quadrant of the matrix. The object-oriented vendor has the following possibilities:

8. Extend an object-oriented DBMS to support object-relational functionality.
9. "Glue" an object-relational engine on top of an object-oriented DBMS.

This chapter focuses on the choices available to vendors that currently sell relational or object-oriented DBMSs but wish to move to object-relational technology to "catch the next wave." This chapter discusses all of the listed options and indicates which vendors have selected each of the possibilities.

12.1   *Strategy 1: Do Nothing*

The first option is always available, that of doing nothing. However, it is a very dangerous strategy for a relational vendor to follow. As noted in Chapter 1, there is an increasing subset of DBMS customers with data processing applications in the upper-left quadrant of the matrix who will add complex data to their environments and thereby move their applications to the upper-right, object-relational quadrant. Certainly, for the foreseeable future there are many applications that will be forms-based bread-and-butter business data processing applications. However, the number that will migrate from the upper-left quadrant to the upper-right, the object-relational side, will be significant.

Doing nothing will ensure that a relational vendor misses this market shift and loses out on the growing upper-right quadrant market. The "do nothing" strategy only makes sense if a company believes there is no significant market in the upper-right quadrant. It is telling that all relational vendors appear to be working on product enhancements that include support for complex data and that not one is doing nothing.

12.2   *Strategy 2: Rewrite a Relational Engine from Scratch*

The second alternative available to a relational vendor is to rewrite its DBMS from scratch. This is innately appealing because it allows designers a clean sheet of paper on which to craft a new system. Unfortunately, it is also a highly risky venture for the following reasons:

- Writing several hundred thousand lines of fresh code is a complex, time-consuming task even under the best of circumstances. Many organizations have failed or been significantly late in delivering new systems because they underestimated the sheer amount of effort involved.

- In order to justify the venture, there is pressure to make the rewrite better than the current system in all ways. The new system must have all the functionality of the old system and offer the same or better performance on all commands the old system can do. In addition, it must promise dramatic new functionality. Because current relational engines have been tuned for several years to offer very high performance in transaction processing applications, the new system must also have this capability.

- The new system must be as reliable as the old system, or customers will not switch. As relational vendors have proved over and over again, it takes a long time to knock all the bugs out of new releases. Stabilizing a new code line appears to take at least a year, and often much longer.

- The new system must be compatible with the old system, or customers' applications will have to be converted to run with the new system. Faced with conversion to a new system, a customer may get itchy feet and begin to evaluate competing products. Obviously, vendors do not wish to give competitors an opportunity to erode their customer base.

- The old system required hundreds of man-years of effort to get to its current state. It is psychologically difficult for management to discard this investment.

A rewrite is a risky and costly proposition; embarking on such a project is not a decision to take lightly. A new system will take years to complete. The experience of Digital Equipment Corporation (DEC) in this area comes to mind.

In the mid-1980s DEC began developing a "from scratch" DBMS, called RDB*, at its Colorado Springs facility. The project was kept completely separate from DEC's RDB group on the East Coast. The initial charter was to develop a relational engine for high-speed parallel hardware, a so-called software database machine. The system was to run on a loosely coupled collection of processors, an architecture that was similar to the Gamma prototype from the University of Wisconsin (Dewitt et al. 1990). This design required a complete DBMS engine for each network node as well as a distributed DBMS to manage the processing of multiple site queries.

A few years later the focus of RDB* shifted to that of a general-purpose distributed DBMS that could run on a network of conventional processors connected by commercial local area network (LAN) or wide area network (WAN) technology.

Within a couple more years the focus shifted again to supporting heterogeneous local DBMSs on the individual nodes of this network. This increase in scope required gateways to various foreign DBMSs.

Because the scope and direction of the project changed several times, by 1992 the group still had not delivered a product. Meanwhile, the RDB group on the East Coast was making consistent steady progress. Ultimately, DEC killed the RDB* project and incurred a financial write-off of many millions of dollars.

A second example of a complete rewrite gone bad is the Sybase Brahms project. Faced with an "elderly" code line that was difficult to significantly enhance, Sybase elected to start a project to investigate a complete rewrite. The Brahms project started off designing a persistent storage system (i.e., a lower-right quadrant system) but moved over time to building an upper-right system. Moreover, the specifications did not include being compatible with the current Sybase relational product. After several years of effort, Sybase gave up the effort, incurring a big write-off.

These are but two examples of the perils of this "cold turkey" strategy. Anecdotal evidence suggests that the strategy of starting from scratch fails approximately three-quarters of the time, usually due to moving specifications and overambitious goals. (A further exposition of these perils is contained in Brodie and Stonebraker 1995.)

12.3   *Strategy 3: Sell Two Systems*

A third strategy is to sell two systems. Computer Associates (CA) has elected this strategy. They have a relational DBMS, Ingres, that they obtained during the ASK acquisition. It is a standard SQL-92 engine with a substantial installed base. CA also acquired an object engine from Fujitsu, which they developed into their second system, Jasmine. Jasmine is an object-oriented DBMS with an SQL system that addresses the right-hand side of the matrix introduced in Chapter 1.

With Ingres and Jasmine, CA sells both a relational engine and a combined persistent language and object-relational engine. (Of course, they also sell additional mainframe legacy DBMSs.)

The challenge to a vendor offering two systems is to address the needs of universal applications. Ingres has been optimized for more than 10 years for the upper-left quadrant of the matrix. But it has only limited upper-right quadrant support, as we will see in Chapter 19. In contrast, Jasmine addresses the upper-right quadrant. Thus neither system completely supports the top row. The obvious challenge to Jasmine is to provide the scalability and OLTP performance required in the upper-left quadrant so that it can support universal applications.

12.4   Strategy 4: An Object-Relational Top on a Relational Storage Manager

A relational DBMS is typically designed to run on top of a storage manager. The storage manager code module provides the following functionality:

- Scans over tables
- Index scans over tables using a B-tree index
- Locking
- Crash recovery
- Page management

On top of this system, a parser, optimizer, and executor are crafted. This architecture was popularized by System R, the early IBM Research relational system from the 1970s, and is illustrated in Figure 12.1. Some object-relational systems, such as Illustra, also use this basic two-level architecture.

There are two vendors who have elected to utilize Strategy 4, Informix and IBM. When Informix purchased Illustra, it elected to utilize this strategy to perform the integration of the two systems. To a first approximation, the Informix storage manager is "byte-oriented": the concurrency control system, table storage, and page management have no information about the types of data they are storing. Therefore, these pieces of the Informix system could be used intact.

Informix added a new top half to its storage manager to produce the Informix Dynamic Server with Universal Data Option (IDS-UDO). This new code borrows substantially from the Illustra system, but contains considerable new code. Specifically, the Illustra function manager, dynamic linking system, and pieces of the optimizer are used intact. IDS-UDO needed to be upwardly compatible from Informix, Version 7. Therefore, the user interface code from V7 was used and extended to accommodate transmission of objects between client and server.

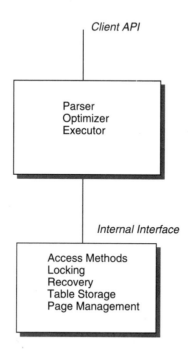

FIGURE 12.1 Typical Relational Architecture

In all, there are some 550,000 lines of new code in IDS-UDO, relative to Informix, Version 7. Essentially all of this new code is in the top half of the system. Informix has effectively constructed a new top on a relational storage manager.

The rationale for this architecture is that the Informix storage manager is a highly parallel, very scalable system, and the goal was to produce an engine that had the functionality of Illustra with the scalability and raw performance of Informix, Version 7. At the current time, IDS-UDO achieves these goals, since it is as fast as Version 7 on relational queries and has the functionality of the Illustra server.

A second company to utilize a new top on a relational bottom is IBM. DB2 6000 was engineered to contain some object-relational functionality, as noted in Chapter 19. Although they have implemented only base type extension and not complex objects or inheritance, IBM still needed to vastly rework the top half of its system. To a first approximation, Release 2 was a new top half on the Release 1 bottom half. They have now moved forward with additional releases and are currently selling Release 5.

When discussing IBM, it is important to note that DB2 6000 is one of at least three IBM relational DBMSs for various operating systems. It has no code in common with the flagship DB2 product available for the MVS operating system. Do not assume that the object-relational strategy for DB2 (if one exists) is the same as the one for DB2 6000.

The advantage of this "new top" approach is that it gets considerable functionality into the system quickly and allows the successful vendor following this strategy to leapfrog any competitors who take a less aggressive tactic such as incremental evolution. However, it is inherently a risky strategy. A vendor must make a great many changes to an existing system in a short period of time and then knock the bugs out of the resulting system. Instead of rewriting a system completely, the vendor is only rewriting half of it; still it is a major undertaking fraught with the risk of failure.

The Informix and IBM engineering teams should be complimented for successfully carrying out a high-risk strategy.

12.5   *Strategy 5: Incremental Evolution*

The fifth option is to incrementally migrate an existing relational DBMS from its current state to an object-relational engine. Incremental migration of an existing system is advocated in Brodie and Stonebraker (1995) as the safest option for obtaining new functionality. Unfortunately, incremental migration will take a relational DBMS vendor several years to accomplish, most likely with a loss of market position to other vendors with more aggressive strategies.

The first vendor to adopt incremental evolution was Ingres Corp., which extended its relational engine in 1988 with base type extension and a rule manager, two of the four features that characterize an object-relational system. Although in both areas its initial offerings lacked needed functionality, Ingres made an early start toward object-relational functionality. Unfortunately, this incremental evolution largely stopped when Ingres Corp. was acquired by ASK in 1990. ASK, in turn, was more recently acquired by Computer Associates, which adopted a new strategy based on Jasmine.

A second vendor to choose incremental evolution is Oracle Corp. Version 7.3, which shipped in 1995, added five specific new data types to SQL-92. More recently, Version 8.0 further added rudimentary support for complex objects. (See Chapter 19 for further discussion on this topic.) In addition, Oracle extended its stored procedure language so that it supports C callouts and a rudimentary form of user-defined functions. More refined support for user-defined functions, as well as base type extension and inheritance, are promised in future releases. Oracle will continue over the next several years to incrementally add most object-relational features to its engine.

12.6   *Strategy 6: Write a Wrapper*

The sixth strategy available to a relational vendor is to write a *wrapper.* Basically, a wrapper is a simulation layer on top of a conventional relational engine. This simulation layer supports an object-relational API by mapping object-relational queries submitted by the user into relational ones, which are executed by a traditional relational engine. This wrapper architecture is shown in Figure 12.2.

Whenever there is a paradigm shift, a vendor with the old technology always has the option of writing a wrapper to support the new technology. This has been the case for years; for example, the IBM 370 line of computers supports an older technology, IBM 1401 programs, by simulating them on top of the 370. Closer to the DBMS space, Cullinet was the dominant vendor in the early 1980s with the then dominant technology (CODASYL). A new paradigm appeared (relational systems), and Cullinet decided to employ the wrapper technology to support it by writing a simulator for the relational model on top of CODASYL, called IDMS-R.

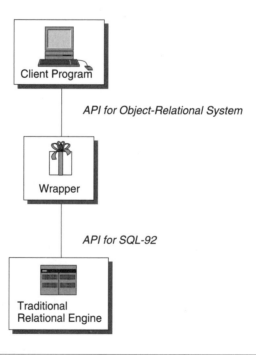

FIGURE 12.2   The Wrapper Architecture

Hewlett-Packard has also adopted the wrapper strategy. It has written an object-relational DBMS wrapper, called Odaptor. Odaptor is implemented as a wrapper on top of Allbase, the HP relational DBMS, as well as on top of Oracle. Recently, HP has deemphasized Odaptor, so its future is unclear at this point.

Wrappers are just as appealing in the 1990s for vendors as they were for Cullinet in the 1980s. They allow a vendor with the old technology to quickly construct an implementation of the new technology. Then, over several years, the vendor can migrate its old engine by adding new function, changing the wrapper at each step to take advantage of whatever functionality is currently available in the underlying engine. Over these years of migration, the wrapper can insulate the user community, and eventually, it can be discarded when the vendor has native support for all wrapper functionality.

The problem with wrappers is poor performance on certain applications. To illustrate, consider the following object-relational table:

```
create table emp (
                name        varchar(30),
                location    point,
                resume      document,
                friends     setof (ref (emp)));
```

This table contains a row for each employee in a given company and records the employee's name, home address, resume, and a collection of references to the employee's friends. This table might be subjected to the following SQL command:

```
select name
from emp
where contained (location, circle ('0,0',2))
and wants (resume) = 'marketing'
and 'Joe' in friends.name;
```

This query retrieves the names of employees who live inside a circle of radius two miles around the origin of the coordinate system, who want a marketing job, and who have a friend named Joe. It typifies the accesses in the upper-right quadrant.

Now consider the implementation of this query using a wrapper. Because point, document, and setof (ref(emp)) are not data types in SQL-92, the wrapper must actually create an SQL-92 table (or tables) with different types. As shown in Figure 12.3, the wrapper could choose to represent the data types as follows:

```
create table emp_92 (
                name        varchar(30)
                location    varchar(20)
                resume      blob
                friends     varchar (100));
```

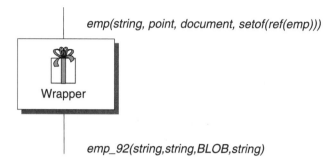

emp(string, point, document, setof(ref(emp)))

Wrapper

emp_92(string,string,BLOB,string)

FIGURE 12.3　The Wrapper in Action

In any case, the wrapper receives an object-relational query on the emp table and must actually run an SQL-92 query on the emp_92 table. Note that in the example above, every clause in the predicate contains functionality not in SQL-92. Therefore, no clause is legal SQL-92, and as a result, the actual query run is

```
select *
from emp_92;
```

The entire query must now be performed in the wrapper, which means that the wrapper must have a second SQL parser, a second optimizer, and a second executor, all performing a simulation on top of a standard relational system.

In this example, the simulation will be extremely slow because a sequential search of all employees must be performed to satisfy the query. In contrast, IDS-UDO can use an R-tree access method to efficiently subset the employees on their spatial location, and thereby utilize indexing to do a lot less work. Additionally, the entire table must be moved out of the relational engine into the wrapper, incurring additional overhead.

A variation on the basic wrapper strategy just discussed has recently been announced by Sybase as their object-relational strategy. After the Brahms project failed in a complete rewrite, Sybase had to select another strategy. Apparently they have rejected incremental evolution and appear to be following a strategy that does not involve changing the server code.

Sybase is extending a middleware system that is already in place to have some object-relational functionality. The architecture of their proposed system is shown in Figure 12.4—a middleware system together with the underlying relational engine. Sybase has designed an open interface, similar to the Informix Virtual Table Interface (VTI) or the Microsoft OLE/DB storage interface, through which external

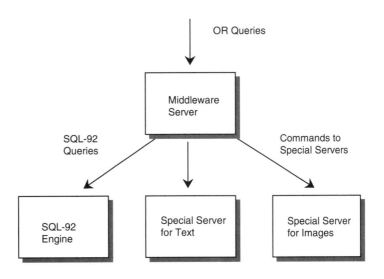

FIGURE 12.4   The Sybase Architecture

storage managers can be attached to the middleware layer. These attachments are intended to be specialized text servers or video servers. The middleware layer has been extended to support calling these attached storage systems and processing the results of records returned from such managers. In effect, Sybase has extended the wrapper architecture of Figure 12.2 to include multiple storage managers in addition to a relational engine.

An open storage manager interface is an excellent idea, as was discussed in Chapter 2. However, this particular architecture has several major disadvantages.

Granularity

A storage manager is required in order to attach a new service to the architecture shown in Figure 12.4. In other words, each special server in Figure 12.4 must have its own storage system with accompanying concurrency control, crash recovery, and access methods. A substantial portion of the lower half of a DBMS must be implemented in order to connect an extension, making the granularity of an extension extremely large.

Of course, it is possible to connect a storage manager to IDS-UDO, using the VTI interface. However, you are not obligated to do so in order to add an extension to it. Instead, you need only specify the semantics of the extension (that is, the data types and functions), not how to store it. It is hard to imagine that the implementor of the Scottish character string data type mentioned in Chapter 2 would be willing to write a storage system to implement this semantic extension.

Multiple Storage Systems

In the approach illustrated by Figure 12.4, there are multiple storage managers, one for relational data and one for each of the extensions. Suppose you have a GIS extension, a text extension, and some relational data. If you specify a query that has a text predicate, a GIS predicate, and a relational predicate, then the middleware will send each portion of the query to its appropriate subsystem, assembling the composite answer from the returned information.

Consider, however, the query from Chapter 1 that required the sunset images within 20 miles of Sacramento. In this implementation, execution of the query requires the relational system to find Sacramento and pass the location of Sacramento to the GIS system, which finds other landmarks within a 20-mile radius. The result of this inquiry must be passed to the text engine to find the appropriate documents with the required keywords. Finally, the result can be assembled and passed to the user. This solution will require the output of a portion of the query to be passed up to middleware and then back down into another storage manager. This data transfer through middleware will hamper the speedy execution of the query. Any time there are multiple storage systems, then this tax will have to be paid for queries that integrate data in multiple storage managers.

In addition, if you insert a new record into this database, then inserts must be performed to the relational system as well as to the specialized servers. This requires concurrency control and crash recovery in each specialized server, facilities that may not be present. If not, then data integrity problems are the obvious outcome. Furthermore, even with transaction support in each server, it is necessary to ensure that all servers commit the transaction in the presence of any kind of failure or failures. To reliably commit a transaction that spans multiple storage systems, you must utilize a two-phase commit protocol. This protocol ensures data consistency, but at the expense of an extra round-trip message between the coordinating middleware and each server. The cost of data integrity is very high.

Optimizer Problems

In an object-relational engine there is a single optimizer that evaluates the collection of possible query plans and selects the most desirable one. This single optimizer has complete information about the query and can select the best way to perform any query, as noted in Chapter 10. In contrast, the Figure 12.4 architecture contains multiple optimizers. There is a relational optimizer for the relational engine, as well as an optimizer in the middleware layer, and there may be an optimizer in some or all of the attached storage managers. Whenever there is an optimizer on top of an optimizer, things get very hard. The "outside" optimizer has no idea what the "inside" optimizer is doing or how much the relational portion of the query costs. Therefore, it has no way of deciding whether to do the storage manager predicates before or after the relational ones. As such, it is likely to produce very poor query plans. This topic is further explored in Chapter 14, where we present benchmark data on the scope of this problem.

In summary, the architecture illustrated in Figure 12.4 is better than a pure wrapper because additional storage managers are presumably more efficient than pure wrappers on top of a relational engine. However, the approach still suffers from excessive granularity, copying excessive data between servers, and an inferior ability to optimize queries. Excessive code on the part of the extension designer and possible poor performance for user queries are the likely results of the approach.

12.7 *Strategy 7: Write a Gateway*

The seventh option is to use gateway technology, which connects an object-relational DBMS to a relational one. The required technology differs somewhat from traditional relational gateways. First we describe this traditional technology, followed by the architecture required in an object-relational system.

The standard relational gateway architecture is indicated in Figure 12.5. Here, you write an application using the API. Instead of processing the SQL commands in the user's program directly, the vendor inserts a relational gateway that maps the SQL commands submitted into the SQL dialect supported by a specific target system. Then, the gateway submits the command to the foreign system, interprets the returned results and error codes, and delivers the result to the user.

The gateway is a simulation layer that converts from one vendor's SQL to a second vendor's SQL. As such, the gateway is a special kind of wrapper whose purpose is the conversion between SQL-92 dialects. Of course, the gateway must also translate error messages and output data back from the foreign system. The architecture in Figure 12.5 is used by essentially all relational vendors to support access to foreign systems. Currently, most vendors have extensive collections of gateways to the popular foreign DBMSs.

Gateway technology can also be used by an object-relational DBMS vendor to support data in foreign DBMSs. Figure 12.6 shows a simplification of the required architecture. Suppose you have the following emp_R table stored in a relational system:

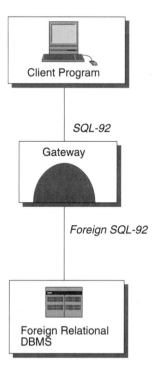

FIGURE 12.5   Relational Gateway Architecture

```
create table emp_R(
                name        varchar(30),
                salary      int,
                startdate   date);
```

And suppose you want to run the following query:

```
select name
from emp_R
where salary = 10000
and vesting(startdate) > 0.6;
```

In this case, the query cannot be translated into SQL-92, because the second clause contains a user-defined function, *vesting*. Some of the query must be internally processed by the object-relational engine, in particular the following clause:

```
vesting(startdate) > 0.6
```

The remainder of the query,

```
select name
from emp_R
where salary = 10000;
```

can be translated by the gateway into the dialect of SQL used in the foreign vendor's system. As a result, your query must be processed by the object-relational engine and decomposed into two parts, one part to be done locally and one part to be shipped through the gateway to a foreign system. As a result, the gateway cannot be at the API level, as was shown in Figure 12.5. Instead, it must be internal to the object-relational system, and the architecture of Figure 12.6 results.

One interpretation of Figure 12.6 is that the object-relational engine plus the gateway implement the wrapper architecture from Figure 12.2. Thus, a relational vendor could partner with an object-relational one to quickly implement a wrapper.

In fact, the actual architecture is somewhat more general and is shown in Figure 12.7. Suppose you have an existing application managed by a relational DBMS. For example, you might have the above emp_R table with existing client programs. To

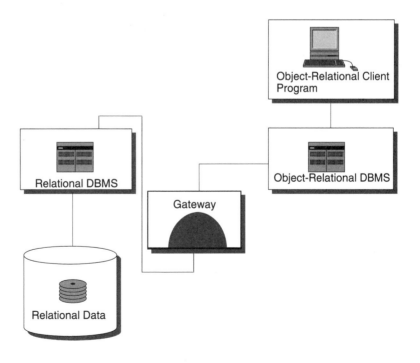

FIGURE 12.6   The Object-Relational Gateway

this table, you might want to add two fields, location and picture, to form the
following table:

```
create type employee_t(
                name       varchar(30),
                salary     int,
                startdate  date,
                location   point,
                picture    image);

create table emp of type employee_t;
```

Unfortunately, location and picture are not SQL-92 data types and cannot be easily
managed by a relational DBMS. One option is to convert the application from a
relational DBMS to an object-relational one to accommodate these extra fields.
However, this requires substantial application maintenance, which would be
resisted by the customer. A better option is to leave the relational data where it is
and then to put the object-relational data in an object-relational system, as shown in
Figure 12.7. The relational system stores the table emp_R, while the object-
relational system stores

```
create table OR_internal(
                name       varchar(30),
                location   point,
                picture    image);
```

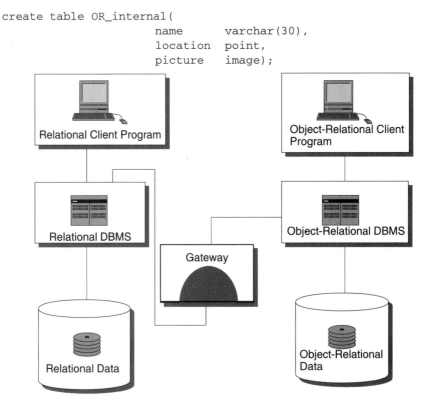

FIGURE 12.7   A Real Object-Relational Gateway Architecture

Furthermore, the table you need can be declared as the following view:

```
create view emp_OR as
select e.*, i.location, i.picture
from emp_R   e, OR_internal i
where e.name = i.name;
```

This view creates a join between emp_R stored in a relational system and OR_internal stored in an object-relational one. Using this approach your current applications can continue to use the relational API without any dislocation, as shown in Figure 12.7. Furthermore, you can utilize the object-relational API for more general commands.

Using this architecture, you have available the full power of the object-relational engine to manipulate the emp_OR table. For example, you can submit the following query:

```
select name
from emp_OR
where salary > 5000
and vesting(startdate) > 0.6
and contained(location, circle ('0,0', 1))
and beard(picture) = 'gray';
```

Using standard view techniques, the object-relational engine transforms this query to

```
select name
from emp_R e, OR_internal i
where e.salary > 5000
and vesting(startdate) > 0.6
and contained(i.location, circle ('0,0', 1))
and beard(i.picture) = 'gray'
and e.name = i.name;
```

This is a conventional object-relational query that can be processed by the parser, optimizer, and executor in the standard way. During execution, the portion of this query that can be processed by the relational system, namely,

```
select name, startdate
from emp_R
where salary > 5000;
```

is forwarded to the relational engine for execution. The remaining predicate on emp_R,

```
vesting(startdate) > 0.6
```

contains a user-defined function. This clause must be solved by the object-relational engine after appropriate data is returned through the gateway.

In summary, the gateway from an object-relational DBMS to a relational one must be inside the executor of the object-relational engine, so that clauses that can be performed by the relational engine can be sent through the gateway, while ones that cannot are performed on the returned data. Moreover, data that cannot be easily modeled in a relational system should be stored locally inside the object-relational storage manager. To implement the architecture of Figure 12.7, you need to be able to declare to the object-relational system that emp_R is a foreign table not stored by the local object-relational storage manager but instead accessed through a gateway. This foreign table interface is exactly the virtual table interface first discussed in Chapter 2.

It is also possible for a relational vendor to use this strategy to quickly achieve object-relational capabilities. For example, Computer Associates formed a relationship with Fujitsu, whereby Fujitsu wrote a gateway from Jasmine to CA-Ingres, and Computer Associates started marketing this partnership. They recently changed direction, however, and are marketing Jasmine and Ingres separately.

Of course, the disadvantage of gateway technology is poor performance. If you implement Figure 12.6, then the gateway plus the object-relational engine are really another kind of wrapper, and your gateway will have the same problems as any wrapper solution.

The architecture of Figure 12.7 is better, because some of the data is "native." However, any query that goes through the gateway will entail

- translation of the outbound query by the gateway
- at least two messages between the gateway and the relational DBMS
- copying all of the returned data from the foreign system to the object-relational one
- possibly reformatting the copied data into the type system of the object-relational engine

Because of these limitations, gateways tend to be slow. This architecture will offer lower performance (perhaps much lower performance) than a native implementation of an object-relational engine.

Gateways have too much overhead to be purposely engineered into an object-relational architecture. However, they are incredibly useful for another purpose entirely, namely as a migration strategy for legacy applications to universal ones. Initially, all data is in a relational engine, and the gateway is used to get object-relational access. In time, new data is implemented in the object-relational system, and the architecture of Figure 12.7 enables object-relational access to both the new and old data. Eventually, you could move the relational data into the object-relational system and move the legacy applications onto the object-relational API. When all your data has been moved into the object-relational system, you can discard the gateway and unhook the legacy system. Of course, this might occur in several steps and perhaps over a substantial number of years.

A gateway from an object-relational system to a legacy system is a good strategy for object-relational vendors; gateways provide you with a migration path to the newer technology without having to dislocate your existing application.

12.8   *Strategy 8: Extend an Object-Oriented DBMS*

As noted in Chapter 1, most of the object-oriented DBMS vendors focus on "persistent languages," that is, systems tightly integrated with a specific programming language such as C++ or Smalltalk. Under the direction of Rick Cattell at Sun Microsystems, the OODB vendors have formed a consortium called the Object Database Management Group (ODMG) with a charter to construct standards for the O vendors. The ODMG has a draft standard for object services, which includes a query language OQL.

OQL has features in common with SQL-3; consider it as an alternative candidate for standardization for upper-right quadrant systems.

There are two possible future outcomes in this arena:

- OQL and SQL-3 will be rolled together into a single standard.
- OQL will be "buried" by SQL-3.

The forces pushing SQL-3 (Informix, Sybase, IBM, and Oracle) are much stronger than those pushing OQL. Therefore, expect SQL-3 to win in the marketplace. This outcome has nothing to do with the technical merits of either standard. It is simply a matter of the size of the "elephants" who are pushing SQL-3.

In any case, most O vendors are moving toward OQL or SQL-3 systems, which require the following steps:

1. Implement an SQL parser.
2. Implement an SQL optimizer.
3. Implement an execution engine for the resulting plans.
4. Bind the result onto their current runtime storage systems.

These O vendors have added a query engine on top of their persistent language system. In effect, they have constructed systems with a top half and a bottom half, as in Figure 12.1. The storage management layer is, of course, architected differently by the O vendors and the R vendors.

Additionally, most of the O vendors currently perform static linking when the DBMS is installed. Thus, their architecture builds in some of the undesirable features discussed in Chapter 2. Fixing these problems entails a fair amount of work.

Moreover, they must address the scalability, reliability, robustness, and high availability requirements of the upper-left quadrant if they want to support universal applications. The relational vendors have typically spent about a decade getting really good at this quadrant. Illustra figured it would take several years of tuning and development to address the upper-left quadrant applications. Addressing universal applications more quickly drove the Illustra/Informix merger. Any new vendor that addresses this space should not assume that it will get there more rapidly.

In summary, several O vendors are using Strategy 8 to address the upper-right quadrant. To that end, they have implemented an SQL engine on top of their storage managers, which is a fair amount of work. Getting the engine to satisfy the requirements of the upper-left quadrant is considerably more work, which will take time to achieve.

12.9 *Strategy 9: Glue an Object-Relational Engine onto a Persistent Language*

It is possible to interface an existing object-relational DBMS onto a persistent language. For example, UniSQL had an internal interface that was close to a persistent language. In other words, it is possible to remove the UniSQL "bottom half" and interface the remaining "top half" onto an object-oriented DBMS. A few years ago Versant formed a partnership with UniSQL to do exactly this. More recently, Versant switched to Strategy 8, using their own SQL engine.

In a sense, this architecture is analogous to that described in Section 12.4. Relational vendors can use their bottom half with an object-relational top half that has a compatible storage manager. Object-oriented DBMS vendors can use their existing systems as a bottom half with an object-relational top half that has a compatible persistent language interface.

12.10   *Summary*

Table 12.1 reviews many of the vendors and their strategies for moving to an object-relational system. Also shown are the issues involved in each strategy. The table lists all the major vendors, with the exception of Microsoft, which has yet to announce its direction in this area. In the meantime Microsoft is touting OLE DB as its approach to objects. However, OLE DB is merely a storage manager interface (similar to the VTI discussed in Chapter 2) and does not empower SQL Server with the object-relational capabilities discussed in this book.

Strategy	Issues	Vendors
1. Do nothing.	You may go out of business.	None
2. Rewrite the engine from scratch.	Dangerous—a high-stakes, "all or nothing gamble."	Sybase and DEC failed at this strategy.
3. Sell two systems.	Does not address universal applications.	CA
4. Implement an object-relational top on a relational storage manager.	Leapfrog strategy, inherently risky because it requires a massive engineering effort.	Informix, IBM
5. Incremental evolution of the current engine to add new functionality.	Safer, but time-consuming.	Oracle, Ingres' strategy in the 1980s
6. Create a wrapper on top of a relational engine.	Possible performance loss.	Hewlett-Packard, Sybase
7. Make a gateway from an object-relational engine to a relational engine.	Possible performance loss. But enables vendor to deliver market-ready product quickly.	Previous CA strategy
8. Extend an object-oriented system.	Will only address universal applications over time.	Many O vendors
9. Glue an object-relational engine to a persistent language system.	Reasonable strategy, if performance is not compromised.	Former Versant strategy

TABLE 12.1   Strategies for Object-Relational DBMS Conversion

CHAPTER 13

More on Object-Relational Architecture

This chapter investigates in more detail the performance implications of two object-relational architectural options mentioned earlier:

- The protocol used to call DBMS extensions
- A middleware object-relational solution (Strategy 6 from Chapter 12)

13.1   Calling Extensions

There is considerable controversy over the proper way to call a DBMS extension. It is possible to call an extension using a local procedure call (LPC). In this case, the extension is linked into the same address space as the DBMS, and the routine is called locally. The overhead to perform an LPC is about 1 microsecond. However, there is one major problem. If the extension fails, it can make the DBMS shut itself down to prevent data corruption.

An alternative strategy is to call the extension using a remote procedure call (RPC) protocol. In this case, the extension is linked into an address space different from the DBMS, on either the same machine or a different machine. Using an RPC, the arguments to the call must be marshalled together into a string of bytes, passed across an interprocess communication channel (IPC), unpacked at the other end, and then passed to the extension using a local procedure call. Moreover, an operating system task switch must occur to start the recipient process. In all, an RPC will cost about 1 millisecond (1000 times the cost of a local procedure call) if the recipient is on the same machine as the caller. If the recipient is on a different machine, the cost is even higher.

Of course, if you choose to utilize a location-transparent RPC system, such as CORBA, then all of the above steps must take place. In addition an object resource broker (ORB) must also be invoked to look up in its directory the machine location of the recipient. This extra overhead makes CORBA about one order of magnitude slower than RPC, which is in turn three orders of magnitude slower than LPC.

Of course, the big advantage of RPC is that an extension failure will only crash the address space in which it is running; and the address space is not the DBMS. The argument between LPC and RPC proponents can be summarized as follows:

- *RPC proponents:* RPC must be used to ensure that extensions do not crash the DBMS. Also, extensions can use a well-known, standard protocol (for example, CORBA).

- *LPC proponents:* The cost of RPC is prohibitive in end-to-end performance degradation. In most cases, this end-to-end degradation is more than one order of magnitude. A six-second query becomes a one-minute query, and a three-minute query turns into a "go out for lunch before you get the answer" query. This performance degradation is unacceptable and has caused the designers of all plug-in systems (such as Visual Basic controls, operating system device drivers, Netscape plug-ins, CICS applications, etc.) to choose LPC. Of course, RPC should be provided for special circumstances, including debugging new extensions, but LPC will be the protocol used by the overwhelming majority of all extensions.

In addition, a sure way for a system administrator to lose her job is to install untested software in a production environment. Rigorously testing all software that goes into a production application is standard practice in a well-run information system shop. This tenet applies equally to DBMS extensions, application programs, and new versions of system software. Extension vendors should, therefore, certify that their extensions have been rigorously tested. A DBMS vendor is the ideal certification agent and should perform this function. There is no safety problem in well-tested, certified extensions.

In order to shed more light on this discussion, the rest of this section quantifies the performance cost of RPC relative to LPC through four simple experiments.

Experiment 1: Bond Time. We treat the situation of bond time mentioned earlier in Chapter 2. Specifically, on Wall Street, the interest on financial bonds is not computed using the Gregorian calendar. Instead a customer gets the same amount of interest during each month, no matter how long the month is. Thus, the SQL-89 notion of date and time does not have the correct semantics.

Recall the table from Chapter 2 that holds

```
create table Bond (
                bond_id        int ,
                coupon_rate    float,
                face_value      decimal(10,2),
                bought         date,
                matures        date,
                value          decimal(10,2));
```

as well as the SQL command to compute the value of the bond:

```
update bond
    set value = face_value + coupon_rate * (matures - bought)
```

We created an example Bond table with 10,000 rows and then ran the update command mentioned above. For each row in the table, the extension corresponding to the operator "-" must be called. Table 13.1 indicates the response time of the update for three different circumstances. First, we used Informix's universal server and called the extension using local procedure call in the same address space as the server. This time is reported in the first row of Table 13.1. Next we forced Informix's system to call the extension in a different address space on the same machine. This RPC time is indicated in the second row of Table 13.1. Finally, we used RPC to call the extension that was running on a different machine than the server, but one connected by a high-speed local area network. This is the third row of Table 13.1.

As you can see, LPC performed the best, while the extra cost of the RPC call resulted in a performance degradation of almost a factor of 15. This performance degradation results because the cost of RPC, which is three orders of magnitude

Call	Response Time (seconds)
LPC	3.1
RPC (same machine)	45.0
RPC (another machine)	104.0

TABLE 13.1 A Performance Analysis on Bond Time

slower than LPC, must be paid once per row in the Bond table. When, an RPC to a different machine was used, the degradation was more than a factor of 30.

The difference in response time is very significant. It is the difference between an acceptable response time and one so frustrating that you want to put your fist through the terminal screen. However, the remaining examples show that this crushing degradation is not isolated behavior.

Experiment 2: Scottish Character Strings. In Chapter 2 we discussed Scottish character strings as illustrative of the need for extended data types. Namely, we discussed the following table:

```
emp (name, startdate, salary)
```

Assuming that name is of type "Scottish string," we then wish to run the following query:

```
select name, salary
from emp
where name > 'McT' and name < 'McU'
order by ascending name;
```

With a Scottish string data type, we require the operators <, <=, =, >, >=, with the proper meanings. To run the query above, we must call Scottish string extensions in the following circumstances:

- *Twice per record to evaluate the qualification:* The extensions for < and > must be called for each possible record to evaluate whether the predicate is true or false for the record.

- *Once per key while descending the B-tree:* If a sequential search of all employee names is to be avoided, then we must build a B-tree index that contains the keys in Scottish name order. To search the B-tree, we use the low key in the range (McT) and scan the root of the B-tree looking for the first key greater than McT. This requires calling the extension <= once per key in the root node. This process is repeated for each descendent page until the leaf level is reached. At the leaf level, keys are accessed until one is found that is greater than McU. For each qualifying key, the corresponding data record is fetched. As can be seen, the extension operators are called with great frequency during index scans.

- *In the sort routine:* To sort the qualifying records in Scottish name order, a polyphase merge sort algorithm is used by most vendors. If N is the number of qualifying records, then the sort routine calls the extension corresponding to the operator <=, about $N * \log (N)$ times. Thus, the extension must be called in the inner loop of the sort routine.

To explore the performance consequences of LPC versus RPC, we ran the above query on an emp table of 26,000 rows using Informix's universal server and timed

Call	Response Time (seconds)
LPC	1.0
RPC (same machine)	22.0
RPC (another machine)	54.0

TABLE 13.2 A Performance Analysis on Scottish Strings

the execution, which is shown in Table 13.2. As can be seen, it executes with a 1.0 second response time using LPC. However, with RPC we observed a response time of 22.0 seconds. Using RPC to access an extension on a different machine causes response time to degrade further to 54 seconds.

Note that the RPC degradation observed in this example is somewhat worse than the Bond time example. The difference is that the extensions must be called with even higher frequency, resulting in proportionally greater overhead. The third example shows another case of extreme degradation.

Experiment 3: Date Intervals. Our third example concerns a typical hotel application dealing with conferences. Specifically, there is a conferences table indicating the collection of conferences that have been booked at a particular hotel:

```
create table conferences (
                    conf_id  int,
                    conf_name varchar(30),
                    duration dateinterval);
```

In addition, there is a reservations table that indicates which hotel rooms are reserved for which dates:

```
create table reservations (
                    Room_id     int,
                    reservation dateinterval );
```

For simplicity, we assume that the guests at the hotel are assuredly attending any conference that overlaps their stay at the hotel. As a result, our example query asks for the names of all conferences booked at this hotel during the months of June, July, and August along with the number of hotel guests that are attending each conference. This query is expressed by the following SQL:

```
select c.conf_name, count(*)
from conferences c, reservations r
where overlaps(c.duration,'06/01/96 to 08/31/96')
and overlaps(c.duration,r.reservation)
group by c.conf_name;
```

There are a couple of points to notice about this query. First, because SQL-92 contains a data type corresponding to time interval, it would be natural to try to solve this query in SQL-92. Unfortunately, the designers of SQL-92 failed to provide an *overlaps* function for two time intervals. As a result, this query is not possible in SQL-92. This is another very good reason for using object-relational DBMSs that allow new functions and operators to be added even for standard data types.

Second, notice that this query contains a restriction on the conferences table that deals with specific months. Such a date range predicate cannot be efficiently solved using B-trees because B-trees only deal with simple numbers or character strings and not with ranges of values, such as are present in this example. Instead an R-tree or other multidimensional access method must be used to accelerate this predicate. This is an example where standard indexing fails to work, and a specialized access method must be provided. An object-relational DBMS must have such an access method, or performance on this query will deteriorate badly because a sequential scan must be used instead of an indexed scan.

As in the Scottish character string example, there will be multiple calls to the *overlaps* function from within the indexing code. In addition, there is a join between the conferences table and the reservations table, which is specified by the predicate containing the *overlaps* function. This is an example where a join clause contains a user-defined function, which must be called for each pair of records that the join engine evaluates. Again, there will be a very large number of calls processed during query execution.

The results of this experiment on a reservations table of size 15,000 and a conferences table of size 300 are shown in Table 13.3. RPC shows serious degradation because of the large number of calls. Again, RPC provides unacceptable response time because of the overhead of the protocol.

Call	Response Time (seconds)
LPC	1.0
RPC (same machine)	26.0
RPC (another machine)	61.0

TABLE 13.3   A Performance Analysis on Date Intervals

Experiment 4: Image Data. Our final example illustrates a large object in the database and is a case where RPC will not suffer as badly. It is included to show that the performance consequences of RPC, in fact, differ widely. Hence, a user must test his own specific circumstances to see what his real performance degradation will be.

Specifically, we use a variation on the California slide library example from Chapter 1:

```
slides (id, date, picture)
```

The slides table contains one row for each picture, giving its ID, the date the picture was taken, and the bits in the image in Kodak Photo CD format. We can run a simple query to find sunset images taken during 1996:

```
select id
from slides
where sunset (picture)
and date > 'Dec. 31, 1995'
and date <= 'Dec 31, 1996';
```

This query contains a pair of date restrictions that are valid SQL-89 clauses and a single expensive user-defined function, *sunset*, on a data type, picture, that consumes a great deal of space—on average, 32 KB of compressed data.

There are three possible execution strategies for this query. First, we could use a B-tree index, if one exists for the date field, to restrict the slides table to the 1996 images. Subsequently, we could evaluate *sunset* for this collection of images. Second, if a functional index exists for *sunset*(image), then we can go directly to this index to find the qualifying sunsets. Subsequently, the executor could evaluate this set for those taken during 1996. The third strategy is appropriate if neither index is present. In this case, the executor must perform a sequential scan of the slides table. Here, it is important that the date clauses be evaluated first and then sunset only be called for qualifying dates. This is an example of *expensive function optimization* mentioned in Chapter 10.

Because there are three different query plans, we tested all of the cases on Informix's universal server with a slides table of 10,000 rows. We used a *sunset* function in which each image evaluated consumed 100,000 instructions. Table 13.4 contains the results of our experiments.

Call	Index on date	Index on sunset	Sequential scan
LPC	237	0.3	242
RPC (same machine)	481	3.1	486
RPC (another machine)	589	10.7	601

TABLE 13.4   A Performance Analysis on Images (response time in seconds)

If the optimizer uses a functional index on *sunset*, then the 80 images that qualify are quickly found and the data range subsequently evaluated, yielding subsecond response time. RPC is a factor of three slower because of the familiar once-per-record RPC tax for the date calls. Remote RPC is another factor of three slower. If this plan is selected, then the results follow the pattern of the previous examples.

In contrast, if an index on date is selected, then the 894 qualifying records can be efficiently found. However, the cost of executing *sunset* balloons the response time to 237 seconds. In this case, RPC has comparable overhead to the cost of the *sunset* function and response time approximately doubles to 481 seconds. Remote RPC adds a corresponding tax. In this case, the cost of the function is comparable to the cost of RPC and the percentage performance penalty is narrowed considerably.

With a sequential scan we notice that expensive function optimization (performing the date predicate first) ensures that *sunset* is only evaluated for the qualifying images. Since this is the vast majority of the work, we observe that the sequential scan performs about the same as an indexed scan on date.

Discussion

As can be seen by three of the four examples, the use of RPC either to a different address space on the local machine or to an address space on a different machine resulted in dramatic performance degradation of at least one order of magnitude. Obviously this kind of performance hit is usually the difference between the application being feasible and being too slow to be interesting. On the other hand, the fourth example showed a case where the difference was a factor of two to three—still quite high, but perhaps acceptable.

Obviously, the actual degradation will depend on the individual circumstances. Therefore, any customer of an object-relational DBMS should carefully do performance testing on any extensions that will use RPC before deploying it. Most of the time (but not always), unacceptable performance degradation results.

13.2 *Middleware*

A second area where there is a heated debate concerns supporting objects in a middleware layer, as in Strategy 6 in Chapter 12. Basically, the argument goes something like this:

- *Middleware proponents:* A relational system is optimized for numbers and character strings. It is foolish to try to overload this functionality with support for objects. Instead you should have specialized servers for the various specialized data types, connected by a middleware object layer.

- *One server proponents:* It is a lot of work to extend a relational engine to store objects. However, the performance and data integrity consequences of a multiple-server strategy are too extreme to be acceptable. The multiple-server option is only being proposed by vendors unwilling to mount a suitable engineering effort to construct a single server.

To examine this trade-off in more detail, we ran the four experiments mentioned above and compared a server implementation with a solution based on middleware.

Experiment 1: Bond Time. Earlier in the chapter, we explored the value calculation for the Bond table using the Informix universal server. This update was a single SQL statement for which control passed from client to server once at the beginning of the query and back to the client at the end of the query.

A middleware implementation of the same query is quite easy because the representation of bond_time can use the standard SQL representation for dates. All the middleware system has to do (whether written by the DBMS vendor or by the user) is to fetch the records, one by one, and perform the appropriate calculation. Hence, middleware will execute the following logic:

```
define cursor C as
select face_value, coupon_rate, matures, bought
from Bond

open cursor C

until (no_more){
    fetch next record
    perform calculation
    update current record with value}
```

System	Response Time (seconds)
LPC/server	3.1
Middleware	27.0

TABLE 13.5   A Performance Analysis on Bond Time

The problem with this code snippet is that control must pass between the application and the DBMS once per record in Bond rather than once for the whole query. Thus, the utilization of a middleware layer results in the performance reported in Table 13.5.

As you can see, this requirement of crossing the client-server boundary once per record, rather than once per query, slows down the system by a factor of nine. Hence, the first difficulty of a middleware implementation is the distinct possibility of excessive numbers of boundary crossings.

Experiment 2: Scottish Strings. Turning to a middleware implementation of the Scottish name search problem, we are immediately presented with two difficulties.

First, if Scottish names are simulated in a middleware layer outside a relational DBMS, then name must be implemented as a character string in the relational DBMS, and not as a Scottish string. Running the original query

```
select name, salary
from emp
where name > 'McT' and name < 'McU'
order by ascending name;
```

of course gives the wrong answer and fails to fetch a superset of the required records to the middleware layer for subsequent filtering.

The simple answer would be to run

```
select name, salary
from emp;
```

but this will result in a sequential search of the whole table with all filtering to be done by middleware code. Such an implementation will be impossibly slow. The smallest possible superset that can be run is

```
select name, salary
from emp
where name > 'MacT' and name < 'MacU' or
name > 'McT' and name < 'McU' or
name > 'M'T' and name < 'M'U';
```

However, it is difficult to imagine that a middleware system could know enough of the semantics of Scottish names to come up with this. In addition, an application programmer would likewise have to be an expert on Scottish names to be able to generate this expression.

Because of this uncertainty, we perform this experiment using both the sequential search query as well as the best possible query.

The second problem concerns the required sort of the result set. Since the names must be sorted in Scottish name order and not in ASCII, we must retrieve all the records to a middleware layer, where they must be sorted. A middleware system that can automatically sort objects in an object-specific order is quite smart indeed. In contrast, it seems equally plausible that the programmer will have to do the work himself. In this case, he must figure out how to call a sort package with the filtered result of his query. Again, a significant amount of manual intervention may be required on the part of the application programmer. This required effort makes a middleware implementation very unattractive indeed from the point of view of the effort required to code a solution.

In this experiment, we utilize the Unix sort package to perform the required sort, and we wrote a C program to specify the required query, filter the returned records, and then sort them in Scottish name order. The result of this experiment is documented in Table 13.6.

Middleware is disastrous when it performs a sequential search and the server does an indexed search. This, of course, results in a performance degradation of more than one order of magnitude. On the other hand, if middleware can perform the best possible query, then the response time is still a factor of five off, and near the threshold of an unacceptable response time. This degradation results from the middleware solution running a query with multiple clauses. This will be slower than a single clause, which the server implementation uses. In addition, the server implementation is sorting the records in the server; the middleware solution must copy them up to the middleware layer and do the sort there.

System	Response Time (seconds)
Server	1.3
Middleware (best query)	6.7
Middleware (sequential search)	31.5

TABLE 13.6 A Performance Analysis on Scottish Names

Experiment 3: Date Interval. The third experiment deals with hotel reservations. A middleware system has three daunting challenges in solving this query, which we discuss in turn.

First, Informix's universal server will begin by filtering the conferences table to find the ones in the required three-month interval. Using an R-tree on the date interval, this will be an indexed search. In contrast, a middleware system will have to perform a sequential search of the conferences table and then do the filtering in middleware. Obviously, this comparison will strongly favor the indexed search, which is unavailable to the middleware solution.

Second, the server will perform the join of the filtered result with the reservations table. In Informix's universal server, this join will proceed by iterating over the filtered conferences table and, for each such record, performing an indexed lookup in the reservations table, utilizing an R-tree on the date interval. If there are K conferences that qualify, then the join will require K indexed lookups in the reservations table.

In contrast, what should the middleware system do? It has three options. First, it can perform the join in middleware. However, this will require a complete join engine in middleware, thereby duplicating the engine that exists inside the relational server. Such required code duplication is one of disadvantages of a complete middleware solution. Alternatively, it can return the data to the server and perform the join there. The problem is that the relational server does not understand the *overlaps* function. The only way the relational server could do the join would be for both the conferences and reservations tables to have the date interval coded as (start_date, end_date). In this case, if temp is the filtered conferences table, then the following query will perform the correct join:

```
select c.conf_name
from temp c, reservations r
where (c.start_date < r.start_date and
c.end_date > r.start_date) or
(c.start_date < r.end_date and
c.end_date > r.end_date);
```

This query is difficult to write and somewhat error prone. Moreover, it will be difficult for the query engine to perform this query other than by exhaustive exploration of all pairs of rows in reservations and temp. A very smart programmer could improve the query to the following:

```
select c.conf_name
from temp c, reservations r
where not c.start_date < r.end_date and
c.end_date > r.start_date;
```

which is the most efficient representation of the join to be done by the relational engine. Of course, it is essentially impossible for a middleware system to have this amount of intelligence. Hence, it seems extremely unlikely that this second option would be available as a join tactic.

Of course, the third tactic would be not to support this kind of functionality at all. In this case, the programmer must perform the join himself. This forces an extreme amount of complexity onto the programmer and is a serious disadvantage of a middleware system. Since it is unlikely that a programmer would want to implement a join engine in his application, we assume that he would return the filtered conferences table to the database and use the most efficient join predicate, as noted above.

The third problem with the middleware solution is performing the aggregation specified in the target list and in the group by clause. If the middleware system was smart enough to have a join engine, then it would have the result of the join in middleware. If so, either it would have to put the result back in the relational DBMS where the aggregation could be performed, or it would have to implement a complete aggregation system. The first alternative will require moving the result of the join from the middleware system back to the DBMS, an overhead-intensive operation. In contrast, the second solution requires an aggregation engine in middleware, thereby duplicating the facilities of the relational system.

Since, we have assumed that the programmer would have put the filtered conferences table back in the DBMS and then performed the join in the DBMS, it is straightforward for him to specify that the aggregation should also be done by the DBMS.

In summary, the middleware solution performs the following steps:

1. Filter the conferences table in middleware using a sequential search, returning the output to the database as a temporary table.
2. Perform the relational join between temp and reservations using the most efficient predicate.
3. Perform the aggregation in the relational DBMS on the answer.

It is impossible to conceive of a middleware system that will do all of these steps automatically. Therefore, the user will have to write these three steps in an application program. This program is tedious to write and the resulting application complexity is a serious disadvantage to the middleware approach.

As expected, performance of the middleware solution is awful, as shown in Table 13.7, because of the sequential scan to do the filtering and the exhaustive evaluation

System	Response Time (seconds)
LPC/server	1.1
Middleware	26.1

TABLE 13.7   A Performance Analysis on Date Intervals

of both tables in doing the join. Between these two effects, the middleware solution is more than an order of magnitude slower than the server solution.

Experiment 4: Image Library. The previous three examples showed the difficulty of *simulating* objects on top of relational tables. The queries were ugly to write, required considerable sophistication to write correctly, and executed with generally bad performance. In addition, it seems implausible that a middleware system could generate the required code automatically unless it was a complete DBMS engine. In this case, a vendor has two of everything, one on top of the other. It would be better in the long run to extend a single engine with the required capabilities!

The final example should be more favorable to the middleware solution, especially one with a specialized server for images. Such a server contains a complete storage manager, concurrency control, and crash recovery system and is optimized for image storage. In this case, we can decompose the slides table into two pieces:

```
image server:  slides (id, picture)
relational DBMS: r_images (id, date)
```

There are now several ways that middleware can perform the user's query, which is repeated here:

```
select id
from images
where sunset (picture)
and date > 'Dec. 31, 1995'
and date <= 'Dec 31, 1996';
```

First, it could do the date restriction to r_images:

```
select id
from r_images
where date > 'Dec. 31, 1995'
and date <= 'Dec 31, 1996';
```

With these IDs, it can interrogate the image server for the appropriate images. In middleware, it could evaluate *sunset* and return the correct answer.

Obviously, this will entail moving a large number of bytes from the image server to middleware to perform the *sunset* computation. It is clearly more efficient if the image server can perform the *sunset* calculation locally. Moreover, we further assume that the image server can optionally perform function indexing, so the result of *sunset*(picture) can be available.

With this in mind, the first strategy would be to filter the r_images table and send the resulting IDs to the image server that would perform the rest of the query. The second strategy is the reverse: that is, find the *sunset* images in the image server, send the result to the relational DBMS, and then do the date restriction. Of course, the last option is to do both in parallel and then do the intersection of returned IDs in middleware.

We call these three strategies: "relational first," "image first," and "both." Depending on whether there is a date index on r_images and/or a function index on sunset, each of these options may be the best choice. It is exactly this information that is used by the Informix's universal server in deciding which strategy it will employ to solve the query. To make this decision intelligently outside the server, the middleware system must include a complete object-relational optimizer, of the sort detailed in Chapter 10. Moreover, this optimizer must be able to get information out of all servers on selectivity estimates and presence of indexes. Although such an optimizer can, in theory, be constructed over time by any vendor, we should merely note that this code is extremely difficult, duplicates the functionality of an existing relational optimizer, and is tougher to write than the extensions to a relational optimizer that would make it an object-relational one. As such, we expect middleware optimizers to be very primitive in the short run, and to be stopgaps for a longer-term rewrite/extension of a server optimizer.

To test the mistakes that are possible using this architecture, we illustrate in Table 13.8 the three cases studied in Section 13.1, namely no indexes present, index on date, and index on *sunset*. For each case, we report the Informix universal server time along with the time recorded by the three possible middleware strategies: relational first, image first, and both.

System	No index	Date index	Image index
All in DBMS	242	237	0.3
Middleware (relational first)	257	256	23.4
Middleware (image first)	2949	2940	1.8
Middleware (both)	2884	2875	14.1

TABLE 13.8   Performance Analysis on Images (response time in seconds)

As can be seen in all three cases, the middleware strategy can come reasonably close to the performance of the server strategy. However, to do so, it must make the correct optimization decision (relational first in the first and second cases; image first in the third), which is a difficult challenge. If it makes an incorrect optimization, the result will be disastrous—one order of magnitude degradation.

13.3   *Summary*

As we have seen in this chapter, the main disadvantage of using RPC as the calling convention for executing extensions is bad performance, typically one order of magnitude or more. The basic problem is the high cost of RPC, given the frequency with which extensions must be called. A more attractive alternative is LPC, together with careful testing to ensure safety.

In a similar vein, the main problem with a middleware implementation of objects is also bad performance. The reasons are varied, as we explored in this chapter, and they include excessive numbers of round-trips between client and server, the inability to make use of new access methods in an object-relational engine, and the possibility of bad query plans.

A single integrated engine, although a great deal of work, is clearly the better technical option.

CHAPTER 14 *Extension Performance: Implementation Makes a Difference*

This chapter continues with our discussion of object-relational engine performance by considering the performance of the extensions themselves. To accomplish this we will discuss spatial extensions in this chapter.

The basic objective is to support standard geographic objects, such as points, lines, polygons, and circles, and the normal functions for these types, such as point in polygon, distance from a line to a line, and so forth.

Currently, there are spatial extensions for the Informix universal server available from several vendors including ESRI, Formida, and MapInfo. Moreover, Informix is retiring its internal 2-D Spatial DataBlade module in favor of these "best of breed" extensions from domain experts. In addition, there is an ESRI extender available for IBM's Data Joiner, which will be in the next DB 6000 release. This extender indexes somewhat differently from the ESRI datablade module from the Informix universal server. Oracle has hard coded a spatial extension called the Spatial Data Option (SDO) into its Version 7.3 server. More recently, they hard coded a different implementation into Version 8.0. When cartridges are supported in a future Oracle server, then SDO will become a true extension. In addition, there are a variety of GIS packages that run outside a DBMS server. We discuss four implementation in this chapter.

The first implementation simulates the desired capabilities using standard SQL-92 facilities. We will see that this solution involves considerable pain and very bad performance. Then, we turn to Informix's 2-D Spatial DataBlade module, which depends on a specialized geographic access method to achieve high performance. It is representative of the performance envelope of most of the spatial datablade modules available for the Informix universal server. The third is a previous implementation of the Oracle Spatial Data Option (SDO). This system was designed for maximum parallelism and did not depend on any indexing. It is included in this chapter because it represents a different performance envelope than the others we consider here. Also, presentation of this option facilitates discussion of the last option we consider, the current implementation of SDO. It was a specialized encoding on top of B-trees and is also widely used by third-party GIS application packages.

We first discuss three examples of spatial queries to focus the resulting discussion. Then, we turn to each of the extensions. This chapter concludes with a qualitative performance comparison of the four options.

14.1   *Examples*

Suppose you wish to store the geographic location of the home address of a collection of employees. This yields a version of the familiar emp table:

```
create table emp (
                name        varchar(30),
                salary      int,
                startdate   date,
                location    point,
                picture     image);
```

The reason to record the location of an employee's address might be to facilitate applications such as car pool programs that need to find employees who live near each other.

Example 1

First, you might like to find the names of all employees who live within a two-mile rectangle centered at a specific bus stop at the position (LAT, LONG). This can be coded as

```
select name
from emp
where contained (location, Box( LAT - one_mile, LONG - one_mile,
                LAT + one_mile, LONG + one_mile));
```

This query constructs a two-mile box around the specific point and then identifies the employees who live within this rectangle using the function *contained*.

Example 2

A second example is to find candidate car poolers for the employee Jones by finding all employees who live within a mile of Jones. This can be expressed using the following query:

```
select e.name
from emp e, emp j
where j.name = 'Jones' and
contained (e.location, Circle (j.location, one_mile));
```

The first clause of the predicate identifies Jones and associates him with the instance variable j. Then, the second clause of the predicate indicates that qualifying employees must reside within a circle of radius one mile centered on Jones's location.

Example 3

The last example concerns the plot map for a specific geographical entity. Suppose a city or county is divided into a collection of parcels; each parcel has an owner, a zoning classification, a center, and an outline. This is represented as the following table:

```
create table parcels(
                 id        int,
                 owner     varchar(30),
                 address   varchar(30),
                 center    point,
                 outline   polygon);
```

There are many applications that use this data; for example, whenever a request for a zoning change is made for a parcel, identified by TARGET-ID, the owners of all parcels within a certain distance of the center of the target parcel must be notified. This requires the following query:

```
select n.id, n.owner, n.address
from parcels n, parcels t
where overlaps (n.outline, Circle(t.center,'some-constant'))
and t.id = TARGET-ID;
```

This query associates the target parcel with t and then finds the other parcels whose outline overlaps a circle of a specific radius around the center of the target parcel.

14.2   *An SQL-92 Solution*

All three of these examples require two additional data types, point and polygon, that are not found in SQL-92. These data types require two user-defined functions, *contained* and *overlaps*. User-defined functions are not supported in SQL-92 either. Obviously, a standard SQL DBMS cannot run the above example queries. You can, of course, simulate this functionality with client application logic. For example, you can utilize the following SQL table:

```
create table emp_sim_1 (
                name        varchar(30),
                salary      int,
                startdate   date,
                location    varchar(20),
                picture     blob);
```

Because point is not an SQL data type, you can simulate it on top of an existing data type, in this case a varchar. For example, you can choose to store location as a comma-separated pair of decimal numbers representing latitude and longitude. The first query cannot be expressed directly to an SQL DBMS because it requires a user-defined function, *contained*. As a result, you must execute

```
select name, location
from emp_sim_1;
```

Then, you must write user logic that will evaluate whether each location is within a two-mile rectangle centered on the bus stop. This simulation is extremely slow because all employee records must be examined to solve this query.

To do better, you can work harder and use a more sophisticated simulation. For example, you can use the following SQL table:

```
create table emp_sim_2 (
                name        varchar(30),
                salary      int,
                startdate   date,
                xloc        int,
                yloc        int,
                picture     blob);
```

In this case, location is represented as a pair of integers, xloc and yloc, for longitude and latitude. If you build a B-tree index on xloc, then you can run the following SQL query:

```
select name
from emp_sim_2
where xloc > LONG - one_mile
and xloc < LONG + one_mile
and yloc > LAT - one_mile
and yloc < LAT + one_mile;
```

By working harder, the search for qualifying records has been reduced from all records at all geographic locations to those within a vertical slice of real estate, as shown in Figure 14.1. The actual search region surrounding the parcel in question is shown in the middle of Figure 14.1. Since there is a B-tree on xloc, the two clauses

```
xloc > LONG - one_mile
xloc < LONG + one_mile
```

can be used by B-tree logic to restrict the search to the vertical slice indicated. Searching the vertical slice is typically much less work than searching the whole space; however, there is still considerable extra unnecessary work being performed.

You may have noticed that it is also possible to build a B-tree on the concatenated field (xloc, yloc). However, this B-tree does not help on the query in question. The concatenated keys will be sorted first in xloc order, and then in yloc order for com-

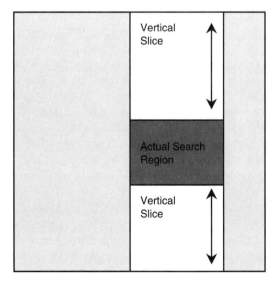

FIGURE 14.1 The Search Region of the Simulation

mon values of xloc. Thus, the keys in the vertical slice of real estate in Figure 14.1 will appear together in the concatenated B-tree, and performance will not improve relative to that obtained from a B-tree on either field by itself.

There are a wealth of other possible simulation options of varying complexity and performance; thus, wrappers of assorted complexity, functionality, and performance can be constructed. To evaluate any wrapper, you need to describe the simulation and then discuss its functionality and how badly its performance degrades. In the next section we discuss the technical approach taken by the 2-D Spatial DataBlade module for the Informix universal server.

14.3   *The Informix 2-D Spatial DataBlade Approach*

The Informix universal server can be extended with a 2-D Spatial DataBlade module, which is a collection of two-dimensional spatial data types along with appropriate operations and functions. The data types include point, line, path, circle, box, polygon, and nested polygon. Operators and functions include *contained* and *overlaps* for all pairs of data types. Using these concepts, the three SQL examples from the beginning of this chapter are legal statements in Informix/SQL augmented by the 2-D Spatial DataBlade.

Informix also allows new access methods to be added to the system, as noted in Chapter 2. Because B-trees do not work well in supporting geographic queries, Informix's 2-D Spatial DataBlade module adds an R-tree access method to the Informix universal server. Gutman (1984) first investigated R-trees, which have been shown to be a very high performance access method for spatial data. An R-tree is a fast access method for point, line, rectangle, and polygon data. It functions something like a B-tree, in that it is a hierarchical structure with nodes corresponding to disk storage blocks. These nodes are split and coalesced dynamically to form a tree structure with leaves that are all the same distance from the root. However, unlike a B-tree, the root node consists of a collection of possibly overlapping rectangles, each with a pointer to a descendent subtree. The root of this subtree further refines the associated rectangle by splitting it into a collection of possibly overlapping rectangles. At the leaf nodes are stored points of interest or bounding rectangles for other geographic types.

To find the employees within a specific bounding box, the R-tree access method code examines the root node of the R-tree to find rectangles that overlap the target area. For each identified rectangle, the system examines the root of the corresponding subtree to find appropriate rectangles and recursively descends the portion of the tree to reach leaf nodes with possibly relevant objects. Data elements at leaf nodes that qualify are then returned to the query execution engine for further processing in the remainder of the query. Thus, the R-tree code explores a set of paths from the root to leaf nodes to identify qualifying spatial objects.

When an insert is made to an R-tree, the access method code descends the tree to find a leaf node on which to store the new object. If the node is full, then the system must split the node in half, creating two nodes. Each node is given a portion of the records and free space is thereby created for the inserted object. When a node is split, then a rectangle in its parent node must be replaced by two possibly overlapping rectangles. Just as with a B-tree, this may cause the parent node to split. Splitting occurs until a parent node is found that is not full or until the root is reached and split. With the Informix universal server, R-trees can be used for any spatial objects in the Spatial 2-D DataBlade module (including point, lines, open polygons, and closed polygons), allowing a high-performance access path for any spatial query.

Moreover, Informix's universal server allows any table to be divided into a collection of storage fragments, each holding a collection of the records in the table. Any query to the universal server is automatically run in parallel on each stored fragment.

The Informix query optimizer examines an incoming query and constructs the heuristically best plan for it. This plan can utilize index scans over R-trees or B-trees, and the best choice is made for each query by the optimizer.

We now turn to a third extension, based on Z transforms, that Oracle used previously in their Spatial Data Option.

14.4   *A Z Transform Solution*

The Z transform solution begins by constructing a table identical to emp_sim_2 from the previous section:

```
create table emp_sim_2 (
                    name       varchar(30),
                    salary     int,
                    startdatedate,
                    xloc       int,
                    yloc       int,
                    picture    blob);
```

When this table reaches a user-specified high-water mark of records, the table is split into four physical tables, emp_new_1, emp_new_2, emp_new_3, and emp_new_4. The records in emp_sim_2 are inserted into one of the four tables, and then emp_sim_2 is deleted. The partitioning algorithm uses the high-order bit of xloc and yloc as follows:

```
xloc-31 = 0, yloc-31 = 0   =>   partition-1
xloc-31 = 0, yloc-31 = 1   =>   partition-2
xloc-31 = 1, yloc-31 = 0   =>   partition-3
xloc-31 = 1, yloc-31 = 1   =>   partition-4
```

Conceptually, this partitioning algorithm divides the two-dimensional plane of longitude and latitude into quadrants, and allocates one table to each quadrant. Whenever any of the resulting tables reaches its high-water mark, it is split four-for-one in the above fashion. The resulting partitioning of the longitude-latitude space might look like Figure 14.2. This figure shows an initial four-for-one split, followed by a four-for-one split in the upper-left corner, followed finally by a last four-for-one split. Notice that Figure 14.2 diagrammatically illustrates the popular quad-tree data structure (Samet 1984).

This solution uses successively lower pairs of bits to perform this partitioning. This means that for any given table, there is a common collection of high-order bits in xloc and yloc shared by all records. This common prefix is stored in a designated table:

```
create table prefixes(
                prefix       long,
                table_name  varchar(20));
```

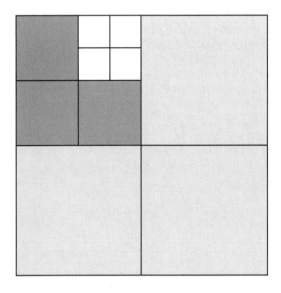

FIGURE 14.2   A Possible Partition

How does this relate to the Z transform? Basically, Orenstein suggested composing the Z transform of a pair of integers as the bitwise merging of the two numbers, so the Z transform is defined for each employee as the bitwise merging of xloc and yloc.

The structure described above is used to process queries in the following manner. Suppose you wish to find all the employees who live within a specific rectangle:

```
select name
from emp
where contained (location, Box(LAT - one_mile, LONG -
one_mile,
                  LAT + one_mile, LONG + one_mile));
```

Then, the following algorithm must be performed:

1. Find the partitions that might hold data of interest. This is accomplished by interrogating the prefixes table to find the names of tables of interest.
2. Issue a query to each table found in step 1. This query will be performed by using a sequential scan of the appropriate table.
3. For each returned record from step 2, the system must ascertain that the geographic predicate is, in fact, true. Hence, the *contained* function must be evaluated on the returned data in each record.
4. Qualifying records from step 3 are then returned to the user.

If K partitions are identified in step 1, then K + 1 queries will be run, one to the prefixes table and K to the partition tables. Parallel execution of the K queries will be performed to minimize a response time.

To deal with polygonal data in this implementation, it is necessary to place each polygon in every partition that overlaps the polygon. The pitfalls of such replication are discussed in the next section. We now turn to a final possible implementation of spatial objects, one that uses B-trees in a clever way.

14.5   *A Final Spatial Extension*

The final implementation of a spatial extension has been suggested as a good implementation of quad-trees (Samet 1984). Basically, quad-trees have been a popular storage system for spatial data utilized by GIS vendors for years. When they wished to run their systems on top of relational DBMSs, they were faced with the poorly performing alternatives discussed in Section 14.2. Alternatively, they could code their quad-trees on top of B-trees, as we now illustrate. Variants on this approach have been used by several GIS systems.

In addition, Oracle uses this technique in the current Spatial Data Option for Oracle V8.0. As you will see in Chapter 18, Oracle V8.0 does not support a base type extension facility. Instead, Oracle has constructed logic for five popular vertical domains and hard-wired it into the Oracle server. This is similar to the tactic used by relational vendors a few years ago when they added hard-wired support for double-byte character strings so that international languages could be supported.

A hard-wired solution, of course, has two serious disadvantages. First, it represents hard-coding by the vendor and cannot be extended by individual users if required capabilities are missing. Second, an extension facility can be used by third-party domain experts to implement a variety of solutions with different characteristics. This facility is used by third-party domain experts for the Informix universal server. In a hard-wired approach, users have only one choice—the vendor's. When Oracle has a base type extension capability, this disadvantage will go away.

The basic idea can be explained with the aid of Figure 14.3. Here we see 10 partitions of a geographic space, each with a common prefix. Suppose we build a B-tree on all the records in the emp table, using the quad-tree prefix as a key. This will pro-

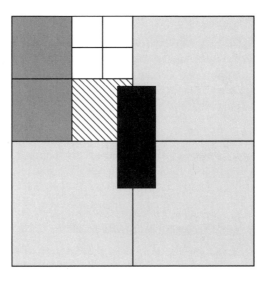

FIGURE 14.3 A Search Region

vide an ordering of the quad-tree buckets, lower-left first, lower-right second, and so forth. The granularity of the quad-tree can be adjusted to make the size of each quad-tree bucket quite small. Whenever a quad-tree bucket is split, then the corresponding prefixes are all adjusted and replaced in the B-tree.

With this structure, the B-tree contains all the prefixes found in a separate table in the previous solution. Thus, searches need to merely have specialized logic to control the examination of B-tree nodes. Required prefixes can be easily found and the associated pointers followed to get the actual records.

The advantage of this scheme is that a fine-granularity quad-tree can be utilized rather than the coarse one used in the previous implementation. Coarse granularity was required in that implementation because the number of database tables could not grow without bound. In contrast, using this implementation there is only one data base table for the emp table and a single B-tree. In this case, the quad-tree can have fine granularity without penalty.

However, this implementation is not without drawbacks. First, consider Example 1 again:

```
select name
from emp
where contained (location, Box( LAT - one_mile, LONG -
one_mile,
                 LAT + one_mile, LONG + one_mile));
```

and reexamine the quad-tree from Figure 14.3 with a possible search region indicated with *'s.

Here we see a search region that overlaps four quad-tree regions. The actual area searched will thereby be the extent of the four shaded regions, which is a much bigger region than the actual search area. Obviously, this cost can be ameliorated by constructing a fine-granularity quad-tree.

However, a second problem exists: namely, the four buckets are not necessarily together in the B-tree, because they are not adjacent in quad-tree prefix order. Four different descents of the B-tree must be made to find the buckets of interest. This will often be slower than an R-tree implementation.

A final issue concerns the modeling of lines and polygons, such as is required in Example 3. What do you do if you want to insert a polygon into a database and the polygon overlaps more than one quad-tree region? This could happen if the search region in Figure 14.3 was added to the data set for which the quad-tree structure of Figure 14.3 was already in place. In this case, you must add the polygon to each quad-tree region that it overlaps. Thus, a spatial object can appear in multiple index blocks. Not only does this increase the size of the index, but it will also slow query processing because the same object will be evaluated by the executor multiple times. This duplication becomes more problematic when spatial joins are involved, such as in Example 3. Finding overlapping polygons becomes more expensive when each one may be replicated several times in the index.

On the other hand, R-tree implementations do not suffer this disadvantage because R-tree index blocks can be expanded to enclose polygonal objects and thereby possibly overlap other R-tree index blocks. In contrast, index blocks in a quad-tree cannot overlap.

14.6 *A Comparison of the Alternatives*

This section provides a brief qualitative comparison of the four approaches discussed in this chapter:

- SQL-92 simulation (Section 14.2 on page 204)
- Informix implementation based on R-trees (Section 14.3 on page 206)
- Z transform implementation (Section 14.4 on page 207)
- Direct B-tree simulation of quad-trees (Section 14.5 on page 209)

We compare the four approaches on the following metrics:

- Speed on point-in-rectangle searches with a small search rectangle (Example 1, page 202 with a small geographic area)
- Speed on point-in-rectangle searches with a large search rectangle (Example 1, page 202, with a large geographic area)
- Speed on rectangle overlaps rectangle (Example 3, page 203)

Our analysis is presented in Table 14.1.

Implementation	B-Tree	R-Tree	Z Transform	Quad-Tree
Small point-in-rectangle	Slowest	Fastest	Slow	Faster
Large point-in-rectangle	Slow	Faster	Fastest	Faster
Rectangle intersections	Slowest	Fastest	Faster	Slow

TABLE 14.1   Comparison of Extension Performance

Small point-in-rectangle searches are fastest using a direct access method, such as R-trees, and are somewhat slower using a quad-tree simulation. The Z transform simulation of quad-trees will be considerably slower because of the coarse granularity of the partitioning and the necessity of searching an entire coarse-granularity bucket. Of course, the crude B-tree simulation requires searching a large vertical slice, as shown in Figure 14.1, and is the slowest of all.

When the search rectangle is large, the analysis is a bit different. The members of the search region will be clustered together on a few coarse-granularity partitions that can be searched sequentially by the Z transform solution. In contrast, an R-tree implementation will be a secondary index, and the actual emp records may be in a different order. Unless the ordering of emp records matches closely to R-tree order, then there will be many random reads to get possibly qualifying emp records, degrading performance. The same comment applies to our quad-tree on top of B-tree scheme discussed on page 209.

Finally, turning to rectangle operations, note that quad-tree solutions contain more than one index entry per object. This will be especially onerous for large rectangles that may be in many quad-tree cells. Since the granularity of index cells for the quad-tree simulation is much finer than for the Z transform, this redundancy, and its resulting performance problem, will be more pronounced in a quad-tree simulation.

14.7   *Summary*

Since the performance and functionality of extensions differs widely, it is necessary for any user to carefully figure out his particular functionality needs and types of queries and to match them against functionality and performance of any given extension. There is no substitute for benchmarking your specific problem on any solutions in which you might have an interest.

Although we have been discussing geographic extensions, this same comment applies to extensions in all vertical market areas.

CHAPTER 15 *Object-Relational DBMS and Application Servers*

Multitier systems are the subject of much talk lately in the industry. Usually the debate focuses on the benefits and pitfalls of thick client versus thin client. *Thick client* means that the business logic is running on the client's desktop and obtains DBMS services from a separate server layer. In contrast, *thin client* means that the business logic is executing in an intermediate application server layer. The term *business logic*, used throughout this chapter, refers to specialized software for a particular business or field; this can range from functions that compute premiums for an insurance company to an image management package used to index and manipulate image files.

Figure 15.1 illustrates the thick client architecture for a traditional client-server DBMS application: the business logic is in the top tier, the client desktop, and the DBMS is in the bottom tier, a remote server.

Unfortunately, there are several disadvantages to the architecture in Figure 15.1, which result from having to administer multiple machines instead of a single, centralized server:

- Memory costs are multiplied. If you have a computationally or memory-intensive application, then each client machine must be beefy enough to run it. The cost of this computing muscle may not be acceptable if there are a large number of client machines.

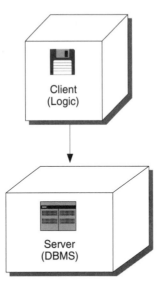

FIGURE 15.1   Thick Client Architecture

- Upgrades can be tedious. Instead of being responsible for upgrading a single application server, the system administrator must find each desktop and install the new software.
- Security must be maintained on several machines, instead of one. Client desktops are often insecure, and information system managers are often reluctant to put proprietary software into an environment where it can be corrupted or compromised.

To circumvent these problems, a thin client three-tier architecture is often proposed. The thin client architecture is illustrated in Figure 15.2.

Placing the business logic in an intermediate tier between the client and the server avoids many of the disadvantages of the thick client architecture:

- Memory is centralized. This strategy puts the business logic on a single "beefy" server, which can be shared by the various clients.
- Maintenance and upgrades are performed on one machine. The software appears just once on the application server, which makes code maintenance much easier.
- Security is managed on a single machine. An information systems group can focus on maintaining security on a single application server, instead of an array of potentially more vulnerable clients.

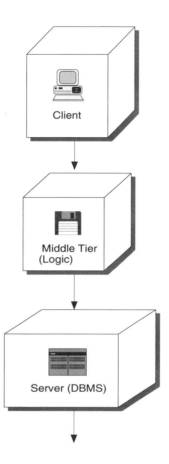

FIGURE 15.2 Thin Client Architecture

The software framework that runs in the middle tier is usually called a *transaction processing monitor* (TP monitor) or an *application server*—simply different names for the same class of products. Examples include Encina from IBM, Tuxedo from BEA, MTS from Microsoft, Jaguar from Sybase, as well as products from NetDynamics (Sun), Forte, and Kiva (Netscape). Such middleware products offer some (or all) of the following services:

- *Function activation*—to run the shared business logic
- *Thread management*—so multiple callers can share a single instance of the logic
- *Security model*—so callers can be authorized to run only certain capabilities
- *Session management*—so the number of sessions open from the middleware to the DBMS is much smaller than the number of client connections to the middleware

- *Queue management*—so that clients can queue requests to the middleware without maintaining a continuous session
- *DBMS connectivity*—so that business logic can obtain DBMS services
- *Load balancing*—so that the load can be spread over multiple middleware servers

Using an application server, business logic that runs in the middle tier is called with one of the standard component protocols such as CORBA or OLE. In turn, the business logic makes use of bottom-tier DBMS services through ODBC, JDBC, or a vendor-specific DBMS protocol. This state of affairs is depicted in Figure 15.3.

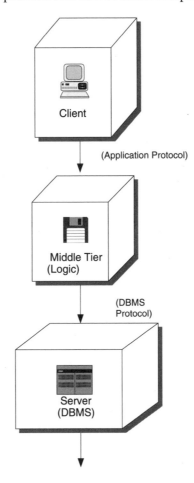

FIGURE 15.3   Thin Client Architecture Revisited

The growing success of object-relational DBMSs as the server-level architecture will impact the picture in Figure 15.3 in two ways. First, it is possible to run business logic inside the DBMS—a "thick database." The following section examines the implications of thick database in more detail. Second, it is now possible to use an object-relational DBMS as an application server. Sections 15.2 and 15.3 discuss two ways an object-relational DBMS can be used as an application server.

15.1   *Implications of a Thick Database on Traditional Application Servers*

If the server level is an object-relational engine, it becomes possible to execute business logic on the client, in the middle tier, or on the server. This section begins with a discussion of the correct location to execute business logic.

Clearly, some business logic modules should run inside the DBMS. For example, consider a data-intensive module such as a data-mining algorithm. This module examines a large amount of data and returns a small collection of "pearls of wisdom." If this module runs in the middle tier, then all this data will be moved from the DBMS to the middle tier module for processing. However, if the module is run inside the DBMS, then this large amount of data movement is avoided. Data-intensive logic should be run as close to the data as possible.

In contrast, consider a module that tracks the location of the mouse on the screen. Obviously, processing mouse events should be done as close to the screen as possible. Otherwise, unnecessary transmission will occur between the client machine and the middle-tier system. Therefore, screen-intensive modules should be deployed as thick client.

Last, memory-intensive or computationally intensive modules may be best run in a middle-tier layer, as discussed in the introduction to this chapter.

> **Guiding Principle 1: Thick client, thick middle tier, and thick database all make sense, and the best choice depends on what the module is doing.**

Moreover, business logic may be reimplemented from time to time, and a new algorithm may be utilized in subsequent implementations. Or, the hardware configuration used in an enterprise can be upgraded, altering either the size of the network pipes between the various layers or the processing capabilities of the various layers. The hardware environment in place clearly influences at which tier the business logic should be run. Because this can change over time, the desirable location where a module of business logic should run also changes over time. In addition, it is desirable to debug a routine on the developer's desktop where a sophisticated debugger can be utilized. When testing is complete, the module can be moved to its correct location in the hierarchy. These considerations lead to Guiding Principle 2.

> **Guiding Principle 2: An information system's organization needs to be able to easily move logic between tiers as circumstances change.**

It is in the best interest of any shop to write the logic *once* and then be able to deploy it as thick client, thick middle tier, or thick database without changing the logic. Subsequent redeployment should have the same seamless movement capability.

Some application server companies, for example, Forte, have made progress along these lines. Forte's architecture allows a user to seamlessly move logic between thick client and thick middle tier. At the present time, we are not aware of any vendor who has extended this seamless movement to thick database.

To support seamless migration among all three levels, a tool kit is required where the business logic can be specified once and then

- compiled for a thick database implementation by adding the DBMS optimizer hints required in the bottom tier. (These hints are discussed in detail in Chapter 10.)
- wrapped in a CORBA or OLE wrapper so that it can be called by popular client or middle-tier systems.

Thus, users can write logic once and deploy it in the bottom tier with the required extra information needed by an object-relational DBMS. Alternatively, they can call it from middle-tier or client systems using one of the popular application protocols.

You might ask at this point about the viability of using an application protocol inside an object-relational DBMS. This would clearly make the environment simpler, and the alternative compilation noted above could be avoided. Unfortunately, extra information is required by an object-relational optimizer in order to execute SQL queries containing user-defined functions effectively (see Chapter 10). This extra information is not required in middle-tier or client systems. As a result, the information required by the bottom tier is different than that required at the middle or client tier. In addition, as noted in Chapter 13, popular application protocols such as CORBA are too slow to be used in the high-frequency call environments of a thick database. As a result, performance and functionality issues dictate that the bottom tier, the DBMS layer, will have a different protocol than elsewhere in the hierarchy.

At least one complication remains in supporting seamless migration between layers; it involves the application that calls a module of business logic. Consider a module of business logic:

```
func_call (a, b, c)
```

If this module is implemented in the client or middle tier, then the caller will use an RPC protocol, specifically CORBA or OLE. In contrast, if the module is implemented in the bottom tier, then the function will have to be called using SQL:

```
select (result = func_call (a, b, c));
```

If the logic is moved from the client or middle tier to the DBMS, then each caller will have to be recoded to convert from an RPC protocol to the SQL protocol. Also, if the logic is moved from the DBMS to the middle or client tier, then the reverse translation must be performed on each caller.

To avoid this disadvantage, an object-relational engine must have a CORBA and an OLE wrapper around the whole DBMS. In this way, the DBMS can accept calls either in the SQL syntax noted above or in an RPC syntax. With this wrapper, the protocol from the middle tier to the lower tier can be the same as the one from the upper tier to the middle tier, and logic can seamlessly move between layers, as illustrated in Figure 15.4.

With the wrapper architecture shown in Figure 15.4, an object-relational DBMS can offer seamless migration of logic between the DBMS and higher tiers of the architecture as long as

- the tool kit at the higher tier supports one of the popular application protocols
- the DBMS has a wrapper for the protocol in question

DBMS vendors differ in their approach to supporting traditional application servers. Oracle and Sybase are building proprietary middle-tier application servers of their own. They have decided to compete in this market segment. In contrast, Informix has elected to partner with traditional middleware vendors instead of writing yet another application server.

The Oracle application server uses its own "cartridge" protocol, which really is merely CORBA. Oracle has elected to support only one application protocol in their middle-tier product. In contrast, we believe the successful middle-tier vendors will be those who support all the popular application protocols, including OLE.

No vendor currently offers seamless migration of logic between all three tiers. In order to get this capability, DBMS vendors will have to get credible object-relational engines and then implement the wrappers discussed in this section. It remains to be seen how long it will take the various commercial DBMS vendors to get these capabilities.

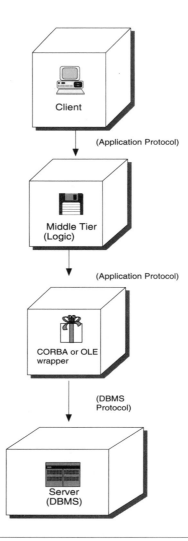

FIGURE 15.4   Another Look at Thin Client Architecture

In short, a user is forced to learn "two of everything." Fortunately, there are simpler alternatives that involve only a DBMS.

The main disadvantage of an application server as a middle-tier system is complexity. The bottom tier is a DBMS, and the middle tier is a different system. Each system has different capabilities in the following areas:

- System monitoring
- User management
- Security

- Crash recovery
- System tuning

In short, a user is forced to learn "two of everything." Fortunately, there are simpler alternatives that involve only a DBMS.

15.2 *Two-Tier Thick Database Model*

Consider again the capabilities of a typical middle-tier system that were mentioned earlier:

- *Function activation*—to run the shared business logic
- *Thread management*—so multiple callers can share a single instance of the logic
- *Security model*—so callers can be authorized to run only certain capabilities
- *Session management* —so the number of sessions open from the middleware to the DBMS is much smaller than the number of client connections to the middleware
- *Queue management*—so that clients can queue requests to the middleware without maintaining a continuous session
- *DBMS connectivity*—so that business logic can obtain DBMS services
- *Load balancing*—so that the load can be spread over multiple middleware servers

With an object-relational engine, business logic can be run as a DataBlade module inside the DBMS. This provides the function activation service mentioned above. Moreover, any SQL DBMS performs the required thread management and security services. Through the use of "callback," a function can execute SQL commands in the object-relational engine.

Furthermore, it is not a difficult extension for a DBMS to perform session management and queue management. Most current DBMSs support a client-server model with a continuous connection (or session) between the client and the DBMS. The client-server connection to the DBMS must be changed to be asynchronous (or message based). In this model, the client sends a message to the DBMS and then relinquishes the connection. The DBMS performs the work and then sends the result back to the client as a message. Using this sort of protocol, a smaller number of sessions can be shared by all the clients of a DBMS. And, the DBMS clearly has to reliably queue any incoming message from a client to assure that it does not get lost when using a messaging protocol. Last, if you run multiple DBMS servers, then it is straightforward for clients to connect to different servers, and thereby balance the load.

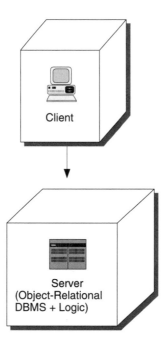

FIGURE 15.5   Two-Tier Thick Database Architecture

In summary, any SQL DBMS can implement most of the services of an application server. By adding a messaging protocol to interact with clients, it can get all of the services except function activation. The switch to an object-relational engine adds this last missing piece and allows an object-relational engine to be a candidate application server. The simplest architecture of this sort is to run a two-tier thick database system, as noted in Figure 15.5.

The idea behind Figure 15.5 is to delete the middle tier completely, moving required function activation into the DBMS. The two-tier thick database model has the following characteristics:

- Function activation occurs inside the DBMS. Clients interact with the DBMS using an SQL protocol, and there is no need for CORBA or OLE.

- Thread management is provided by the object-relational engine.

- Security model is provided by the object-relational engine.

- Session management is provided if the object-relational engine supports a messaging protocol.

- Queue management is provided if the object-relational engine supports a messaging protocol.

- DBMS connectivity is provided by the object-relational engine through callback.
- Load balancing is provided if the client manually selects a server for processing.

The advantage of this two-tier architecture is simplicity. There is only one server to deal with rather than two. Also, there is only one protocol for getting service—clients activate business logic using SQL, and business logic requests database services through callback using the same SQL protocol.

However, one advantage of a three-tier architecture has been lost: if you wish to spread the load over servers, then it is necessary for a client to manually connect to a "good" one. Also, if there are multiple servers, then the database must be partitioned among them so that each transaction runs within one partition and the client connects to the correct server. Alternatively, the database must be replicated over all servers and a multiple-copy protocol used to sort out conflicting updates. Last, all the servers can be connected to a common set of disk drives through a shared-disk architecture. In this way, each server can access all of the database.

All of these solutions may have flaws. For example, it is difficult to construct an application to access the correct partition in a partitioned database, especially if the number of partitions can be varied over time. Also, it is extremely expensive to ensure transactional consistency between multiple replicas. Without such consistency, it may not be possible to write an application with the correct user semantics. Last, a shared disk architecture has limits to the amount of scalability that can be achieved. The next section explores a solution to some of these problems—a more scalable architecture that uses an object-relational engine in both the bottom and the middle tier.

15.3 *Three-Tier Thick Database Model*

In this architecture, the middle-tier component of a three-tier architecture is replaced by an object-relational DBMS, and the bottom tier, which is also an object-relational engine, is retained. This three-tier architecture is shown in Figure 15.6.

Clearly, we wish to have function activation occur in the middle tier and database services to be provided in the bottom tier. Moreover, for load-balancing purposes, we might like to run multiple middleware servers. This requires the middle-tier object-relational DBMS to perform two services not found in a traditional DBMS:

- *Remote callback:* It must be possible for a function activated in the middle tier to obtain DBMS services in the bottom tier. This requires that callback be extended from the local machine to a remote server.

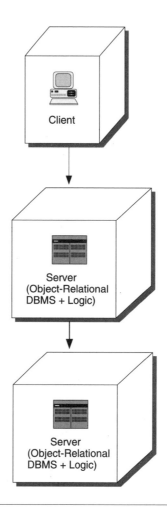

FIGURE 15.6   Three-Tier Thick Database Architecture

- *Remote function activation:* It must be possible for a client to specify a function call to the middle tier and have that activation routed to a different middle-tier machine for load-balancing purposes.

Both of these features are best addressed by extending an object-relational DBMS to be a distributed DBMS, which will run in the middle tier. To further explain this concept, consider a schema in which the emp table is at site A and the dept table is at site B, as noted in Figure 15.7.

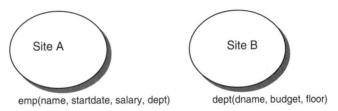

emp(name, startdate, salary, dept)   dept(dname, budget, floor)

FIGURE 15.7   A Distributed DBMS

Further assume the user wishes to run the following query:

```
select name
from emp
where dept in
     (select dname
     from dept
     where floor = 1);
```

Here, the tables to be joined are not collocated, and a traditional SQL DBMS will not perform the desired operation. A distributed middle-tier DBMS is required with the following capabilities:

- *Distributed SQL processing:* A middle-tier query optimizer and executor is required, which can process the above query by decomposing it into pieces and sending each piece to the correct site. A possible query plan for the above query might be the following:
  1. Restrict dept at site B.
  2. Send the result to site A.
  3. Do the join with emp.
  4. Send the ultimate result to the site of the user.
- *Distributed transactions.* If a user submits a transaction that spans multiple sites, the middle-tier system should supervise the execution of the transaction so that it is either committed at all sites or aborted at all sites. Distributed transactions are a complex subject that entail using a two-phase commit protocol. See a book on transaction processing such as Bernstein et al. (1987) for further information on this topic.
- *Replication:* If site A is down, it would be desirable to process the above query by using a replica of the emp table at a second site. Keeping the two copies in synchronization as updates occur is the service desired of a distributed DBMS. Again, algorithms to perform this function are complex; see Bernstein et al. for more information.

Suppose the software system used in the middle tier of Figure 15.6 is a distributed object-relational DBMS. In this case, if the client generates an SQL query such as

```
select (result = func_call (a, b, c));
```

In this case, if func_call is registered on the local machine, then a local activation will take place and the local middle-tier server will perform the function call. Otherwise, the SQL query will be directed to some remote machine containing the code for the desired function. Thus, function activation can be directed to a remote machine in the middle or bottom tier. Moreover, it is possible for there to be multiple sites on which func_call is registered and for the distributed DBMS to load-balance among them.

Suppose func_call is now running at some site performing its logic. If func_call requires DBMS services, it merely performs a callback. Rather than calling back to a single-site DBMS, it calls back to a middle-tier distributed DBMS. This system merely processes the required query as if it had been submitted by an end user.

With a distributed object-relational DBMS, we can organize the hierarchy of Figure 15.6 in several ways. First, we can put all the data on a collection of bottom-tier machines and install all the functions on a set of middle-tier machines. The distributed DBMS will ensure that correct processing is accomplished. We can also organize the collection of machines as a pool. Data and functions are intermixed on each machine, and it is up to the distributed DBMS to optimize execution. The collection of machines are each performing both middle-tier and server-tier tasks. Undoubtedly, there may be other ways to organize this machine collection to produce the desired results.

The benefits of the three-tier thick database shown in Figure 15.6 include all the benefits of the two-tier thick database model, plus several additional features:

- Load-balancing is straightforward.
- Code modules can be location transparent. Therefore, the client does not need to know the machine on which modules will be run. Moreover, once inside a function, location-transparent data service can be obtained using callback. Thus, a distributed three-tier object-relational DBMS supports location transparency for both code and date. In contrast, an application server can support location transparency for code modules by incorporating an object resource broker (ORB). However, once inside a function, the designer must know which server machine to request DBMS services from. In other words, the traditional application server architecture provides location transparency for code modules but not for data.

- Dedicated machines are not required. You do not need to organize a network of computers so that some are dedicated to middle-tier activities and some to server activities. In a distributed object-relational DBMS, machines can be partly allocated to each activity, and a more flexible environment results.

15.4 *Summary*

This chapter discusses three different architectures: a three-tier traditional, a two-tier thick database, and three-tier thick database. To work well in a traditional three-tier architecture, an ORDBMS must support seamless movement of modules between thick client, thick middleware, and thick DBMS implementations. This requires a tool kit whereby a user can specify the logic once and have it compiled for thick DBMSs with appropriate optimizer hints or have it compiled with an OLE or CORBA wrapper for thick client or middleware implementation. Moreover, to avoid requiring the program that calls the logic to change when the logic moves between levels, the DBMS itself must have CORBA and OLE wrappers around it. We expect that DBMS vendors will move in this direction over time.

A two-tier thick database or a three-tier thick database architecture is superior to the traditional architecture. In fact, there are four significant disadvantages to the traditional three-tier architecture:

- Two different protocols must be understood by application designers. A client module uses OLE or CORBA to interact with middleware, but a middleware module uses ODBC or JDBC to interact with the DBMS. This is extra complexity.
- Two different component systems must be understood. The DBMS uses an SQL plug-in framework, but the middleware uses CORBA or OLE. This is extra complexity.
- Two different system management environments must be learned, each with recovery, naming, and location services. This is extra complexity.
- There is location transparency for code modules but not for data. For example, if some of the data required by a module is moved from one site to another, then the module may have to be recoded. Specifically, if the module is performing a join between two tables, A and B, then it would issue the appropriate SQL command if A and B are collocated. If one of the tables is moved to a different site, then the service must be recoded to perform the join manually in the application. This absence of data integration is a serious disadvantage to the traditional three-tier architecture.

The advantages of using an object-relational DBMS in middleware architecture are compelling—watch the marketplace move in this direction over time. But, there are developments that must take place to enable this technology to work well, including a messaging interface to the front of the DBMS and the integration of distributed DBMS capabilities. Hence, it may take vendors a few years to put the necessary structures in place. In the meantime, DBMS vendors as well as traditional middleware vendors need to support the seamless movement of modules between thick client, thick middle tier, and thick database. This requires tool kits that can compile a single module to two or more different target environments.

CHAPTER 16

Multiquadrant Problems

This chapter discusses *hybrid* DBMS applications—problems that have characteristics of more than one quadrant in the DBMS matrix introduced in Chapter 1.

As you will recall, this is how the matrix is used to classify DBMS problems:

- The lower-left quadrant of the matrix requires no searching on simple data and is best served by file systems.
- The upper-left quadrant requires queries on simple data and is the domain of business data processing. It is well served by relational DBMSs.
- The lower-right quadrant requires support for complex data but not queries. This box is well supported by object-oriented DBMSs.
- The upper-right quadrant requires queries on complex data and is best supported by object-relational DBMSs.

The matrix is a useful tool for classifying a DBMS problem and deciding which technology should be used to solve the problem. But what do you do if parts of your application fit into more than one quadrant? As noted in Chapter 1, universal applications are both upper-left and upper-right problems. However, there are three- and even four-quadrant problems that occur in the real world.

This chapter discusses two such examples, a video service application and an insurance industry application, and explains why they are three-quadrant applications. Then, Chapter 17 presents possible solutions for such applications.

16.1   *A Video Service Application*

Consider a cable television service that delivers movies on demand to people's homes. Through this service, customers can choose a video at any time and then play it through their set-top cable box on their television. The service offers movie previews for customers who want to sample a movie before ordering it. The service also maintains an online catalog of movie reviews that can be browsed by viewers who want a critical opinion of movies. Finally, because this service specializes in international films, it offers its customers the ability to identify films by their location of filming, for example, Cape Breton Island in Nova Scotia.

Assuming that an object-relational DBMS is available, the following tables are appropriate to support this application. The first table stores the video for each movie along with assorted attributes of the movie:

```
create table movie (
                mid         oid,
                mname       varchar(30),
                release     date,
                genre       varchar(30),
                studio      varchar(30),
                stars       set(varchar(30)),
                supporters  set(varchar(30)),
                length      int,
                contents    mpeg);
```

The movie table contains an identifier for each movie, its name, the date it was released, the genre of film (action, mystery, etc.), the studio that produced the film, the stars and supporting actors and actresses in the film, the running time of the movie in minutes, and finally the contents of the video in MPEG format. There is one row in movie for each available film supported by the service. The cable service anticipates that it will eventually need to support thousands of films.

The second table stores previews of films:

```
create table preview (
                mid         ref(movie),
                length      int,
                contents    mpeg);
```

In preview, a reference is stored to the movie in the movie table that each preview describes, along with the length of the preview and its contents in MPEG format.

The third table stores reviews of movies for customers to browse:

```
create table review(
                 mid          ref(movie),
                 reviewer     varchar(30),
                 affiliation  varchar(30),
                 rating       rating_type,
                 review       document);
```

Each review describes a particular movie, identified by an mid, and contains the name of the reviewer and media affiliation (for example, the *New York Times*). Additionally, each reviewer uses a rating system to describe a film (three stars, thumbs up or down, excellent, and so forth). For each review, the rating given to the film by the reviewer in the reviewer's specific rating system is stored. This requires a new data type, rating_type, capable of storing a value from the rating system of any reviewer. The actual text of the review is also stored.

The last table describes the locations where each movie is filmed. This information typically appears in the credits at the end of the film.

```
create table location(
                   mid        ref(Movie),
                   location   point);
```

Here, location is coded as a (latitude, longitude) pair that indicates the coordinates of the filming location. For simplicity, movies that are filmed in more than one place have multiple entries in this table.

With these tables in place, a collection of queries that naturally fall in three of the four boxes in the application diagram can be described.

A Lower-Left Quadrant Example

The most common operation in a video service is for a customer to request the service to play a selected movie. This query can be expressed in standard SQL as follows:

```
select contents
from movie
where mname = 'Dirty Harry';
```

Although this is certainly a legal statement in most relational and object-relational systems, video services still use a file system to implement this functionality today. Specifically, if all you need to do is identify an object by name and then retrieve the entire object onto a network connection for delivery to a customer, you hardly need a DBMS. In fact, this command can be thought of as the video equivalent of the text editor operation used as an example in Chapter 1, where the application reads an object by name in its entirety and then operates on it.

In the commercial marketplace all providers of video-on-demand services use a file system to implement this functionality. Specifically, Silicon Graphics used its file system in the Orlando, Florida, video-on-demand pilot system trials. Moreover, the Oracle media server is marketed as a DBMS solution, but in fact it is a high-speed file system with a custom application delivering bits to network connections. The Oracle DBMS is used only to store the attribute data about each movie. Microsoft has implemented a high-performance file system for video, called Tiger. Again, there is no DBMS involvement in this functionality. Playing a video is a lower-left quadrant application, one that requires no searching on simple data and that is best served by a simple file system.

Upper-Left Quadrant Examples

If this application is implemented on a relational DBMS, then the schema needs to be changed somewhat because of the absence of references, sets, and user-defined types:

```
create table movie_R (
                mid        int,
                mname      varchar(30),
                release    date,
                genre      varchar(30),
                studio     varchar(30),
                length     int,
                contents   blob);


create table star_R (
           mid      int,
           star     varchar(30));


create table supporter_R (
                mid         int,
                supporter   varchar(30));


create table preview_R (
                mid        int,
                length     int,
                contents   blob);


create table review_R (
                mid          int,
                reviewer     varchar(30),
                affiliation  varchar(30),
                rating       int,
                review       blob);
```

In this version of the schema, identifiers must be created for all movies, and it is assumed they are integers. In addition, the movie table must be decomposed into three tables storing movie information, star information, and information about supporters. Furthermore, the contents of the movie must be stored as a BLOB, since MPEG is not a data type in a relational system. In the review table, rating must be simulated using an existing data type, such as an integer. The same comment applies to the review field, which is assumed to be a BLOB. (Because it requires a fair amount of user-level logic, this example does not attempt to model the location information.)

The following two examples fit into the upper-left quadrant of the matrix. An easy query is to find the running time of *Dirty Harry*, which is coded as follows in a relational engine:

```
select length
from movie_R
where mname = 'Dirty Harry';
```

As a second example, suppose you want to find the action movies starring Clint Eastwood filmed in 1993. This can be expressed in Informix universal server SQL as

```
select mid
from movie
where category = 'action'
and ('Clint Eastwood') in stars
date >= '1/1/1993'
and date < '1/1/1994';
```

Similarly, it can be expressed in relational SQL as

```
select M.name
from movie_R M, star_R S
where M.category = 'action'
and M.mid = S.mid
and S.star = 'Clint Eastwood'
and M.date >= '1/1/1993'
and M.date < '1/1/1994';
```

Although it is a little easier to express in an object-relational system, this query can be readily expressed in a relational engine. Because it entails only simple data types, it can be considered an upper-left quadrant query. Additional upper-left quadrant queries include the following:

- How many movies in the video service star Sean Connery?
- Did Clint Eastwood star in movies from multiple studios during the 1980s?

Both of these example queries are readily expressible in either a relational system or an object-relational system. In some cases, the object-relational query is simpler, while in other cases, the two expressions are the same. These example queries fall in the upper-left corner of the matrix.

Upper-Right Quadrant Examples

The examples in this section lie in the upper-right quadrant. As a first example, suppose you want to find the movies that movie critics Siskel and Ebert like. This is expressed in Informix universal server SQL as

```
select  deref (mid).mname
from review
where reviewer = 'Siskel and Ebert'
and liked (rating);
```

In this example, a user-defined function on rating_type, called *liked,* is required. This function will return true if the movie got a rating that could be quantified as the critic liking the movie. Without the function *liked*, this functionality must be provided in a user program. Thus, in a relational system, you can find the movies reviewed by Siskel and Ebert in SQL, but then you must perform the rest of the query in a user program.

The next example is even more difficult for a relational system. Suppose you want to find action movies that contain the word "fabulous" in at least one of their reviews. This is expressed in Informix universal server SQL as

```
select deref (mid).mname
from review
where contains (review, 'fabulous')
and deref (mid).category = 'action';
```

In this case, a function, *contains*, examines the text of a review for the word "fabulous." In Informix's universal server, there is a *contained* function that is defined in the Document DataBlade module. Moreover, instances of the document data type have a keyword index built on the stems of all words appearing in the document that are not on a stop list. Keyword indexes can use a variety of techniques to make searching sets of documents efficient. This means that the reviews that contain the word "fabulous" can be found very rapidly. There is no such functionality in a standard relational DBMS to provide similar indexing for BLOBs. As a result, the user must write substantial user-space logic to implement this functionality.

The last example in this section is the most difficult query of all for a relational system. Suppose you wish to find the movies that were shot within 50 miles of San Francisco during 1994. This is readily expressed in Informix universal server SQL as

```
select deref (mid).mname
from location
where year (deref (mid).date) = 1994
and distance (location, make_point ('San Francisco')) < 50;
```

To implement this query in a relational system, you must implement geographic locations (somehow) in user logic and then be able to efficiently find the points within a 50-mile radius of a specific city. On the other hand, this functionality is directly available in the Informix 2-D Spatial DataBlade module.

The video service application contains queries that fit in three of the four quadrants of the DBMS classification matrix. There is no single system that performs well on all aspects of the video service problem. In this case, you are left with a dilemma concerning which kind of a DBMS to utilize. The remainder of this chapter gives a second example application with the same dilemma.

16.2   *An Insurance Application*

Consider the insurance application from Chapter 1, which contains customer and claims information:

```
create table customer_R (
                    cname        varchar(30),
                    caddress     varchar(40),
                    last_premium money,
                    date_paid    date,
                    start_year   int);

create table claim_R (
                 cname        varchar(30),
                 amount       int,
                 date         date);
```

This sort of information is easily represented in a traditional relational system. For example, whenever a customer makes a premium payment, a transaction must be posted to the customer table updating the last_premium and date_paid fields. Similarly, whenever a claim is made, an insertion must be made to the claim table. In an industrial-strength version of this example, there would be many more fields and additional transaction types, including sending out payment notices to customers and commission checks to agents. Additionally, this database is accessible online by all of the insurance company's agents so that many transactions and inquiries are submitted from many terminals to a common database.

So far, this application is a conventional business data processing problem that fits in the upper-left quadrant. Most insurance companies have implemented such systems either on a relational DBMS or on some sort of legacy mainframe DBMS. Relational DBMS vendors have spent many years tuning their engines to perform well in these kinds of environments.

However, most insurance companies want to extend their traditional database with new information. What they really want are tables like the following:

```
create table customer (
                cname           varchar(30),
                caddress        varchar (40),
                last_premium    money,
                date_paid       date,
                start_year      int,
                location        point);

create table claim (
                id              ref(customer),
                amount          int,
                date            date,
                police_rpt      image,
                dented_car      image,
                location        point);
```

Notice that the geographic location of the home of each customer is added to the customer table. The location of the accident that each claim is associated with, along with the picture of the dented car and the scanned image of the police report, are also new in the claim table. With this extra information there are numerous things that an insurance company would be able to find out. For example, perhaps it would like to find customers who have had accidents close to home. This query finds customers with a claim less than a mile from where they live:

```
select deref (c.id).cname
from claim c
where distance (c.location, deref(c.id).location) <1.0;
```

Further, suppose the insurance company has written an expert system that examines the picture of a dented car and guesses the amount of the associated claim. If this is a user-defined function, *Guess*, then the following query finds the claims that are suspicious in nature because they cost substantially more to fix than the expert system estimates:

```
select id
from claim
where amount  - Guess (dented_car)  > 3000;
```

Such queries are extremely difficult for a relational DBMS to perform and clearly belong in the upper-right quadrant. This is an example of an application that has a component in the upper-left quadrant and a component in the upper-right quadrant.

Basically, the application begins with a transaction processing problem. To this base will be added an ever-increasing collection of multimedia data types and their associated decision support queries. Such decision support queries will be used to identify fraudulent claims, hot spots of activity, repair shops that charge high prices, and so forth. Over time, this component of the application will grow very rapidly, and it is entirely upper-right quadrant activity. The end result is that this application will move quite rapidly from being mainly an upper-left quadrant application to being mainly an upper-right quadrant application.

There is also a desired lower-right quadrant activity. Consider the task of inserting a new customer into the customer table. This task can be pseudocoded as follows:

1. Interrogate screen for cname, caddress, and last_premium.
2. Calculate date_paid as today's date and start_year as current year.
3. If necessary, translate data types.
4. Insert values into Customer_R values.

In this case, the user does data entry and the program interacts with him to obtain a new customer record. Then, the program must perform an SQL insert to put the data in the DBMS. Moreover, since the DBMS uses some SQL data model and the program uses a data model for Visual Basic, Java, or C++, the program must also translate the values from programming language data types to DBMS data types. In general, there is data entry, translation, and a manual insert.

This is the current structure of most application programs that interact with DBMSs. However, note that this program does not query the database; it merely performs an insert. There is an easier way to specify the interaction:

1. Create a new customer object.
2. Interrogate the screen for cname, caddress, and last_premium, and assign to new object.
3. Calculate date_paid as today's date and start_year as current year, and assign to new object.
4. Commit the transaction.

In this case, we allocate a Customer_R record, fill it with data, and then commit the insert to the database with the final statement. Although this is a very simple application, it is clear that it is easier to program using some sort of persistent language interface, so that the programmer simply specifies data structures in the application, fills in the data structures, and then commits the result to the database. In other words, the programmer requires a lower-right quadrant application with a persistent language interface.

16.3   *Summary*

There are several observations that we can draw from the above discussion:

Observation 1. Business data processing databases are about to increase in size by three orders of magnitude as users put multimedia objects (video, audio, images, geography) into their databases.

Observation 2. The average byte will be video or image data (since these types are by far the largest ones). Unless users have a lavish hardware budget, the average byte will live on near-line storage. Tape or CD robots and stackers are expected to form the majority of the devices supporting such tertiary memory.

Observation 3. The average business CPU cycle will be used for decision support queries on multimedia objects. Transaction processing rates are going up at perhaps 10% per year. As such, the upper-left quadrant piece of the application is increasing in scale slowly. In contrast, the upper-right quadrant is exploding, and the computational demands are severe. Over time the major component of a DBMS application will be in the upper-right quadrant.

Observation 4. There are many applications with demands in the bottom row of our matrix. Although these demands are often less important than the ones in the upper row, it is nevertheless desirable for a DBMS to have bottom row capabilities.

An ideal DBMS should optimize for the various quadrants as shown in Table 16.1

Over a substantial period of time most upper-left quadrant applications will become less and less important. As noted earlier, transaction processing workloads are going up slowly, perhaps at 10% per year. For example, a typical insurance company has at most 10% more customers this year than last year. Similarly, a healthy airline sells 10% more seats this year than last year. Because CPUs, disks, and memory are getting cheaper at almost a factor of two per year, the cost of executing

Priority	Now	Future
First concern	Upper-left	Upper-right
Second concern	Upper-right	Upper-left
Third concern	Bottom row	Bottom row

TABLE 16.1   DBMS Priorities

a workload is declining at, say, 40% per year. Over time, the cost of transaction processing hardware will become insignificant. In this scenario, the performance of a DBMS on the upper-left quadrant workload will be much less important, and perhaps become irrelevant.

An example of this trend is the Sabre airline reservation system. Originally, this system was coded for the largest available computer at the time, in assembler, with a specialized operating system and data manager, the Airline Control Program (ACP), recently relabeled the Transaction Processing Facility (TPF). Sabre engineers suggest that the current workload could be run on a large conventional SMP server running a general-purpose operating system and DBMS. At some point in the future, it may be possible to run Sabre in an even less demanding environment. Thus, one of the world's most demanding OLTP environments has become less demanding over time.

Even though running on conventional hardware and software is feasible, the major obstacle faced by Sabre is the migration. Sabre engineers must write a new system and then figure out how to cut over to it without ever going offline. Legacy system migration problems haunt most large information technology organizations.

In contrast, there will be applications with extreme OLTP requirements well into the next century. We expect the most severe requirements will come either from telephony or from the Internet.

Today, telephone switching is performed using realtime main memory databases because the transactions rates are way too high for anything more conventional. Basically, data records are stored in the switches on a per-call basis. Also, optimizing routing must be done even more frequently. In short, telephony is in the same state today that airline reservation systems were in 15 years ago— "specialized everything" is the only solution with acceptable performance. It is possible that telephony will become a very demanding general-purpose DBMS application at some point in the future.

Another example is Web crawlers. Right now, many of the major vendors (Alta Vista, Lycos, Inktomi, etc.) do not use conventional DBMSs to process Internet searches. Although relational or object-relational engines could perform the workload, these vendors find them too slow and have elected to utilize specialized solutions for performance reasons. At some point in the future Web crawlers may be a very demanding client of DBMS services.

Electronic billing and commerce over the Internet provide yet another example of an area that may well become very demanding of DBMS services. Although current Internet services are almost all supported by advertising revenue, we do not expect this situation to be the common future case. We expect most Internet services will move to a pay-per-view business model or to the expectation of an electronic commerce transaction. In such a situation, Internet billing will become a very demanding application, which will stretch OLTP capabilities of future DBMSs.

CHAPTER 17

Solutions to
Multiquadrant Problems

This chapter discusses possible solutions to the multiple-quadrant problems introduced in Chapter 16. These are problems that do not fit neatly into just one quadrant of the DBMS matrix. As noted in Chapter 1, the main market will be for so-called universal applications, which require DBMS services in both quadrants of the top row of our matrix. Relational vendors are moving to address these needs, as will be noted in Chapter 19. All will support object-relational DBMS functionality as soon as possible. However, what should you do if you require services in additional squares of the matrix? This chapter addresses that question.

17.1 *Supporting File System Aspects of an Application*

There are several approaches to supporting files in a universal server, and we discuss the more interesting ones in this section. First, we focus on ways to store files inside the DBMS, and then follow that discussion with techniques that store file data outside the DBMS.

Option 1: Use relational BLOBs.

The simplest mechanism is to implement file objects as relational BLOBs and to use standard relational capabilities to access them. To retrieve a file you simply run an SQL query that retrieves the BLOB of interest. While this implementation does give you access to the file object, it is nowhere near as flexible or efficient as a file system. Specifically, to operate on a file, you have to retrieve the whole BLOB to a client application and then filter the retrieved object. This is much less efficient than a file system that allows selective retrieval. Therefore, we are led to discuss alternative options.

Option 2: Use a large object data type with appropriate methods.

The simplistic mechanism in Option 1 can be improved upon substantially by utilizing the object-relational capabilities of a universal server. Informix has implemented a "smart BLOB" data type, and user-defined functions for this data type can be developed that mimic file system operations. For example:

```
create type file_object (
                    internallength = variable);

create function read (file_object, integer, integer)
returning file_object
as external file '$INFORMIX DIR\extend\file.bld (VFS_read)'
language 'C';
```

Now consider a table that looks like this:

```
create table file (
                name  varchar(30),
                owner varchar(30)
                file  file_object);
```

Now you can read 1000 bytes from a file object stored in the file table beginning at byte 10,000 using the following commands:

```
select   read (file, 10000, 1000)
from file
where name = 'foo';
```

You now have selective read capability. However, the syntax of the calls is not very appealing. This leads us to a third option.

Option 3: Cover Option 2 with appropriate programming language wrappers.

An improvement to Option 2 is to cover up the system with something more appealing. Using this technique, a set of familiar file operations like read, write, and so forth are included in the DBMS's client libraries. Instead of operating over file system objects, these new calls simply run the SQL commands of Option 2 behind the scenes.

Option 3 gives the user a familiar bytestream style of interface. In addition, all the capabilities of the DBMS (such as transactions) are available for file data stored in a DBMS. The last two options store file system data outside the DBMS.

Option 4: Use a data type that stores actual bytes outside the DBMS in the file system.

In this case, you can construct a data type that stores a value that is a file name and has an input cast routine that stores the actual bits in a file outside the DBMS. On output, the converse routine reads the bits and returns them to the user. This achieves the effect of storing file names in the DBMS and data storage directly in the file system.

In this case, you can access a file using the DBMS as noted above. To achieve high performance, you can also directly access the bytes in the file system by making direct file system calls. Thus, there are two accessing mechanisms, one using the DBMS and one that directly accesses the bytes using the file system. The second mechanism, of course, offers exactly the same performance as a file system, because that is the underlying implementation.

Figure 17.1 shows this option with the two different access mechanisms.

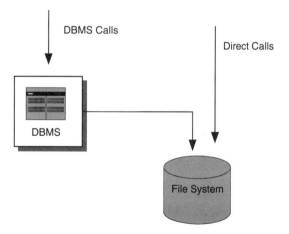

FIGURE 17.1 The Architecture of Option 4

Option 5: Use the virtual table interface.

A second mechanism to generate exactly the same effect is to use the virtual table interface (VTI) mentioned in Chapter 2. Using VTI, you construct a file table as noted earlier:

```
create table file  (
                name  varchar(30),
                owner varchar(30)
                file  file_object);
```

and then use the operating system file system as the storage manager for this table. A VTI adaptor is required to convert from VTI calls to those of the file system. Again, this solution offers the ability to access the bytes either through the DBMS or directly through the file system as shown in Figure 17.2.

The problem with using separate storage for files (Options 4 and 5) is one of data integrity. With Options 1–3 you can construct DBMS transactions that update both file data and other DBMS data. In this case, the standard DBMS transactional properties are assured. Specifically, all updates in the transaction are either committed or rolled back (durability) in the presence of arbitrary failures. In addition, all transactions are serializable; that is, updates of each transaction logically appear to be applied either before or after all other concurrent transactions (atomicity). If separate storage is used (Options 4 and 5), then storage is provided by the file system. Unfortunately, there are few transactional file systems, so the consistency properties provided by DBMSs are not available.

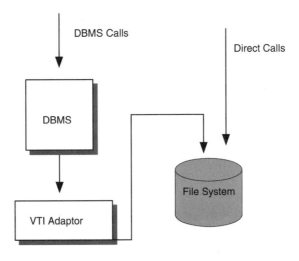

FIGURE 17.2   The Architecture of Option 5

In this situation, serious data integrity problems can arise. A crash at an inopportune time will cause a DBMS transaction that is "in flight" to be rolled back. However, the file system updates from the same transaction may have been written to disk. In other words, the transaction is not atomic. In this situation, it is up to a human (the programmer or system administrator) to restore data integrity between the two storage systems.

In time, file systems may offer more widespread support for transactions. If so, it is possible to guarantee consistency among the two storage systems using a two-phase commit protocol. Hence, Options 4 and 5 may offer better integrity at some point in the future. In the meantime, the implementor must choose between high file system performance (outside storage—Options 4 and 5) and guaranteed data integrity (inside storage—Options 1, 2, and 3).

17.2 *Supporting Lower-Right Quadrant Applications*

We now turn to universal applications that also require persistent language support. These are applications that require services in the upper-left, upper-right, and lower-right quadrants of the matrix introduced in Chapter 1. As noted in Chapter 1, there appear to be no systems that work well in both upper-left and lower-right quadrants. However, over time we expect both object-oriented and relational DBMSs to improve their support for other quadrants.

In this section we discuss two mechanisms for supporting a persistent language in a universal server. Neither solution is very elegant and should only be considered a placeholder for future technology.

Option 1: Simulate persistent storage on top of an object-relational DBMS.

The first choice is to use a wrapper to simulate a lower-right quadrant system on top of an object-relational DBMS, as shown in Figure 17.3. For every class in a C++ application, we require an object-relational representation. Then, the wrapper must perform the following functions:

- For every access to a persistent object, generate the appropriate SQL query to fetch the object.

- Convert the result to C++ format and store it in virtual memory. Provide a runtime library so that accesses to components of the object "do the right thing."

- For every store to a persistent object, generate the appropriate SQL update or insert statement to perform the required action. In the process, map from C++ representation to SQL representation.

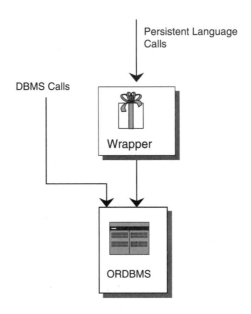

FIGURE 17.3   The Architecture of Simulation

There are aspects of C++ that are easy to handle in this fashion such as base types, records, sets, and references, because each has a counterpart in a full function object-relational engine. However, there are C++ constructs that are very difficult to simulate. These include templates, variant records, and union types. Such facilities have no counterpart in the Informix universal server or in other object-relational engines.

To illustrate this problem, we briefly discuss support of union types. Suppose we have an employee table:

```
create table emp(
    name      varchar(30)
    salary    int
    dept      varchar(20),
    age       int);
```

and suppose that an employee is either in a department or on loan to a customer. If he is in a department, then we record the number of the department. Alternatively, if the employee is on loan to a customer, then we record the name of the customer in the dept field. Because it is a union type, dept records either a number or a character string.

Although simple in concept, union types raise significant processing issues. For example, suppose we want to build a B-tree on the dept type. If so, we require a B-tree implementation capable of supporting union types. This requires two separate physical indexes, one for character strings and one for numbers, that appear logically as a single index. Complexity in the B-tree system is the obvious result.

Moreover, suppose that a user generates a query of the form

```
select name
from emp
where dept = '111';
```

In reality, this is two queries: one to find the employees in department 111 and the other to find employees on loan to customer 111. The execution engine is complicated by dealing with such issues.

Last, suppose we require the names of employees in the same department:

```
select e.name, f.name
from emp e f
where e.dept = f.dept;
```

Again this query must be decomposed internally into two queries: one to find all the employees in the same department and another to find employees on loan to the same customer. The complexity this implies for the join engine are substantial.

Because of these difficulties, no object-relational engine developer is contemplating supporting union types. However, the designer of a persistent language must either disallow union types or support union types in his wrapper. Disallowing this (and other hard-to-support constructs) will make the wrapper a lot simpler, but at the expense of supporting only a subset of a persistent language. Alternatively, simulating such constraints in the wrapper typically can only be done with severe performance consequences. This discussion is reminiscent of the performance consequences of simulating object-relational capabilities on top of relational engines mentioned in Chapter 12.

There is a second significant design decision to be made concerning wrappers, involving the treatment of caching. Most object-oriented DBMSs maintain a significant cache of objects in the address space of the application, as noted in Chapter 1. Such a cache is required to ensure good performance for persistent language commands. In contrast, relational and object-relational DBMSs do not currently maintain a cache of data in the address space of the application. Instead they maintain a cache of disk blocks in the DBMS address space.

Good wrapper performance requires a cache. However, if there are 500 users, then there will be 500 caches, one in the address space of each user. Cache coherency on updates will be a serious performance issue in this environment. To avoid a multiplicity of caches, you must move to running all persistent language applications in a multithreaded application server. Requiring a three-tier architecture complicates the system administration environment. Also, ultimate scalability requires multiple middleware servers, as mentioned in Chapter 15, thus reintroducing the cache coherency problem. The conclusion to be drawn here is that wrapper cache design and optimization is a challenging problem.

There is another option proposed by some vendors: to push the caching problem onto the application designer. For example, one vendor's wrapper requires a user to specify a collection of SQL queries that will bring data into the wrapper where it remains until discarded. Such data is *locked* in the DBMS until discarded from the cache. In this case, an object that has a write lock can appear in only one cache. An object with a read lock can appear in multiple caches; however, it cannot be modified. As a result, cache coherency is never a problem, since conflicts are handled by the DBMS locking system.

Unfortunately, the user must specify a collection of SQL queries to fill the cache. If the user caches a lot of data, then concurrent updates cannot be processed because of the read locks for cached objects. Alternately, if the user caches too little data, then the wrapper will have to run an SQL query for each object requested. Obviously, this results in very poor performance. As a result, user-specified caching is very tricky.

Another problem with user-specified caching concerns predictability. If the user access pattern is predictable in a manner that allows a SQL command to specify desired objects, then the user is equally able to specify his complete problem in SQL. There is no need for a navigation interface if the user can specify declaratively what he wishes to do. Put differently, if the user has a predictable reference pattern, then he has an upper-right quadrant application and should use SQL for its solution. The approach of pushing the problem onto the application appears to be an undesirable solution.

Simulating a persistent language on top of an object-relational DBMS is difficult and there are likely to be performance problems. Therefore, we next turn to an alternative option, placing an object-relational DBMS on top of a persistent language. This can be accomplished by using the SQL engine on top of several object-oriented DBMSs. Alternatively, you can interface the SQL engine from a universal server onto an object store; this is the next option we discuss.

Option 2: Use a virtual table interface to allow access to an object store from a universal server engine.

In this situation, we utilize the architecture of Figure 17.4. Here we place object data in some sort of an object store. This could be a commercial OODBMS or a specialized software system. In either case, it should have the characteristic that it caches a large number of objects in native format in main memory. The object store manages a collection of classes of the form

```
class_name (item-1, . . . , item-n)
```

The instances of this class can be thought of as an object-relational table. As such, a virtual table interface can be used to allow object-relational access to this data. All you need is an adaptor from the VTI interface to that of the specific object store. As shown in Figure 17.4, the persistent language user can access the object store directly, thereby obtaining superb performance. The object-relational user can access the same data using SQL by going through the adaptor.

Unfortunately, there is no free lunch. Lower-right quadrant accesses are accelerated because they are natively supported; however, upper-left and upper-right accesses will be adversely affected because they will go through the adaptor, which will degrade performance.

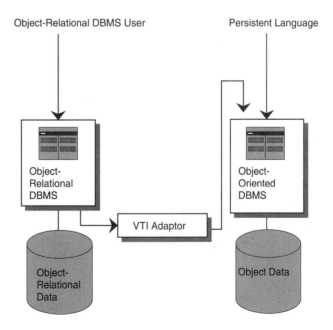

FIGURE 17.4 Using VTI to Support a Persistent Language

17.3   *Summary*

This chapter has discussed how to support lower-quadrant applications in a universal server. File system support appears straightforward, and there are several reasonable solutions to lower-left quadrant requirements. In contract, supporting a persistent language is more difficult, and current approaches are simply interim workarounds. In our opinion, the best technical approach is to design a persistent language interface into the DataBlade module interface. In this way, a DBMS extension can interface efficiently to lower-level interfaces in the system and is not forced to go through an SQL layer.

An interesting observation can be drawn from this discussion: as object-oriented DBMSs add rich SQL layers to their systems and address scalability and OLTP concerns, they will increasingly offer better multiquadrant support. Similarly, relational vendors will enrich their SQL systems and engineer efficient persistent language support with the same overall objective—good multiquadrant application support. As a result of these transformations, we expect future systems from both classes of vendors to offer increasingly overlapping services.

In the meantime, the adage from Chapter 1 should be repeated here. It is crucial that any user decide in which quadrant the majority of his problem resides, and then obtain the correctly architected DBMS for that quadrant. Other quadrants can be dealt with his system of choice, but performance may be inadequate.

CHAPTER 18

Database Design for Object-Relational DBMSs

Many users have a great deal of trouble with database design, and poor schema design is responsible for the failure of many applications. In an effort to shed some light on this vexing area, this chapter begins with a presentation of some basic relational database design concepts, and then extends those principles to object-relational database design.

18.1 *Relational Database Design*

Good database design is challenging even for SQL-92 databases. This section looks at the traditional algorithm for relational databases. The procedure discussed here can be found in any text on database design, such as Toby Teorey's well-known book (1994).

Most design products use an entity-relationship (ER) model to assist users with database design. The ER model was first introduced by Peter Chen (1976) and has found universal acceptance in database design, but it is rarely used as the data model for an actual DBMS.

ER database design tools offer a "boxes and arrows" drawing tool that assists you in constructing a graphical ER diagram to represent your data. The basic construction process is the following:

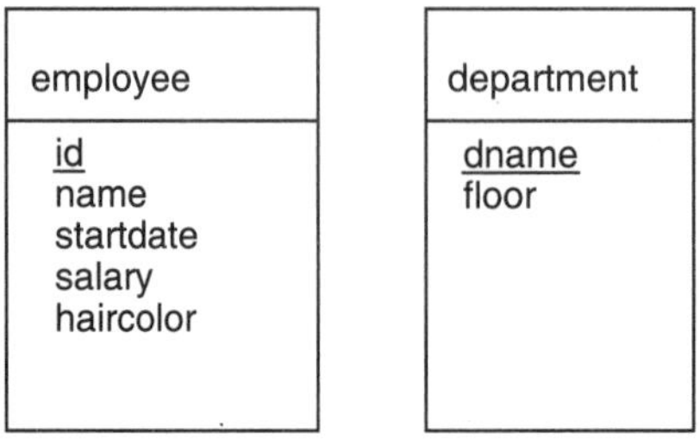

```
┌─────────────────────┐   ┌─────────────────────┐
│  employee           │   │  department         │
│ ┌───────────────┐   │   │ ┌───────────────┐   │
│ │ id            │   │   │ │ dname         │   │
│ │ name          │   │   │ │ floor         │   │
│ │ startdate     │   │   │ │               │   │
│ │ salary        │   │   │ │               │   │
│ │ haircolor     │   │   │ │               │   │
│ │               │   │   │ │               │   │
└─────────────────────┘   └─────────────────────┘
```

FIGURE 18.1   A Typical ER Diagram

1. Identify the *entities* of the application.

These are objects that have an existence that does not depend on other constructs in the application. Alternatively, they are objects for which a unique identifier is appropriate, as well as ones for which it is natural to create and delete. Employees, persons, departments, and automobiles are all natural entities.

An entity is represented with a box in the ER drawing tool. Typically the name of the entity is used to identify the box. The sample application in this chapter uses the entities employee and department, as shown in Figure 18.1.

2. Identify the *attributes* of each entity.

Attributes are the fields that describe the entity. Relevant attributes for the employee entity might be name, start date, salary, and hair color. Attributes for the department entity might be name and floor number. Each identified entity should have a data type.

Typically, the attributes of each entity appear inside the box containing the entity, or perhaps in a pop-up window activated by clicking on the box. Figure 18.1 shows each entity's attributes.

3. Give each entity a *unique identifier*.

It is important to be able to distinguish between instances of an entity. Sometimes it is reasonable to assign one attribute or group of attributes as their identifier. On other occasions, it is more practical to use a system assigned object ID (OID) or to employ some scheme for creating them.

The unique identifier is a primary key in relational terminology and is typically underlined in the ER diagramming tool. In Figure 18.1 dname is the primary key for department, while a new field, id, fills this need for employee.

4. Entities can participate in *relationships*.

A relationship is an association between two entities. For example "manages" is a relationship between an employee and a department, "works-in" is a different relationship between an employee and a department, and "friend of" is a relationship between pairs of employees.

Relationships are indicated by drawing a line between the two entities that participate in the relationship. The three example relationships are shown in Figure 18.2.

For each relationship, indicate whether it is

- *one-one:* An entity on each side can only be related to one entity on the other side. Generally speaking, "manages" is a one-one relationship because an employee can manage only one department and a department is managed by only one employee.
- *one-many:* An entity on one side can be related to many entities on the other side, but an entity on the second side can only be related to one entity on the first side. For example, "works-in" is a one-many relationship because an employee works in only one department, but a department may have many employees working in it.
- *many-many:* An entity on each side can be related to many entities on the other side. For example, "friend of" is a many-many relationship.

The status of each relationship is drawn on the ER diagram. A line between the two entities indicates a one-one relationship, while a "crow's foot" at one end of the line indicates a one-many relationship. Crow's feet at both ends of the line indicate a many-many relationship.

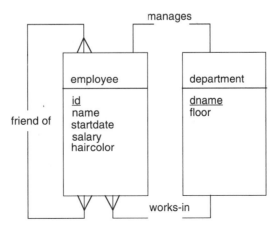

FIGURE 18.2   A Further Elaboration of the ER Diagram

5. Relationships can have *attributes*.

For each relationship, identify the attributes of the relationship. For example, "works-in" can have attributes regarding an employee's length of employment and seniority status, while "manages" might have an attribute corresponding to the rating of the manager by his employees.

After you have completed these five steps, you have an ER diagram that represents your data. The complete ER diagram for the employee and department application is shown in Figure 18.3.

The idea behind the ER drawing tools is that you will construct your ER diagram and then iteratively modify it until you capture the desired semantics of your application. When your diagram is adequate for your application, the ER tool typically can be instructed to generate a normalized collection of relational tables that correspond to the diagram. The algorithm to do this originally appeared in Wong and Katz (1979) and is repeated here.

1. Construct a table for each entity, containing all the attributes of the entity and having a primary key of the identified unique ID. The result of this step is the following two tables:

    employee(id,name,startdate,salary, haircolor)
    department(dname,floor)

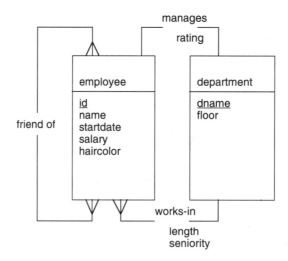

FIGURE 18.3 The Complete ER Diagram

2. Construct a table for each many-many relationship containing the unique identifier for each side of the relationship along with the attributes of the relationship. The friend_of table shown below results from this step.

3. For each one-many relationship, add the unique identifier from the "one" side to the table corresponding to the entity on the "many" side, along with all the attributes of the relationship. As a result of this step, dname, length, and seniority are added to the employee table to capture the semantics of the "works-in" relationship.

4. For each one-one relationship, add the unique identifiers from either side to the table for the other side, along with the attributes of the relationship. As a result of this step, id and rating are added to the department table to capture the "manages" relationship.

The end product is a collection of relational tables, which are normalized according to relational normalization theory, and a good relational database design. This collection is

```
employee(id,name,startdate,salary,haircolor,dname,
        length,seniority)
department(dname,floor,id,rating)
friend_of(id_1, id_2)
```

Relational database design is straightforward. Simply follow the above procedures, either manually or with the help of an ER diagramming tool, and a good relational schema will result.

So why do users have so much trouble with database design? The next section looks at some reasons.

18.2 *Reasons for Problems*

There are at least six reasons why people have a lot of trouble with database design:

- Excessive focus on formal modeling of the application
- An unwillingness to iterate the design
- Unrealistic application design
- Difficulty capturing the rest of the schema
- Difficulty tuning the database
- Failure to test early and appropriately

Excessive Focus on Formal Modeling

One of the authors recently visited a large customer who was two years into a three-year development project. As part of the tour, the visitors were ushered into a converted conference room and shown "The Schema." It covered the room's long wall: 650 tables, 7500 columns, and 1390 relationships. Accompanying "The Schema" was a four-inch stack of paper, which included a mathematical treatise that demonstrated that the entire schema was in at least project-join normal form, and that most of it was in fifth normal form!

The developers had spent six months analyzing tools, two months arguing that nothing on the market met their needs, six months building their own, and twelve months modeling "The Schema." With a year before the system was scheduled to go live, not one line of actual code had been written.

In all too many projects, teams spend too much time either on ancillary problems or on impractical applications of theory. The bottom line to remember from this vignette: "If a little analysis goes a long way, then a lot of analysis goes nowhere."

Unwillingness to Iterate the Design

An unfortunate fact of life is that users change their minds, make mistakes, vacillate, and sometimes lie. A second unfortunate fact of life is that developers are strangely unwilling to iterate their designs to accommodate the first fact.

It is essential to recognize that schema design is an iterative process and that you will work and rework aspects of the schema design as circumstances change. Moreover, whenever the schema changes, it will be necessary to perform at least some application changes. It is almost always a mistake to freeze the schema early in a project to avoid this maintenance. If the schema is wrong, the downstream headache is almost always worse than the incremental maintenance.

Put your best talent on schema design and you will reap long-term rewards. Expect this task to consume significant project resources—between 10 and 20%—and don't skimp in this area. Ensure that there is at least one person whose sole responsibility is schema design. Assume that schema design is never finished.

Unrealistic Application Design

Called in to explain why a DBMS was so slow, it didn't take long for one of the authors to spot the problem: 40 tables and *200 triggers*. The database development team was in love with the feature to the point of delirium. For example, they were using triggers to ensure that all surnames contained no spaces and had the first letter capitalized. They had even gone so far as to create two separate but identical table schemas—one for read and one for write— which they were keeping consistent with triggers.

The general idea is that you should use features appropriately. In the situation above, the edit check was moved into client code, and the two schemas were combined. The repaired system still used triggers to enforce several quite complex constraints, and the overall performance was quite acceptable.

In object-relational DBMSs, one obvious candidate for this kind of abuse is collections. With nested collections of composite types, it is possible to create a schema that looks a lot like a hierarchical database. This is normally a bad idea. For example, it is tempting to model a schema where employees are employed by departments that are combined into divisions as a three-level hierarchy. Unfortunately, this means that any query involving only employees will need to navigate through the entire hierarchy. This is one of the key complaints about hierarchical systems such as IMS: queries that do not exploit the hierarchy are very slow. In general, you should always use good taste in deciding how and where to use any given DBMS feature.

Difficulty Capturing the Rest of the Schema

The fourth problem concerns capturing nonstructural aspects of the database schema. Clearly, there will be a variety of business rules that must be enforced by the application. For example, in the employee and department example earlier in this chapter, it is reasonable to enforce the following business rule:

> Every employee must work in a department.

There are a variety of ways to enforce this rule. For example, when an employee is added with a nonexistent department, then any of the following actions are plausible:

- Refuse the insertion.
- Create a new department with a supplied name.
- Put the new employee into a null or default department (special projects).

Similarly, when a department is deleted, the following actions are all reasonable:

- Refuse the deletion if there are employees still in the department.
- Cascade the deletion. That is, fire employees in the deleted department.
- Put the orphaned employees in the null or default department.

The user needs to describe which of these actions is appropriate. In general, a large number of business rules must be enforced in an application. Here are a few examples:

- Employees must have a positive salary.
- Employee names consist of a last name and a first name.
- Managers can have at most 10 direct reports.
- Departments lacking managers are managed by the president (who is exempt from the previous rule).

The difficulty of capturing these business rules poses additional problems in database design. Typically, it is difficult to get users to explain these rules in a way developers can understand. Moreover, if the system in question is replacing a legacy application, these rules may be enforced somewhere in the undocumented legacy application's code. There are few more unrewarding tasks than decrypting antique code.

Difficulty Tuning the Database

Every DBMS consultant has a version of the following story. The consultant is engaged to work on an application experiencing performance problems. Upon arrival, the consultant is shown a sample query— often an apparently straightforward retrieve that takes several hours to run. For example:

```
select count(*)
from dept d, emp e
where e.dname = d.dname
and d.floor in ( select b.floor
                 from building b
                 where b.blg = 5);
```

The consultant then does at least one of the following fairly obvious things:

1. Rewrites the query into a slightly different form. For example, the query above is equivalent to

```
select count(*)
from dept d, emp e, building b
where e.dname = d.dname
and d.floor = b.floor
and b.bldg  = 5;
```

   Unnesting queries is almost always a good idea in current systems because the optimizer for nested queries is invariably worse than the one for unnested queries. In fact, most systems automatically unnest certain classes of nested queries. Just in case the optimizer does not unnest your query, you should do it manually.

2. Creates an index. In this case, depending on the number of rows in the dept table, creating an index on dept.floor may dramatically speed up the query performance.

3. Runs a DBMS maintenance script that gathers information about the data in the tables.

4. Modifies the table structure to include the building information in the dept table, thereby turning a three-way join into a two-way join. This is called *denormalization*, and results in enhanced performance at the expense of data replication.

5. Finally, the consultant may tweak one of the vast array of tuning knobs in the DBMS's configuration file.

As a result of these efforts, the example query should run in minutes instead of the original hours.

The point of this example is that this kind of tuning requires experience and intuition. Such characteristics are found in the "four-star wizards" who understand application design and the performance characteristics of the specific DBMS in use.

Most application developers lack this level of expertise. Their focus instead is on understanding the problem domain, and as a result they often create schemas that are not well optimized.

There are not enough four-star wizard types to go around. If you don't have one, retain one as a consultant. Although consultants are typically more expensive than regular employees, good ones are worth the expense.

Failure to Test Early and Appropriately

The final problem relates to meeting, or failing to meet, performance expectations. A classic case is that of a large consulting company that agreed to build a transaction processing application for a customer who was a public service agency in an eastern state. In the specification, the customer demanded two-second response time on 95% of the transactions in the system. The consultants proceeded with the design and were most of the way through coding when they realized that they were a factor of four away from meeting the response time specifications. Their schema design was fine; however, the choice of hardware, application programming system, and DBMS architecture was too slow to meet the application's demands.

In this situation, the developers failed to heed a basic principle of database development:

> **Load a production-sized database early and test it under production conditions.**

It is only by heeding this principle that problems can be uncovered early enough to do anything about them.

18.3   *Challenges in Object-Relational Database Design*

Because of its greater sophistication, database design in an object-relational DBMS is considerably more challenging than in relational systems. You face increased complexity in three areas:

1. Choosing from the multitude of options
2. Choosing procedural or data representation
3. Choosing rule or data representation

The following sections discuss the challenges posed in these areas.

More Options—More Potential Confusion

Clearly, an object-relational DBMS is a superset of a relational DBMS. All of the problems mentioned in the previous section also occur in an object-relational world. However, they are all more complex in an object-relational system.

For example, there are many more ways to deal with integrity constraints. It is possible to implement the employee and department tables mentioned earlier. In addition, you can implement dname in the employee table as a ref (department) type. You can also implement the works-in relationship by storing a set of references to employees in the department table. Furthermore, you could define your own data type that connected employee and department in some other way.

The same issue of increased complexity arises in denormalization. If you implement the employee and department schema, and then find that the SQL query is not fast enough, then you can denormalize the schema by combining the tables into an emp_dept table. However, you can also implement dname in the employee table as a ref (department) type. These both offer higher performance than the employee and department schema.

In addition, you can choose to implement a *floor(employee)* function that retrieves the floor of any employee when called. By itself, this will not increase performance. However, some object-relational systems allow you to specify that you want the result of a function to be precomputed and indexed. As a result, a B-tree index can be built on the result of the *floor* function. This index remains correct as employees change departments. Using function indexing, you can achieve very high performance on certain classes of queries.

In a good object-relational DBMS, you also have inheritance, base type extension, as well as a variety of complex objects available to use in schema design. It truly requires art and a lot of well-educated intuition to know how to use these concepts most effectively.

An object-relational database design contains all the hazards and remedies available in SQL-92 database design. In addition, because of the richness of the data model, database design is correspondingly more difficult.

Procedural versus Data Representation

The second problem concerns procedural versus data representation. Consider the salary and bimonthly paycheck amount for an employee. In a relational system, you must decide which one of these to store or, alternatively, to store both using a trigger for data consistency. Thus, you must decide on the representation of the data when there is more than one alternative.

However, in an object-relational system data can be encoded procedurally. As a result, it is possible to store either salary or paycheck as a data field and then compute the other using a function.

Whenever procedural representation is utilized, you must decide whether to compute the corresponding functions on demand when they appear in a query (lazy evaluation) or to compute the function at data load time (eager evaluation) by utilizing function indexing. This performance and space trade-off must be understood and optimized by an object-relational database administrator.

Rule versus Data Representation

The third problem concerns the possibility of using rules to represent information. Return to the rule example from Chapter 7, which dealt with two employees, Jane and Mike, and the requirement that both have the same salary. In a relational system the obvious alternative is to store both salaries as data elements, and then enforce the rule with the following trigger:

```
create rule Mike_Jane_salary_synch as
on update to emp.salary where current.name = 'Mike'
do   update emp
     set salary = new.salary
     where name = 'Jane';
```

However, there is another way to accomplish the same goal in an object-relational DBMS, namely, with a query-query rule:

```
create rule Jane_Mike_salary_synch as
on select to emp.salary where current.name = 'Jane'
do   instead
     select salary
     from emp
     where emp.name = 'Mike';
```

Using this scheme, Jane's salary is never stored, but is computed when required using the rule. Clearly, both representations are available in a good object-relational DBMS. Unfortunately, making the choice between them requires substantial sophistication. There are two aspects to this choice.

First, the performance characteristics of the two choices are different. If Mike receives many raises, but it is rare to query for Jane's salary, then the trigger system will fire on each raise and propagate the new salary from Mike to Jane. However, if queries that request Jane's salary are rare, then this overhead is wasted. Instead, you would prefer the second implementation, where Jane's salary is computed by the rule when it is required in a query. Alternatively, if Mike receives few raises and Jane's salary is often queried, then the opposite choice is appropriate. An object-relational database administrator must understand the application and the performance envelope of the DBMS in order to intelligently make this trade-off.

In addition, there is a second somewhat devious aspect to the choice between these two rule-based alternatives: namely, they have slightly different semantics. Suppose Mike is deleted from the emp table. In this case, using the trigger implementation, Jane's salary will be equal to Mike's salary at the time he left the company. In contrast, using the second implementation, Jane's salary will be null after Mike is deleted.

The object-relational database administrator must understand these subtle distinctions and decide which rule-based choice is usable.

18.4   *Summary*

Relational database design is difficult, and developers struggle with this fact all too frequently. But object-relational database design is harder yet. The great wave of object-relational DBMSs may be threatened by the challenges real users will face when they try to create reasonable database designs.

Traditional database system vendors have done a clear disservice to the application community. In response to demand from sophisticated shops, they have created products with an enormous number of tuning knobs in them. A sophisticated user (the four-star wizard) can use these knobs to optimize a given application.

However, there are not enough four-star wizards to go around, and current systems have a built-in dependency on this level of sophistication. DBMSs will have to become much easier to use in the future. The course is clear: a system must be able to perform automatic tuning. An internal expert system can watch the workload being performed and then alter the tuning knobs automatically to achieve best performance. In addition, a second expert system can be built to explain to users the performance consequences of their design choices. This movement from human wizards to internal expert systems appears necessary in order for object-relational DBMSs to be truly usable by ordinary mortals—and thus to become broadly accepted in the business world.

CHAPTER 19

The Next Great Wave in DBMS Technology

This chapter begins with an overview of the book and concludes with a review of commercially available object-relational products. In this book you have seen why the object-relational DBMS's power to handle complex data will make it the next great wave in database technology. There are already signs that the object-relational database will eclipse relational technology as most of the major commercial vendors make a play for market share—and more importantly, as the user community begins to appreciate and require the features an object-relational database offers.

19.1 *Overview of the Book*

This book begins by pointing out the need for a new kind of DBMS that meets the requirements of the upper-right quadrant of the two-by-two application matrix. Chapters 2 through 7 define the four cornerstone *characteristics* of a good object-relational DBMS:

1. Base type extension
2. Complex objects
3. Inheritance
4. A rule system

The *features* required to support the four basic characteristics are outlined below:

1. Base type extension

    a. Dynamic linking of user-defined functions

    b. Client or server activation of user-defined functions

    c. Integration of user-defined functions with middleware application systems

    d. Secure user-defined functions

    e. Callback in user-defined functions

    f. User-defined access methods

    g. Arbitrary-length data types

    h. Open storage manager

2. Complex objects

    a. Type constructors

    • set

    • record of

    • reference

    b. User-defined functions

    • dynamic linking

    • client or server activation

    • secure user-defined functions

    • callback

    c. Arbitrary-length complex data types

    d. SQL support

3. Inheritance

    a. Data and function inheritance

    b. Overloading

    c. Inheritance of types, not tables

    d. Multiple inheritance

4. Rule system

    a. Events and actions are retrieves as well as updates

    b. Integration of rules with inheritance and type extension

    c. Rich execution semantics for rules

    d. No infinite loops

These characteristics and their detailed features provide a yardstick to evaluate any object-relational DBMS so that you can distinguish the pretenders from the real thing.

Chapters 8 through 11 discuss the construction of an object-relational DBMS and explore the requirements for implementing an object-relational parser, optimizer, and rule engine. Chapter 12 describes why major surgery is required on a traditional relational DBMS to extend its functionality to the four basic characteristics of an object-relational DBMS. Also discussed is the fact that considerable extension is required to turn an object-oriented DBMS into an object-relational one.

The strategies available to the existing commercial relational and object-oriented DBMS vendors are the following:

- Do nothing.
- Rewrite the engine from scratch.
- Sell two systems.
- Implement an object-relational top on a relational storage manager.
- Incremental evolution of the current engine to add new functionality.
- Write a wrapper on top of a relational engine.
- Implement a gateway from an object-relational engine to a relational one.
- Extend an object-oriented DBMS to support object-relational functionality.
- "Glue" an object-relational engine onto the top of an object-oriented DBMS.

Chapter 12 identifies the vendors that utilize each of these strategies.

Chapters 13 and 14 deal with basic performance issues. Chapter 13 treats the overhead of supporting methods in a separate address space using RPC and the overhead of supporting methods in a middleware layer. In both cases, the result is ruinously bad performance. Chapter 14 considers the performance of different implementations of geographic information system (GIS) functionality. The performance envelope of the various options exhibit vastly different characteristics. Both chapters conclude that performance of a given object-relational application may vary wildly depending on these underlying issues.

Chapter 15 considers the topic of how middleware relates to object-relational DBMSs. It is expected that a good object-relational DBMS will be a serious contender for future middleware application frameworks.

Multiquadrant applications are the subject of Chapter 16. Discussed first are two examples of applications that exhibit characteristics of three quadrants in the two-by-two matrix. Because most DBMSs work well for applications inside their respective quadrants and poorly or not at all on other problems, multiquadrant applications are not likely to be well served by just one DBMS. Solutions available to users with multiquadrant problems are the topic of Chapter 17.

The inherent difficulty involved with database design for object-relational applications is discussed in Chapter 18. Because of the challenges posed by object-relational database design, it is imperative that users begin to seriously develop and cultivate their database design and administration capabilities.

19.2   *Overview of the Object-Relational Marketplace*

A brief survey of the systems available in the commercial marketplace is next. The following tables indicate how well current systems comply with the characteristics and detailed features of a fully object-relational system. Also indicated is the architecture that each vendor is following. We discuss systems with the following characteristics:

- The system is currently released. (Most vendors have a "next system" that is "available soon.")
- The vendor markets the product as an object-relational one. Although several O vendors have products with some object-relational capabilities, they do not want to label their products this way. Hence, we do not include them.
- The product includes functionality in the server and not in a middleware layer outside the server. For this reason, we did not include the Sybase products or a variety of other middle-tier products.
- The company exists. (UniSQL, for example, is not included because it appears to have ceased operation.)

The following systems satisfy these criteria:

- CA-Ingres
- Cloudscape

- DB2 6000 Release 5
- Informix IDS-UDO V9.1
- Oracle V8.0

The characteristics of these systems are summarized in Table 19.1. Each entry in this table is a "yes" or "no," indicating whether the system has the corresponding characteristic. For some systems it is difficult to ascertain if they have a specific characteristic. In this case, a "?" appears in the table.

There are three entries in the table that merit discussion. DB2 6000 supports base type extension in that it allows new base data types and user-defined functions. However, they have not extended their B-tree system to support user-defined operators. Unless a new type can use the operators form one of the built-in types, then B-trees will be unavailable to optimize access to instances of the type. Although we put a "yes" in this entry, users note that they may fail optimization issues.

A second entry where "partial" is recorded concerns complex objects in Oracle V8.0. This system supports all of the complex objects mentioned. However, in two of the cases (set of, reference to), the system only supports one level of objects. Thus, you can have a set of objects, but not a set of sets of objects. Similarly, Oracle V8.0 allows references to objects but not references to references. Hence, the complex object features are not type constructors but merely a one-level implementation. Certainly a one-level implementation is a good start, but it is not a full-function implementation. Hence, "partial" is the appropriate entry in the table.

System	Strategy	Base Type Extension	Complex Objects	Inheritance	Rules
CA-Ingres	Evolution	Yes	No	No	Yes
Cloudscape	Native Implementation	Yes	Yes	No	No
DB2 6000	New top	Yes	No	No	Yes
IDS-UDO (Informix)	New top	Yes	Partial	Yes	Yes
Oracle	Evolution	No	Partial	No	Yes

TABLE 19.1 Characteristics of Object-Relational DBMSs

A third "partial" entry is Informix V9.1, which supports type constructors for records and sets, but does not have a reference (pointer) type.

Systems that are fully object-relational must have all four characteristics of an object-relational DBMS given on page 267. As you can see, there is still a lot of work to do to get systems to have all four features.

Next, this chapter takes a more detailed look at the features displayed by the systems that are currently available in the marketplace. Tables 19.2 through 19.5 examine in turn the features of today's commercial systems. Each table deals with one of the four basic characteristics of an object-relational DBMS: base type extension, complex objects, inheritance, and rule systems.

Because it is difficult to get information from some of these vendors, a question mark indicates wherever there is an unknown parameter. Also, each table omits any vendor's system that does not have the characteristic at all. Last, the specific features of each product are likely to change rapidly. Therefore, check with each vendor for the most current information.

As Table 19.2 shows, several systems support base type extension. Moreover, the quality of some of the implementations leaves room for improvement. In the case of DB2 6000, IDS-UDO, and Cloudscape, expect future releases to fill in the missing features. On the other hand, Computer Associates has announced that their future

Feature	DB2 6000	IDS-UDO (Informix)	CA-Ingres	Cloudscape
Dynamic linking	Yes	Yes	?	No
Client or server activation	No	No	No	No
Secure user-defined functions	Yes	No	No	Yes (Java)
Callback	No	Yes	?	Yes
User-defined access methods	No	Yes	No	No
Arbitrary length data types	Yes	Yes	?	Yes

TABLE 19.2   Features of a Fully Object-Relational DBMS in Support of Base Type Extension

object-relational strategy entails using the Jasmine DBMS. Thus, it is unknown whether CA-Ingres users can look forward to any improvement in object-relational features.

In Table 19.3, notice the poor support by many commercial systems for needed features of user-defined functions. However, because all of the systems listed are under active development, you can expect better compliance with the required features in future releases.

Feature	IDS-UDO (Informix)	Cloudscape	Oracle
Type constructors			
set_of	Yes	Yes	Partial
record_ of	Yes	Yes	Yes
reference	No	No	Partial
User-defined functions			
Dynamic linking	Yes	Yes	Yes (separate process)
Client or server activation	No	No	No
Secure user-defined functions	No	Yes (Java)	Yes (separate process)
Callback	Yes	?	No
Arbitrary length complex data types	Yes	Yes	Yes
SQL support for complex objects	Yes	Yes	Yes

TABLE 19.3   Features of a Fully Object-Relational DBMS in Support of Complex Objects

In Table 19.4 notice the compliance level of the two commercial systems supporting inheritance.

Notice in Table 19.5 that most vendors have primitive trigger systems with impoverished semantics. Hopefully this state of affairs will improve in future releases.

As the tables show, most vendors have very restricted compliance with a limited number of the object-relational characteristics. Over the next several releases of these products, expect the compliance of the various systems to improve considerably. After all, many are relatively new systems. In addition, expect the number of object-relational systems to increase as additional vendors try to "catch the next great wave."

Feature	IDS-UDO (Informix)	Cloudscape
Data and function inheritance	Yes	No
Overloading	Yes	Yes
Inheritance of types, not tables	Yes	Yes
Multiple inheritance	No	No

TABLE 19.4   Features of a Fully Object-Relational DBMS in Support of Inheritance

Feature	DB2 6000	IDS-UDO (Informix)	CA-Ingres	Oracle
Events and actions are retrieves as well as updates	No	Yes, with restrictions	No	No
Integration of rules with inheritance and type extension	Type extension only	Yes	Type extension only	No
Rich execution semantics for rules	No	No	No	No
No infinite loops	Yes	Yes	Yes	Yes

TABLE 19.5   Features of a Fully Object-Relational DBMS in Support of Rules Systems

19.3 Integration of Object-Relational Features with Database Services

The previous section enumerated the details of object-relational feature compliance by the various vendors, which gives an indication of the characteristics provided in any given implementation. In this section, we turn to the matter of how well the various vendors have integrated their object-relational features with other DBMS services. The ones we are concerned with are enumerated below.

- *Transaction support:* All relational vendors provide support for transactions in their engines. In this way, users are assured of concurrency control and crash recovery services. Clearly, vendors of object-relational systems should provide the same transaction support for objects that they provide for relational tables. The compliance of the various vendors with this goal is indicated in Table 19.6.

- *Parallelism:* Most commercial relational engines support intraquery parallelism, through which a user query is decomposed into constituent pieces and the pieces run in parallel on as many processors as available. A popular mechanism is to decompose a table into horizontal partitions and then run each user query in parallel on each partition. Assuming the partitions are stored on separate disk drives and there are sufficient processors to perform each constituent piece, then the user will see a response time that improves monotonically with the number of partitions. For decision support queries that might run a very long time, intraquery parallelism provides vastly improved response time; hence it is a desirable feature in such environments and has been added to most relational engines.

  When a vendor extends its engine to support object-relational functionality, it is desirable to obtain intraquery parallelism on object-relational queries. In this way, the same service would be available for object-relational queries as for relational ones. Unfortunately, it is a challenge to support this service because parallel execution of user-defined functions must be supported. As noted in Table 19.6, some vendors have taken the time to perform this integration, while others have left out this capability.

- *Replication:* Most relational vendors offer a replication system whereby a replica of a relational table can be declared at a remote site. The vendor then includes code in his system to move committed updates from the primary site to the site of the replica. Vendors' products differ in functionality and architecture, but all have the purpose of providing replication to users.

  Obviously, we would like to have this feature available for objects as well as relational numbers and character strings. To completely support replicated objects, you must support replication of user-defined functions as well as replication of OIDs. Vendors have typically not taken the time to integrate these features into their replication systems.

Feature	IDS-UDO (Informix)	DB2 6000	Oracle	Cloud-scape	CA-Ingres
Transactions	Yes	Yes	Yes	Yes	Yes
Parallelism	Yes	Yes	?	No	No
Replication	No	No	No	No	No

TABLE 19.6   Integration of Object-Relational Features

19.4   *A Brief Historical Perspective*

One note of history is important at this point. In the 1970s the mainstream technology available in the marketplace was hierarchical and network systems. Relational technology was just being investigated in the research labs. Prototype systems were developed at the University of Toronto, the University of California, and IBM Research. In the 1980s relational technology came out of the research labs and into the commercial marketplace, causing a paradigm shift that displaced network and hierarchical systems as the dominant DBMS technology.

During the same decade, the research labs were hard at work on object-relational systems. Prototypes were constructed at the Microelectronics and Computer Corporation (MCC), the University of Wisconsin, IBM Research, and the University of California. In the 1990s these systems have come out of the research labs and will cause another paradigm shift to this technology. By the year 2000, expect that relational systems will be the new legacy systems and that the mainstream vendors will be marketing object-relational technology. What will the next great wave in database technology be after object-relational systems? From a historical perspective we should simply look in the research labs in the 1990s for the answer. Unfortunately, there is no clearly identifiable "next great wave" from this direction, and we will have to wait and see what ideas will emerge. Table 19.7 summarizes these observations.

Technology	1970s	1980s	1990s
Research lab	Relational	Object-relational	Not yet identified
Mainstream commercial	Hierarchical and network	Relational	Object-relational
Legacy		Hierarchical and network	Relational

TABLE 19.7   A Lesson from History

19.5 *Summary*

Expect object-relational DBMSs to be the next great wave in database technology. This will be caused by the twin forces of

- rightward migration of business data processing applications
- new DBMS applications, especially multimedia Web-oriented ones

As a result of the first force, expect the majority of the $10 billion relational market to shift from the upper-left quadrant to a mix of upper-left and upper-right quadrants of the two-by-two matrix over the next decade. Within a few years, such universal applications will be mainstream and require object-relational DBMS technology. By then, most of the major relational vendors will have a credible object-relational implementation, and relational systems will become the new legacy systems, joining hierarchical and network systems in this sunset category.

As users capture the 85% of information that is not yet computerized, there will be a huge new class of mostly upper-right quadrant applications, including digital library applications, electronic commerce, online catalogs, digital publishing applications, and asset creation and management—the second force behind the great wave.

The next great wave of the object-relational DBMS will be at least as dramatic as the last great wave, which saw relational systems replace network and hierarchical DBMSs in business data processing applications.

References

Ault, Michael. 1998. *Oracle 8 Black Book,* Coriolis Group Books, Albany, NY.

Bernstein, P. A., Hadzilacos, V., and Goodman, N. 1987. *Concurrency Control and Recovery in Database Systems,* Addison-Wesley, Reading, MA.

Brodie, Michael L., and Stonebraker, Michael. 1995. *Migrating Legacy Systems: Gateways, Interfaces, and the Incremental Approach,* Morgan Kaufmann, San Francisco.

Brown, Paul. 1996. "Spatial Indexing in Modern Database Systems," Informix White Paper.

Cattell, R. G. G., et al. 1997. *The Object Database Standard: ODMG 2.0,* Morgan Kaufmann, San Francisco.

Chamberlin, Don. 1998. *A Complete Guide to DB2 Universal Database,* Morgan Kaufmann, San Francisco.

Chen, Peter. 1976. "The Entity-Relationship Model—Toward a Unified View of Data," *ACM Transactions on Database Systems,* June.

Cloudscape, Inc. 1998. *Cloudscape Developers Guide,* Cloudscape, Oakland, CA (*www.cloudscape.com/support/doc/html/dgoIt.htm*).

Date, C. J. 1985. *An Introduction to Database Systems*, 4th ed., Addison-Wesley, Reading, MA.

Date, C. J., and Darwen, Hugh, 1994. "An Optimization Problem" in *Relational Writings 1989-1991*. Addison-Wesley, Menlo Park, CA.

Dewitt, David, et al. 1990. "The Gamma Database Machine Project," *IEEE Transactions on Knowledge and Data Engineering*, March.

Gray, Jim (editor). 1993. *The Benchmark Handbook for Database and Transaction Processing Systems*, Morgan Kaufmann, San Francisco.

Gray, Jim, and Reuter, Andreas. 1993. *Transaction Processing: Concepts and Techniques,* Morgan Kaufmann, San Francisco.

Gutman, A. 1984. "R-trees: A Dynamic Index Structure for Spatial Searching," *Proc. 1984 ACM-SIGMOD Conference on Management of Data*, Boston, June.

Haderle, Don. 1990. "Database Roles in Information Systems: The Evolution of Database Technology and Its Impact on Enterprise Information Systems" in *Database Systems of the 90s,* Springer-Verlag, Berlin.

Hellerstein, J., and Stonebraker, M. 1993. "Predicate Pushdown for Expensive Functions," *Proc. 1993 ACM-SIGMOD Conference on Management of Data*, Philadelphia, May.

Knuth, Donald. 1973. *The Art of Computer Programming,* Vol. 3, *Sorting and Searching,* Addison-Wesley, Reading, MA.

Koch, George, and Loney, Kevin. 1998. *Oracle 8: The Complete Reference,* Oracle Press/Osborne, Redwood Shores, CA.

Korth, Henry, and Silberschatz, Abraham. 1986. *Database System Concepts*, 2nd ed., McGraw-Hill, New York.

Lucas, B., et al. 1992. "An Architecture for a Scientific Visualization System," *Proc. 1992 IEEE Visualization Conference*, Boston, October.

Melton, Jim (editor). 1997. ANSI SQL3 Papers. ISO/IEC 9075 Third Edition. International Standards Organization, New York.

Moore, Geoffrey. 1995. *Crossing the Chasm: Marketing and Selling High-Tech Products to Mainstream Customers*, Harper Collins, New York.

Nievergelt, J., et al. 1984. "The Grid File: An Adaptable, Symmetric Multikey File Structure," *ACM Transactions on Database Systems*, March.

Ogle, Virginia E., and Stonebraker, Michael. 1995. "Chabot: Retrieval from a Relational Database of Images," *IEEE Computer*, September.

Oracle Corporation. 1995. "Oracle7 Multidimension, Advances in Relational Database Technology for Spatial Data Management," Oracle White Paper.

Orenstein, J., 1986. "Spatial Query Processing in an Object-Oriented DBMS," *Proc. 1986 ACM SIGMOD Conference on Management of Data*, Washington, D.C., May.

Organick, E. 1972. *The Multics System: An Examination of Its Structure*, MIT Press, Cambridge, MA.

Rasure, J., and Young, M. 1992. "An Open Environment for Image Processing Software Development," *Proceedings of 1992 SPIE Symposium on Electronic Image Processing*, February.

Robinson, J. 1981. "The K-D-B Tree: A Search Structure for Large Multidimensional Indexes," *Proc. 1981 ACM-SIGMOD Conference on Management of Data*, Ann Arbor, MI, May.

Samet, H. 1984. "Quad Trees, a Dynamic Access Method for Spatial Data," *ACM Computing Surveys*.

Sarawagi, S., and Stonebraker, M. 1994. "Efficient Organization of Large Multidimensional Arrays," *Proc. 1994 IEEE Data Engineering Conference*, Houston, February.

Selinger, P., et al. 1979. "Access Path Selection in a Relational Data Base System," *Proc. 1979 ACM-SIGMOD Conference on Management of Data*, Boston, June.

Teorey, Toby. 1994. *Database Modeling and Design: The Entity-Relationship Approach, Second Eddition,* Morgan Kaufmann, San Francisco.

Ullman, Jeffrey. 1980. *Principles of Database Systems*, Computer Science Press, Potomac, MD.

Upson, C. 1989. "The Application Visualization System," *IEEE Computer Graphics and Applications*, July.

Wahbe, Robert, Lucco, Steven, Anderson, Thomas, and Graham, Susan. 1993. "Efficient Software-Based Fault Isolation," *Proceedings of the 14th Symposium on Operating System Principles*, Asheville, NC, December.

Widom, Jennifer, and Ceri, Stefano. 1995. *Active Database Systems*, Morgan Kaufmann, San Francisco.

Wong, E., and Katz, R. 1979. "Logical Design and Schema Conversion for Relational and DBTG Databases," *Proc. of the International Conference on the Entity-Relationship Approach*, Los Angeles, December.

Index

A

access methods, user-defined, 47–51,
    142–144
activation
    client or server, 42–43
    server-side, security
      recommendations, 45–47
    See also function activation
aggregates, user-defined, 40–41,
    148–149
aggregation, array storage optimizing,
    81, 82–86
alerters, 104, 157–158
API. *See* application program interface
    (API)
application design, unrealistic, 258–259
application program interface (API)
    client-server activation, 47
    gateways, 175–177, 179
    rules extension, 157

wrapper support, 170
application server
    thick database implications, 220–226
    thin client architecture, 218
arguments
    inheritance of function, 93–94, 97
    in SQL operator and function, 38–40
    temporary, 125
arrays, storage optimizing, 81–86
ASCII
    conversion to INT function, 34–35
    non-ASCII characters
      alphabetization, 30–31
ASK, 166, 169
avg aggregate operator, 40

B

B-tree
    access methods, 48–50, 143
    collating sequences identification, 31

B-tree *(continued)*
  compared to R-tree, 33–34
  geographic queries, 206
  persistent language updates, 13
  persistent storage simulation, 249
  and quad-tree, 209–212, 213
B-tree index
  clustered or unclustered, 121–122
  database design, 262
  image data, 191
  for image-query database, 18
  object-relational optimizer, 133–135,
    137, 145, 146
  Scottish character strings, 188
  SQL-92 solution, 204–205
  on startdate, 122–124
  on table_R, 119–122
  triggers execution, 152
  See also indexed scan
base data type extension
  base type collections, 72–73
  and complex objects, 73–75
  creation of, 34–35
  examples
    geographic information systems,
      21–22, 55–57
    image type library applications,
      58–59
    quantity data type, 59–60
  fully object-relational type
    extensions, 41–53
    arbitrary-length types, 51
    callback, 47
    client or server activation, 42–43
    dynamic linking, 41–42
    integration with middleware,
      43–45
    open storage manager, 51–53

  security, 45–47
  user-defined access methods,
    47–51
  need for, 27–33, 263, 268, 273
  user-defined functions and operators,
    36–41
  See also complex objects;
    extensions; object-relational
    optimizers, extensions
base types, inheritance, 97–98
binary large object (BLOB)
  data type length, 51
  file system support, 243–244
  video-on-demand storage, 235, 236
  See also images
bond market calendar, 28–29
  calling extensions, 187–188
  middleware, 193–194
business data processing applications, 4
  data warehousing, 5–6
  insurance industry, 20–21, 237–239
  system requirements, 7, 240
  transaction processing, 5
  as universal applications, 24
  See also transaction processing
business logic
  datacentric, 43–44
  defined, 215
  execution locations, 220–226
  middleware, 219

C

C
  function opacity, 144
  user-defined functions, 37–38
C++
  persistent language performance,
    11, 13, 14, 181

persistent storage simulation,
    247–250
row objects, 74
cache coherency
    TPC-C environment, 14
    and wrapper performance, 249–250
callback
    alerters, 104
    object-relational type extension, 47,
    224
    remote, 226
calling extensions, 185–193
cast function
    definition syntax, 98
    extensible data type system, 35
certification, server-side activation
        security, 46–47
character sets, alternate, 30
chunking, arrays, 82, 84, 85
client tools
    business logic migration, 221, 222
    compaction routine, 11
    middleware integration, 43–45
    query-oriented database, 17
    simple data with queries, 4–5
    SQL DBMS, 6
client-server connection, asynchronous,
    224
Cloudscape, 163, 270, 272, 273, 274
collections
    base types, 72–73
    and client-server communication, 73
    effect on performance, 259
    type constructors, 63
columns
    for parsing, 114
    in tables, 62
commercial DBMS vendors,
        architectural options
    in general, 163–164, 183–184, 269

strategy 1: do nothing, 164–165, 183
strategy 2: rewrite relational engine,
    165–166, 183
strategy 3: sell two systems,
    166–167, 183
strategy 4: object-relational top on
    relational storage manager,
    167–169, 183
strategy 5: incremental evolution,
    169–170, 183
strategy 6: write a wrapper, 170–175
strategy 7: gateways, 175–181, 183
strategy 8: extend object-oriented
    DBMS, 181–182, 183
strategy 9: glue object-relational
    engine onto persistent language,
    182, 184
See also O vendor market
commit protocol, two-phase, 228
commit time, execution of triggers,
    153–154
commutators, object-relational
        optimizer, 136–137
compaction routine, 8–10
comparison operators
    in B-tree indexes, 134
    in extended data types
    in SQL, 38
    See also operators
complex objects
    and base types, 73–75
    collections and client-server
      communication, 73
    DBMS technology support, 263,
      268, 274
    "flattening" queries, 144–145
    functions and support for, 76
    size restrictions, 76
    type constructors, 61–73
    See also base data type extension

composite types, data inheritance, 87–88, 97

Computer Associates, 13
Ingres, 166–167, 180, 270, 272, 273
Jasmine, 166–167, 169, 180, 272
object/relational DBMSs, 166–167

concatenated field, B-tree index, 205–206

constraints, data type definition, 35

contained function/operator, 39, 203, 204, 206

CORBA
middleware, 218
for remote procedure call, 186
thick database implementation, 221–222, 230
wrapper, 44

cost function estimation
index scan, 120
joins, 124–129
optimization, 117–118

count aggregate operator, 40

crashes
recovery from, 5, 153
security issues, 45–46

Cullinet
IDMS-R, 170
IDMS, 52
wrappers, 170, 171

D

data conversion and ordering, 75

data corruption, local procedure call, 185

data representation, vs. rule representation, 263–264

data type extension. *See* base data type extension

data types
for external byte storage, 245
for parsing, 114

data warehousing, business data processing, 5–6

data mining, 220

database design, object-relational, 253–259
challenges, 262–264
problems, 257–262

database design, relational, 253–257

database procedure, as function, 39–40

DataBlade. *See* Informix

date intervals
calling extensions, 189–190
middleware, 196–198

DBMS
footprint and linking, 42
See also object-oriented DBMS;
object-relational DBMS;
relational DBMS

DBMS connectivity
business logic middleware, 218, 224
two-tier thick database, 225

DBMS matrix
classification matrix, 1–2
multiquadrant problems
file system support, 243–247
in general, 231–233
insurance application, 237–239
quadrant 3 applications support, 247–252
video-on-demand, 232–237
quadrant 1, simple data without queries, 2–3
quadrant 2, simple data with queries, 3–8

quadrant 3, complex data without
    queries, 8–15
quadrant 4, complex data with
    queries, 15–20
universal application, 19, 20–24
decision support applications, 21
decision support query
    business data processing
        application, 240
    data warehouse, 6
deletion, foreign key values, 69
denormalization, database design, 261,
    262
deref function, 69–70, 71, 76
Digital Equipment Corporation (DEC),
    DBMS development, 165–166
discrimination network, 160, 161
disk pointers, compared to main
    memory pointers, 9
document management systems, 3, 53
dot notation, 97
dynamic linking, object-relational
    DBMS, 41–42

E

electronic computer-aided design
    (ECAD), 9, 12
encapsulation, and base types, 74–75
entity-relationship (ER) model,
    253–257
    attributes identification, 254
    entities identification, 254
    relationships, 255–257
    unique identifier assignment, 254
equality search, object-relational
    optimizer, 133
extensions
    calling extensions, 185–193

general rules, 156–157
type, object-relational DBMS, 41–53
See also base data type extension;
    object-relational optimizers,
    extensions
extensions performance
    alternatives comparison, 212–213
    examples, 202–204
    implementation, 201–202
    Informix 2-D Spatial DataBlade,
        206–207
    spatial extension, 209–212
    SQL-92 solution, 204–206
    Z transforms, 207–209, 212, 213
    See also performance

F

fields, inheritance, 88–89
file system
    data storage, 53
    performance capability, 3
    support for application, BLOBs,
        243–244
    video-on-demand, 233–234
finalization, user-defined aggregate, 40–
    41
firewalls, server-side activation, 45–46,
    47
floats, comparison operators
    application, 38, 138
foreign key, use with references, 68–71
formal modeling, excessive focus on,
    258
Forte, 44, 218, 221
FORTRAN-style arrays, 82–83
fourth-generation languages (4GLs)
    examples and applications, 4–5
    for SQL DBMS, 6

from clause, functions, 64–65, 66
function activation, 42–43
  business logic middleware, 218, 224
  remote, 226, 228–229
  two-tier thick database, 225
  See also activation
function index
  database design, 262–264
  object-relational DBMS, 137–138
  See also B-tree index; indexed scan
functions
  aggregate, 81
  and arguments, 97
  from clause, 64–65, 66
  for geographic queries, 56
  image type library applications, 59
  for parsing, 115
  for quantity data type, 60
  signatures, 115–116
  user-defined, 36–41, 64, 66, 96
    create function command, 41
    parsing, 114–115
    in rules, 112

G

gateways, object-relational/relational
      DBMS connections, 175–181
geographic data, storage and access,
      48–50, 237, 238
geographic information systems (GISs)
  base type extension, 55–57
  support and implementation, 201–
      202
  universal application, 21–22
global positioning systems (GPS), 25
grafting, query plan, 153
granularity
  B-tree and quad-tree, 123, 210–213
  storage manager, 173–174

grid file
  access methods, 142
  spatial clauses acceleration, 18

H

hashing, access methods, 48, 143
Hewlett-Packard, 6, 8
  Odapter, 171
  wrappers, 171
histograms
  image analysis and retrieval, 59, 139
  optimization, 120

I

IBM, 6, 19, 163
  Data Joiner, 201
  data types, 33
  DB2 6000, 167, 168–169, 201, 271,
      272, 273, 276
  Encina, 218
  IMS, 52
  System R, 167
  wrappers, 170
Illustra
  Informix IDS-UDO, part in creating,
      167–168
  market demands, response to, 18–19
image type library
  applications, 58–59, 142
  middleware, 198–200
  operators, 58
images
  access methods and optimization,
      137–138
  data types length, 51
  image data calling extensions, 191–
      192
  query-oriented database, 15–20
  storage with histogram, 139
  See also binary large object (BLOB)

index, relation to performance, 260
indexed scan
    compared to sequential scan, 192
    object-relational optimizer, 132, 136,
        137, 148
    on table_R, 119–122
    triggers execution, 152
    See also B-tree index; function index
infinite loops, from chain rules,
        108–109, 112
Informix, 6, 18–19, 26, 163, 182
    DataBlade modules, 33, 44, 79–81,
        206–207, 252
    function codes, 38
    IDS-UDO, 167–168, 173–174, 273,
        274
    universal server representation,
        91–92, 201, 207, 210, 235, 236
    Virtual Table Interface (VTI), 53,
        172, 173–174
Ingres, 28–29, 169
inheritance, 87–99
    data, 87–93, 98
    DBMS technology support, 263,
        268, 274
    functions, 93–98
    multiple, 99
    overloading support, 98
inheritance hierarchies
    optimization over joins, 147–148
    scans, object-relational optimizer,
        147
initialization, user-defined aggregate,
        40–41
insertion, foreign key values, 68–69
instead keyword, 105
INT-to-ASCII function, 35
integers, comparison operators, 38
integrity problems
    base type collections, 72
    rows as type constructor, 68

storage systems, 174, 246–247
integrity support, update-update rules,
        103
interprocess communication channel
        (IPC), extension calling,
        185–193
iteration, importance of in database
        design, 258
iteration, of user-defined aggregates in
        SQL, 40–41

J

Java
    function definition, 36
    ORDBMS products, 13
    server-side activation security, 46
joins
    compared to restrictions, 118, 141
    effect on query, 68–69
    four-way, 128
    methods for processing, 124–129
        hash-join algorithm, 126–129
        merge-join, 125–126, 127
        nested loop, 125, 127, 148
    optimization over inheritance
        hierarchies, 147–148
    three-way, 127

K

K-D-B tree
    access methods, 48, 142
    spatial clauses acceleration, 18
keyword indexing, access methods, 142

L

left-only trees, 128
legacy systems
    data storage, 52, 53
    migration strategy, 180–181, 241

legacy systems *(continued)*
 relational systems as, 278
 replacement, 260
lines, modeling, 211–212
listen statement, 104
literals, conversion to new data type, 34
load balancing
 business logic middleware, 218, 224
 three-tier thick database, 229
 two-tier thick database, 225
local procedure call (LPC)
 compared to remote procedure call,
  186–187, 189, 200
 extension calling, 185–193
location transparency, thick database,
  229, 230
locked data, cache, 250
locking
 access methods, 143
 two-phase, 5
low-level hooks, trigger support,
  151–152
LPC. *See* local procedure call (LPC)

M

mapping layer, relational DBMS, 23–24
matrix. *See* DBMS matrix
max aggregate operator, 40
memory
 tertiary, 240
 thick client architecture, 215
 thin client architecture, 217
 See also storage
metadata, tables as, 115
methods. *See* functions
Microsoft
 DBMS products, 6, 11
 Excel, 53

MTS, 218
OLE DB, 172–173, 183
 Tiger, 234
middleware
 capabilities, 218, 224
 integration, base type extensions,
  43–45
 object-relational architecture,
  193–200
  bond time, 193–194
  date interval, 196–198
  image library, 198–200
  Scottish strings, 194–195
 and optimizers, 174–175
 thick database, 222, 230
 thin client architecture, 218
 and wrappers, 172–173
migration
 business logic, 221–222
 legacy systems, 180–181, 241
min aggregate operator, 40
mouse-tracking module, 220
multitier systems, 215

N

names, function sharing, 115–116
naturalness, and base types, 74
negation operation, optimization, 123
negators, 123, 136
new, keyword, 102
not optimization, 123, 136

O

O vendor market
 players, 13–15
 standards consortium, 181–182
 See also commercial DBMS
  vendors, architectural options

Object Database Management Group
(ODMG), 181
object resource broker (ORB)
in CORBA/RPC, 186
location transparency, 229
object-oriented DBMS
extensions, 181–182
markets and players, 13–15, 25, 26
object-relational DBMS
aggregation support, 85–86
and application servers
in general, 215–219
thick database implications,
220–226
three-tier thick database model,
226–229
base data types creation, 34–35
calling extensions, 185–193
characteristics, 267–270
collections, 73
database design, 253–259
database services integration,
275–277
function definition, 36
inheritance support, 88
markets and players, 18–19, 25, 26,
270–275
middleware, 193–200
persistent storage simulation,
247–250
references, 69–70
time series data, 81
type extensions, 41–53
object-relational optimizers
extensions, 131–132
access methods on function of
data, 137–138
access methods, user-defined,
142–144

aggregates, user-defined, 148–149
B-trees and user-defined
comparison operators, 133–135
commutators, user-defined,
136–137
expensive functions, 140–142
"flattening" complex object
queries, 144–145
"in-line" sets, 145–146
indexes of attributes on sets, 146
inheritance hierarchies scans, 147
joins over inheritance hierarchies,
147–148
negators, user-defined, 136
operator and function notation,
132–133
selectivity functions,
user-defined, 135–136
smart ordering of predicate
clauses, 138–140
See also base data type extension
image library, 198–200
See also optimizers; relational
optimizers
object-relational parser
compared to relational parser, 113
defined, 114–116
OIDs
and complex objects, 75
and system assigned object ID, 254
OLE
middleware, 218
thick database implementation, 221,
222, 230
wrapper, 44
online analytical processing (OLAP),
aggregation operations, 82, 86

online transaction processing (OLTP), 26, 252

operational data stores (ODS), 52

operators
  for image type library applications, 58
  for parsing, 115
  for quantity data type, 59–60
  user-defined, 36–41
  See also comparison operators

optimizers, 167, 179, 181, 240
  expensive function, 191
  for image-query database, 18
  for nested vs. unnested queries, 260–261
  storage manager problems, 174–175
  thick database, 221
  See also object-relational optimizers; relational optimizers

OQL systems, requirements, 181–182

OR SQL, function definition, 36, 38, 40–41

Oracle, 6, 19, 163
  "cartridge" protocol, 222
  data types, 33
  Developer 2000, 4
  media server, 234
  Spatial Data Option (SDO), 201, 202, 210
  Version 7.3, 169–170
  Version 8, 271, 274, 276
  wrappers, 171
  Z transforms, 207–209

ORB. *See* object resource broker

overlaps function
  calling extensions, 190
  date intervals, 196–198
  SQL-92 solution, 204

P

page management, access methods, 143

parallelism, database services integration, 276

parser, 167, 179, 181

parsing, object-relational, 113–116

pattern recognition, 114–116

performance
  arithmetic operations in SQL, 32
  gateways, 180
  indirection affecting, 57
  for query-oriented database, 18
  relation to security concerns, 11–13
  relational DBMS, 14, 23
  for simple data with queries, 5–6
  testing, importance of, 261
  wrappers, 171–172
  See also extensions performance

persistent language
  architecture, 12
  for compaction application, 10
  markets, 25
  object-relational engine onto, 182
  updates, 13
  vendors, 13–15, 181–182

persistent storage simulation, object-relational DBMS, 247–250

point data type, application, 33

pointers. *See* references

points, storage, 57

poll mechanism, alerters, 104

polygon
  modeling, 211–212
  storage, 57
  Z transforms structure, 209

polymorphism, 95

polyphase merge-sort algorithm,
    Scottish character strings, 188
positive-integer data type, 98
predicate clauses ordering,
    object-relational optimizer,
    138–140
predicate migration, joins and
    restrictions, 141
predicates
    canonical form, 124
    in execution, 152
    optimization, 123
predictability, caching, 250
primary/foreign key relationship, 68–71
proximity searching, access methods,
    142

Q

quad-tree
    access methods, 48, 142
    and B-trees, 209–212, 213
    and spatial extensions, 209
    Z transforms, 208
quantity data type, operations on, 59–60
query
    join effect on, 68–69
    nested vs. unnested, 260–261
query modification, trigger support,
    151–152, 154–156
query plan
    after grafting, 153
    predicates checking, 152
query-query rule, 105–107, 156, 263
query-update rule, 103
queue management
    asynchronous client-server
        connection requirements, 224

business logic middleware, 218, 224
two-tier thick database, 225

R

R-tree
    access methods, 48, 50, 142, 144,
        172
    date intervals, 196–198
    spatial clauses acceleration, 18
    spatial modeling, 212
    2-D Spatial DataBlade, 33–34,
        206–207
recovery, access methods, 143
ref function, 70, 76
references
    as type constructors, 63, 74, 76
    collections of, using, 71–72
    using, 68–71
relational DBMS
    database design, 253–257
    mapping layer, 23–24
    markets, 25
    rewrite requirements, 165–166
    trigger implementation, 151
    See also DBMS; object-oriented
        DBMS; object-relational DBMS
relational optimizers
    defined, 117–118
    join processing methods, 124–129
        bushy trees, 128–129
        left-only trees, 128
    performing restriction on table_R,
        119–124
    See also object-relational optimizers;
        optimizers
relationships, database design
    attributes, 256

relationships, database design
    (continued)
    many-many, 255, 257
    one-many, 255, 257
    one-one, 255, 257
remote procedure call (RPC)
    activation, 42–43, 45–46
    business logic, 221–222
    compared to local procedure call,
        186–187, 189, 200
    compared to middleware, 200
    extension calling, 185–193
replication
    database services integration, 276
    denormalization, 261
    thick database, 228
restrictions
    compared to joins, 118, 141
    on table_R, 119–124
retrieval
    content-based, images, 58–59
    rules support for, 111
risk assessment and fraud detection,
        insurance industry, 20–21
rows
    manipulating, 64–68
    as type constructors, 61–62, 74, 76
RPC. *See* remote procedure call (RPC)
rule representation, vs. data
        representation, 263–264
rules
    business rules, 259–260
    execution, immediate vs. deferred,
        110–111, 112
    general form, 101–102
    implementation
        extension to general rules,
        156–157
        scalability, 157–160
        triggers support, 151–156

integration, 111–112
    query-query, 105–107, 156, 263
    query-update, 103
    semantics
        aborting action part terminates
        transaction, 110
        chain rules and infinite loops,
        108–109, 112
        firing of rules, 110–111
        multiple rules from same event,
        107–108
    update-query, 104
    update-update, 102–103
rules data structure, 160, 161
rules system, DBMS technology
        support, 268, 275

S

scalability
    and middleware, 250
    rules extension, 157–160
Scottish character strings, 30–31, 174
    calling extensions, 188–189
    middleware, 194–195
security
    business logic middleware, 218, 224
    grant/revoke system, 106
    server-side activation, 45–47
    thick client architecture, 216
    thin client architecture, 217
    three-tier thick database, 225
    two-tier thick database, 223
security/architecture
    client-server architecture, 6, 45–47
    compaction routine, 11
    decomposed DBMS, 11–13
    for query-oriented database, 18
selectivity functions, object-relational
        optimizer, 135–136
semantics, rules, 107–111, 264

sequential scan
    compared to indexed scan, 192
    object-relational optimizer, 132, 133, 139
    on table_R, 119
    See also B-tree index; indexed scan
session management
    asynchronous client-server connection, 224
    business logic middleware, 218, 224
    three-tier thick database, 225
    two-tier thick database, 223
sets
    "in-line," 145–146
    indexes of attributes, 146
    as type constructors, 63
signatures, functions, 115–116
spatial clauses, acceleration, 18
spatial extension, 209–212
SQL
    business logic, 221–222
    distributed, 228
    not used in text editor, 2
    primary/foreign key relationship, 68
    support for complex types, 77
SQL-3
    base data types, 98
    object-relational DBMSs, 18–19
    requirements, 181–182
    type constructors, 63
SQL-89
    date and time semantics, 187
    query language requirements, 4
SQL-92
    aggregate operators, 40–41
    alternate character sets definition, 30
    clause computation expense, 141
    data type restrictions, 27–28
    dialect conversion, 175–176

extensions performance solutions, 204–206, 212
    foreign key references, 68–71
    standard data types, 4
static linking, compared to dynamic linking, 41–42
storage
    indirection, 57
    persistent storage simulation, 247–250
    See also memory
storage manager interface, 173
    multiple storage systems, 174
    open storage manager, 51–53
    optimizer problems, 174–175
stride, array indexes, 82
subtype, inheritance from supertypes, 88–89, 92, 94, 96
sum aggregate operator, 40
sunset function, 17, 18, 42–43, 47, 192, 198–199
supertypes, inheritance to subtypes, 88–89, 92, 94, 96
Sybase, 4, 6, 19
    Brahms project, 172
    Jaguar, 218
    PowerBuilder, 4
    wrappers, 172–173
System R (Selinger), 117

T

table hierarchy, 90
tables
    for inheritance, 89–93, 98, 147, 148
    for parsing, 114
    relational, 256–257
    for row type, 62
    rules application to, 152

tables *(continued)*
  security for, 106
  for time series data, 80–81
testing, database design, 261–262
text editors, DBMS service levels, 2, 9
text servers, 173
thick client
  choices, 220
  compared to thin client, 215, 216
thick database
  application server implications,
    220–226
  business logic middleware, 219
  choices, 220
  three-tier model, 226–229, 227, 230
  two-tier model, 224–225, 230
thin client
  architecture, 223
  compared to thick client, 215
  three-tier architecture, 216–217
thin client/thick client, middleware
    integration, 43–45
thread management
  business logic middleware, 218, 224
  three-tier thick database, 225
  two-tier thick database, 223
tick interval, 80
time series data
  object-relational DBMS, 81
  type constructors, 79–81
tools. *See* client tools
transaction management, business data
    processing, 5, 239
transaction processing
  database design, 261
  rate of increase, 240, 241
  See also business data processing
    applications

Transaction Processing Facility (TPF),
    241
transaction processing monitor (TP
    monitor), thin client
    architecture, 218
transaction support, database services
    integration, 276
triggers, 103
  effect on performance, 258–259
  immediate vs. deferred execution,
    153–154
  rule systems support, 111, 151–156
    executor modification, 152–154
    query modification, 154–156
2-D data types, geographic queries, 55–
    56
2-D geometric objects, encoding, 33
two-phase locking, business data
    processing, 5
type constructors
  arrays, 81–86
  defining, 74
  references as, 63
  rows as, 61–62
  sets as, 63
  support for, 76
  time series data, 79–81
  using, 63–73
    base types collections, 72–73
    manipulating row collections,
      66–68
    manipulating row types, 64–66
    references, 68–71
    references collections, 71–72
type hierarchy, modified, 94, 95, 96
types, parsing, 114

U

union table, nested loop join, 148

union types, persistent storage simulation, 248–249

unique identifier, assignment in database design, 254

UniSQL, 18, 182, 270

universal applications, 19, 20–24

    human resources application modernization, 21

    markets, 25, 26

    multimedia and GIS systems, 21–22

    part number tracking, 22–23

    risk assessment and fraud detection, 20–21

universal server, 19, 20, 139–140

unwinding, functions in SQL, 37, 38

update

    executor modification, 152

    persistent language, 11–13

    query modification, 154–156

    ref function coding, 70

    rules application, 157–160, 161

    text editor, 2

    virtual table interface, 246–247

update-query rules, 104

update-update rules, 102–103

upgrades

    thick client architecture, 216

    thin client architecture, 217

user-defined functions and operators, 36–41

    support for, 39–40

    user-defined aggregates, 40–41

V

values, extensible data type system conversion, 35

varchar data type, extensible data type system conversion, 35

Versant, 13, 182

vesting function, 116, 176

video servers, 173

video-on-demand (VOD)

    DBMS applications, 232–237

    file system technology use, 3

views, security, 106

virtual data elements, 97, 105

virtual table interface (VTI)

    file system support, 246–247

    persistent language simulation, 251–252

    See also Informix, Virtual Table Interface (VTI)

Visual Basic, function definition, 36

W

Web servers, data storage, 53

wrappers, 170–175, 177

    action sequence, 172

    architecture, 170

    BLOB appropriate programming language, 244–245

    persistent storage simulation, 247–250

    thick database implementation, 221–222, 230

    See also gateways

write-ahead log (WAL) technology, business data processing, 5

Z

Z transforms, 207–209, 212, 213

zoning changes, 203